Charles R. Henderson

An Introduction to the Study of the Dependent, Defective and

Delinquent Classes

Charles R. Henderson

An Introduction to the Study of the Dependent, Defective and Delinquent Classes

ISBN/EAN: 9783337178710

Printed in Europe, USA, Canada, Australia, Japan

Cover: Foto ©Andreas Hilbeck / pixelio.de

More available books at **www.hansebooks.com**

AN

INTRODUCTION TO THE STUDY

OF THE

Dependent, Defective and Delinquent Classes·

BY

CHARLES RICHMOND HENDERSON, A.M., D.D.
ASSISTANT PROFESSOR OF SOCIAL SCIENCE IN THE
UNIVERSITY OF CHICAGO

BOSTON
D. C. HEATH AND COMPANY
1893

PREFACE

We discuss here the subject of the Dependent, Defective and Delinquent Classes as a part of sociology. Why? Evidently because there is no place for them in any of the special sciences which deal with social phenomena. Indispensable as are the results of economic science, the social treatment of these classes involves elements far transcending the range of economics under its most liberal definitions. Ethical science and philosophy are essential in this inquiry, but the word "ought" has not much to do with idiots or with Lombroso's "L'Uomo Delinquente" of the lowest stratum. Political machinery must be invoked, but statecraft waits for the theoretical issues of several sciences and for the organization of personal philanthropy to make its efforts effectual in helping pauper and criminal.

Who are these Dependents, Defectives and Delinquents? Anthropology and historic sociology declare that they are "outcast" survivals of an imperfect past race, living out of their time in a civilization to which they are not adjusted, or degenerate offspring of an injured and a defeated stock, or examples of an arrested development, unfit to endure the strain of modern competition. And yet they are brethren of a common race, in whom are latent powers akin to those of the highest. In the region of religion we discover the rational ideals of social treatment of these forlorn "children of Ishmael," while economic science gives the industrial laws, morality orders the rules of conduct, political and legal science advise in respect to the agencies of government. Since all science and all arts must contribute, and since each alone is defective though necessary, a new science must be invoked to harmonize and direct to an adequate action. This science, youngest of all, is called "Sociology." The progress of

the other sciences has made its appearance inevitable and neces -
sary, just as the development of the banking system has called
forth the Clearing House of the metropolitan centers.

This book is the fruit of twenty years and more of study and
experience and lecturing on the subjects treated. The contents
have been substantially presented and tested in class work.

The writer believes that in form and contents it is suitable for
a text book in college and University work, for clubs of women
or men seriously engaged in the study of social problems, for
ministers who are perplexed by difficult questions in parish work,
and are seeking light to give on the topics here offered, and for
directors of many kinds of charities in city and state. It may be
used as the basis of correspondence studies for those who wish to
keep in close relation with University life, while busy with the
exacting duties of church or business.

My honored friend, Rev. Oscar McCulloch, called the National
Conference of Charities and Corrections the "Church of the
Divine Fragments." This book is offered as a janitor or verger
to guide visitors about the place made holy by suffering and
philanthropy.

And here I may set down with gratitude a few among many
names of persons to whom I am indebted for help and inspira -
tion in this study: Rev. G. W. Northrup, D.D., LL.D., one of
the first teachers of theology to introduce these subjects into the
theological seminary; Rev. H. L. Wayland, D.D., also my
teacher and counsellor; Hon. F. Wayland, LL.D.; Hon. W. P.
Letchworth; Mr. C. D. Kellogg of New York; Mr. N. S.
Rosenau; Rev. F. H. Wines; A. MacDonald, Ph.D.; Mr. Joseph
Nicholson, Superintendent of Detroit House of Correction; Hon.
A. G. Porter, who aided me in inquiries in Rome. To name all
would be impossible; but I thank those who have through many
years counselled and helped me with knowledge and with practical aid in connection with causes that lay heavy on my heart.

The encouragement of President W. R. Harper and of my
genial colleague and Head Professor, A. W. Small, Ph.D., has
been an element too important to leave unmentioned.

I acknowledge here my obligations to members of various boards with whom I have been associated as Director; and especially the Directors of the Rose Orphan Home and Charity Organization Society of Terre Haute, Indiana; the Directors of the Detroit Association of Charities, and of the Michigan Home of Industry for Discharged Prisoners (and "Mother" D'Arcambal with them), the Councils of the various Charities of Detroit.

I have indicated what I regard the most important works for the study of these subjects. "The Reader's Guide" (Putnams) will direct to other literature, and the bibliographies in such works as R. M. Smith on "Emigration and Immigration," and MacDonald on "Criminology" will give exhaustive lists in their special lines. For the use of others than specialists such bibliographies are not helpful. General readers must have selected lists. Most of the books named are in public libraries. In small communities a book club can be formed for the purchase of the necessary material for study. Specific personal direction can be had by correspondence with the University Extension Department of the University of Chicago, and the methods employed by them greatly facilitate such study. The work is conducted by the instructors in the University.

THE UNIVERSITY OF CHICAGO, May, 1893.

TABLE OF CONTENTS.

PART I.—DEPENDENTS, ESPECIALLY IN THE UNITED STATES.

vii

PART II.—DEFECTIVES.

PART III.—CRIME AND ITS SOCIAL TREATMENT.

PART IV.—SOCIAL HYGIENE AND THERAPEUTICS.

————————

ABBREVIATIONS.   The only abbreviated forms necessary to explain are N. C. C. (Reports of National Conference of Charities and Corrections) and N. P. A. (Reports of National Prison Association).

DEPENDENT,

DEFECTIVE AND DELINQUENT

CLASSES

INTRODUCTION.

"Masses indeed: and yet, singular to say, if, with an effort of imagination, thou follow them, over broad France into their clay hovels, into their garrets and hutches, the masses consist all of units. Every unit of whom has his own heart and sorrows; stands covered there with his own skin, and if you . . . prick him, he will bleed." . . .

Dreary, languid do these struggle in their obscure remoteness, their hearth cheerless, their diet thin. For them in this world rises no Era of Hope. . . . Untaught, uncomforted, unfed. . . . Especially it is an old truth, that wherever huge physical evil is, there, as the parent and origin of it, has moral evil to a proportionate extent been."— CARLYLE.

1. The Aim of this Course. — It is not possible to give full instruction and training for administrative offices in institutions of charity by means of lectures. Nurses of the sick, physicians to the insane, and secretaries of charity organizations must find their discipline in the actual work of their offices and in special schools for technical preparation. It is here our effort and aim to give educated leaders of society such a method of study and such codified results of past study and experience that they may think effectively and act wisely. Those who shape and direct public opinion, and who are inspired by philanthropic purpose, need the outlook of sociological methods of regarding these complicated and difficult problems.   While experts can not be fully prepared by class work and books, they may receive in this way a more scientific direction than if they are confined to the discipline of daily experience in some particular institution.

2. Method. — The material of our study lies scattered in many books and reports and pamphlets.   We shall here attempt to state in the most condensed form possible the elements of the subject, and the most important received conclusions of the most reliable authorities, with somewhat full bibliography for future readings on special points.   We profess to give nothing more than an introductory essay on a subject of world - wide interest.   An indexed note book may well be used to gather facts and reasonings, and keep them in accessible form for use.   It is wise for a student to make an inventory of his own knowledge of this subject before he enters the field.   One must proceed from his known to the less known and the unknown.

3. Personal Interest. — Progress will be promoted by asking oneself : Why should I take up this difficult and sometimes repulsive theme ?   What are the sources of personal interest in this mournful subject ?   Let no one enter here who is not prepared to meet difficulties of many kinds.

A sustaining purpose of high order is required for the study of dependency, because a thorough knowledge demands of us that we submit our senses of sight, hearing, and smell to very disagreeable phenomena.   Investigation cannot be entirely by proxy.   Mr. Booth prepared himself for his great work on East London by taking lodgings among the people whose life and labors he determined to know and reveal. Mr. McDonald's recent book on Criminology is enriched by illustrations gathered from prisoners in their cells. Indignation, disgust and pity succeed each other. Sympathy is pain. The subject is full of intellectual difficulties. One must expect to meet disappointments. There is no ready-made solution of these problems. If careful thinking and boundless self-denial could remove pauperism, the world ere this time would not contain a beggar.

But if one is fond of knotty questions that put thought to strain; if horrors fascinate the philanthropic disposition; if there is much of the "mind that was in Christ Jesus," then the study of dependency will arouse curiosity and attract eager interest.

PART I.—DEPENDENTS.

CHAPTER I.

DEFINITIONS.

All human beings are dependent in infancy. Nothing is more helpless than a babe. But the children of capable families are not "dependents" in the sense of the word used in this Introduction. In a certain sense adults of the most civilized communities are most dependent on each other. Increase of unlikeness of parts carries with it increased dependence of parts. The savage makes all he requires, but the civilized man makes one article and buys ten thousand articles of all the world. Nor are all the poor "dependents." Most people are relatively poor. A poor Yankee would be rich in China. A poor Irishman would be wealthy in Patagonia. "Dependents" are those members of society who cannot or will not support themselves without aid of others. It is easy to see that Dependency admits degrees. It shades off upward into the simple poverty of misfortune, and downward into beggary and crime. In its extreme form among adults, dependency may be called Pauperism, a word which carries with it a suggestion of reproach. The pauper is a social parasite who attaches himself to other members of the community, and, by living at the expense of others, like a Hermit Crab, suffers loss of faculty by atrophy and disuse. Pauperism

5

is a loathsome disease, more difficult of cure, many think, than crime.

CHAPTER II.

SOURCES OF KNOWLEDGE.

1. **Observation** is the prime source of real knowledge. He who would have genuine impressions, by which to vivify and correct his reading, must go into the homes of the extremely poor, and have actual dealings with them. One may go with visitors of relief societies and poor authorities of city or town ; or with a city physician called to treat a "county case ;" or resort to pauper hospitals and poor-houses; or walk in forlorn regions with mission workers who know the haunts and ways of the destitute. So Mr. Dugdale studied at first hand the habitats and customs of "The Jukes" in New York, and so Mr. McCulloch studied the "Tribe of Ishmael" in his Indianapolis parish.

2. **Art.** To deepen and widen and refresh the fading impressions of observation the *representations of art* are valuable. Painters and sculptors recall jaded spirits to feel the reality of poverty. Writers of fiction suggest new fields of research, and intensify the moral reaction against morbid social conditions. "Ginx's Baby" stings us with satire ; Dickens attracts us to walk with him in his descent into the Inferno and Purgatory of human sorrows ; Bellamy's "Looking Backward" has at least the merit of arousing the selfish from dreams of luxury ; Mrs. Browning's "Cry of the Children" thrills the sensitive heart,

and her "Aurora Leigh" opens all philosophies, and all wounds, and all modes of cure; Hood's "Song of the Shirt" has not become antiquated where Sweaters toil; and Hugo's "Les Miserables" still creep along the alleys of our towns to unhealthy dens.

It is true that such works of art have their limitations. They often describe scenes that no longer exist, they seldom offer scientific analyses of causes or offer adequate remedies. The novelist is free to fly in air, but the sociologist must walk on solid earth, close to facts, and the reformer must deal with reality and not with dreams. Still the "Children of Gibeon" appeal to us as if they were at our doors, and "All Sorts and Conditions of Men" are our near contemporaries. Such is the power of strong imagination that we can go with Meriwether in his "Tramp at Home" and learn many facts that thus unhelped would never come to our notice. Mr. Riis in "How the Other Half Live" and "Children of the Poor," by the aid of written words and photography leads us, even though little willing, to almost converse with the inhabitants of the dolorous tenements of our metropolis.

> Crabbe's Poems: "The Village" (English Almshouse).
> Hogarth's Pictures.   ·
> Barrie's "Little Minister."
> "Fraternity."
> Abbé Le Roux, "Thoughts of a Parish Priest."

3. Records. During the past fifteen years the Associations of Charity have piled up records of actual cases which are a mine of information in respect to particular persons and families. The reports of charitable institutions, the reports of state boards of charities and corrections, the government tables and consul reports, are rich treasuries of exact information.

4. Statistics. These impressions of special forms of dependency require the aid of statistics. The chief uses of statistics are,—to secure accurate and mathematical measurement of the extent of the evil of pauperism and kindred social diseases ; to map out the geographical situation of the worst plague spots ; to disclose the causes of the phenomena at their spring ; to reveal the tendencies of the current of poverty and distress, the fluctuations, eddies, changes in the turbid stream. Models of such investigation are found in Mr. Dugdale's "The Jukes," McCulloch's "Tribe of Ishmael," and Booth's "Life and Labor."

5. The Special Sciences contribute facts, laws, reasonings. One great reason for past failures to deal successfully with pauperism is that it has been attacked at a single point and regarded from a single standpoint. The conviction is growing upon all competent workers in this field that such fragmentary and partial methods are doomed to failure. He who would study Dependency with the best results must first master the principles of biological science. He may not be an expert in physical science, but he must know the laws of heredity in the animal world, the imperative commands of sanitary science and art, the laws of food and habitation. Psychology must contribute a special study of the general laws of thinking and feeling, and those special modes of thinking and feeling which are peculiar to dependents and defectives. The Political Economist must be asked to tell us what industrial conditions are most sure to produce or increase a tendency to dependency, and what economic principles must be observed by philanthropists if they wish to do good and not harm.

Ethical science must tell us the fundamental obligations of society to the broken members and the grounds of voluntary or governmental action. The Historian must be drawn upon for an account of the past social conditions out of which these evils have grown, and of the efforts and experiments of philanthropy in other times.

Political science will show the methods of government in dealing with the class under consideration, the organs of the state adapted to this end, and the limits of the powers of lawmakers and judges and magistrates. And then our theory and practice will be greatly affected by our real convictions in respect to God and the relations of men to each other as children of a Common Father.

At last all these forms of knowledge must be coördinated in sociology, their proper place and relative value found and estimated, and practical conclusions drawn from the entire series. He who imagines that any amiable impulse will answer for science is sure to blunder. The pages to follow, imperfect as they must be, are inspired by a profound conviction that the time is ripe for a more thorough and adequate treatment of these subjects. If we can succeed in one field of social study the same method will help us forward in other fields.

If more than twenty-two years of almost daily contact with the poor in an attempt to help them by personal, parish, institutional, and governmental means; if constant study of the greatest writers in medical, sanitary, economic, ethical, religious, political and social science, if long journeys for research in many towns and cities, in America and in Europe, if years of converse and discussion and correspondence with wise and generous men and women over these themes; if constant experience as an organizer, administrator, trustee and director of important charities; if all this entitles one to offer a humble contribution to this subject, then this course of essays may claim a small corner for its own. Without such experience and study the author would not feel justified in offering one more book to a long-suffering public.

CHAPTER III.

INTEREST AND IMPORTANCE OF THE SUBJECT.

1. **Pauperism is Costly.** The economic effects of dependency deserves study and consideration.

Mr. McCulloch (N. C. C., 1891, pp. 12-13) makes the following estimates, which must be compared with the results of the last census and other recent sources. In 1880 the census reported 481,240 as belonging to the dependent, defective and delinquent classes. This did not include those in jails, nor was it in anyway correct as to those receiving out-door relief. The view presented in the glowing pages of Mr. Carnegie's " Triumphant Democracy " is based on the confessedly imperfect figures of the census of 1880, and is not reliable. But, taking the figures as they stand, they represent a half-million. Marshalling them in regiments, we should have these results :

ADULTS. Idiotic, 76,895 ; Insane, 91,997 ; Blind, 48,-928 ; Deaf-mutes, 33,665 ; Paupers, 88,665 ; Prisoners, 59,-255 ; Total, 400,000.

CHILDREN. Deaf-mutes, 6,617 ; Blind, 2,032 ; Orphan, 59,161 ; Feeble-minded, 2,472 ; in Reform Schools, 11,-340 ; Total, 81,622.

Nor would this include the vast number of children cared for by Children's Aid Societies and the neglected children of the street. But this number, large as it is, would be immensely swelled by the more careful statistics of 1890.   Mr. Ely, in *North American Review*, April, 1891, taking the report of the conference for 1887 as a basis, estimates an average of 250,000 out-door and 110,000 in-door paupers per year.   This is on the authority of Mr. H. H. Hart and Mr. F. B. Sanborn.   Mr. Kellogg estimates that 3,000,000 have been supported in whole or in part by the United States in any one year.   Mr. McCulloch esti-mates the cost in money, $50,000,000 in maintenance and $50,000,000 in loss of productive power.   Every human being who cannot or will not support himself must be sup-ported at the expense of other persons more industrious and capable.   Professor Tucker (And. Rev. 1889 and after-wards), gives some comparative estimates which are instruct-ive.   " There are in Great Britain over 1,000,000 paupers, supported at an annual cost of $40,000,000.   The annual charge for the army is $90,000,000, of the navy $60,000,-000, law and justice, $30,000,000, education, $30,000,000. Michigan has 45,000 paupers, out-door and in-door, sup-ported at an annual cost of $650,000 ; 2,500 insane, sup-ported at a cost of $500,000.   Ohio has 54,000 paupers, supported at a cost of $1,100,000 ; insane 6,000, cost $800,-000.   The whole cost of dependent, defective and delin-quent persons in the state of New York is over $12,000,000. Massachusetts has 62,000 paupers, who cost $2,000,000 ; insane, 6,800, cost $900,000.

Mr. Dugdale closes his account of " The Jukes" with this remark : " Over a million and a quarter dollars of loss in seventy-five years, caused by a single family 1,200 strong, without reckoning the cash paid for whisky, or taking into account the entailment of pauperism and crime of the sur-vivors in succeding generations, and the incurable disease, idiocy, and insanity growing out of this debauchery, and reaching further than we can calculate.   It is getting to be

time to ask, Do our courts, our laws, our alms-houses and
our jails deal with the question presented?" Mr. Round
very aptly states a suggestive paragraph of Mr. Dugdale:
" He had sometimes a moment of scorn for the hurrying
crowd who will not stop and think about the problems
with which their lives and interests are entangled. It was
but the longing of the true reformer for sympathy and help
that made him once cry out: I am informed that twenty-
eight thousand dollars was raised in two days to purchase a
rare collection of antique jewelry and bronze recently discovered in classic ground forty feet below the *débris*. I
do not hear of as many pence being offered to fathom the
débris of our civilization — however rich the yield."

"The number of paupers in London in 1815 was about
what it was in 1875, although the population has increased
threefold, 100,000. But it cost about five times as much
and living is cheaper. This seems to mean that paupers
have better care, as demanded by the ideas of what is necessary in the classes above them in the social scale."

> Riis', "How the Other Half Lives"; facts relating to New York
> City.
> Mulhall, "Dictionary of Statistics: Pauperism."
> D. A. Wells, "Recent Economic Changes," p. 334 and 414.

2. **The Moral Cost of Dependency** cannot be measured
nor stated in figures; but it is this which is far more important than the cost in wealth. A rich country may long be
able to support a pauper population even larger than the
vast army we now endure; but it is absolutely intolerable
to think of the misery, the degradation, the moral hideous-
ness of these forlorn and depressed children of poverty.
Then consider the portentous fact that the men of these
classes can vote, and the vote of one of them counts with

the vote of the president of a college or of a railroad.   Consider further that pauperism leads on toward crime, prepares the nest out of which all loathsome diseases of body and soul are hatched, and that evil is contagious.   No marble walls can separate our children from the contaminating influence of pauperism.   In spite of the great mortality among dependents, they are so prolific that heredity has a chance to work on through many generations.   Before a degraded family has become extinct, its collateral lines replenish and recruit the host of incompetents.   There is not a community in the land but has an increasing stock of people in whose blood runs the corrupt tendencies of past weakness and depravity.   They count without facts who trust to the inherent and natural forces of society to root out this threatening element.   Meantime, while we wait for the slow and murderous processes of unassisted nature, millions suffer and inflict their evil upon us all, and transmit to their descendants and to ours a burden that menaces the very existence of the race.   A distinct type of man is forming among us, armed with all the power of universal suffrage, supported largely at the cost of the sober and industrious, who already have as much as they can do to sustain themselves in life's stern battle.

CHAPTER IV.

CLASSIFICATION AND SOCIAL AFFILIATIONS.

All the members of society may be classed, for the present purpose as, relatively, Progressive and Stationary or Retrogressive.

1. **The Progressive Class** includes, we may hope, a majority of the people of the United States. In all ordinary circumstances most families are self-supporting, self-respecting, law-abiding, industrious, and under the educational influences of schools, churches, newspapers and the public sentiment of Christian civilization. The majority of bread-winners not only support themselves, but a great army of social parasites of all kinds, the non-productive, idle classes, rich and poor.

2. **The Stationary or Retrogressive Class** may be divided into three sections : *a*) Dependents. These are persons who are unable or unwilling to support themselves without aid from others. Here belong helpless infants, infirm old people who are without means of subsistence, paupers of all grades and kinds. *b*) Defectives. These are also generally dependents, but are considered apart because of the nature and origin of their disability. *c*) Delinquents. In this section are placed for study all those who have forfeited their place in society by reason of violating laws which are designed to protect life, personal security, property and character. These are of all grades, from the passionate youth of respectable parentage who has been caught in a moment of sudden temptation and whirled along among thieves, to the confirmed instinctive criminal with whom robbery is a craft in which he finds pleasure and glory.

There is a very close and organic connection between these classes. They cannot be studied or treated as if they belonged in separate compartments with impervious walls between them. Very often one family will impose upon society the burden of degraded children who will be classed among dependents, defectives and delinquents. The feeble members will go to asylums for incurables, the women will

furnish recruits to the host of outcasts, the men will swell
the ranks of thieves and vagabonds.   In the last days, if
they reach old age, the county poor house shelters them all.
There are two paths open to members of each class, one
upward into the progressive class, and one downward into
lower depths of weakness, vice and misery.   The fact that
society is organically one body, with a common life, has
these two sides, dark and light.   These considerations show
that progressive members of society cannot ignore the retrogressive members.   The moral energies of evil are not
merely negative.   A cancer feeds on the body in which it
is rooted.   We cannot forget misery, and we cannot exter-
minate the wicked.   Even capital punishment settles
nothing.   If our humane sentiments permitted us to recur
to the severe penalties of old England before the days of
Elizabeth, and inflict the death penalty for begging, still we
should not reduce but increase the stock out of which
beggars grow.   The policy of letting pauperism alone is as
foolish and wicked as the policy under which the legal
punishment was a worse crime than the deed punished.

CHAPTER V.

STUDY OF TYPICAL CASES.

At this important point the book cannot supply material
for study.   All social studies must rest upon actual experience.   We must deal with concrete realities.

1. **Sources.**   We may, however, indicate how such typical cases may be sought and found.   Unfortunately there is

only too much clinical experience in every community. Those who are at all likely to use these chapters have already met more or less of destitution. Memory is a storehouse of facts, although they may be rudely thrown together and unrelated. This personal knowledge may be extended by visits with physicians to the poor, with friendly visitors of Associations of Charity, with investigators of local state aid to paupers, with pastors and Sunday School workers in towns and cities. In all communities of considerable population there are various institutions for the relief of the indigent. Those who are bent on thorough knowledge may pursue their studies by friendly visits among these lonely and miserable persons, doing good to them by conversation and eliciting from them stories of scientific importance.

2. **Kinds of cases to be sought.** *a*) Destitute children, foundlings, orphans, half-orphans, deserted children, children of vicious or criminal parents. Facts should be set down, but not in the sight of those who are directly interested, in respect to age, home surroundings, school, church relations of parents, origin (city or country), and as to parents, living or dead, and their conditions and character. *b*) Destitute adults. The questions asked by relief societies and charity investigators are usually important. These cover facts relating to age, nationality, heredity, occupation, income, number of children, dwelling, rent, references, and the immediate cause of dependency, as sickness, accident, inability to get work, sudden misfortune, old age, widowhood. It is also desirable to find out from all sources whether the case is recent or chronic. *c*) Defectives. These are usually found in special institutions. A careful study may be given to feeble minded children, deaf-mutes,

insane, blind, epileptic. The characteristics of each class should be noted.

Indexed note-books are of great value, and this value increases with years of observation. The authority for the facts, with dates, should be scrupulously set down with the name, and all statements should be sifted by rules of evidence applicable to the situation.

CHAPTER VI.

A STUDY OF THE CAUSES OF DEPENDENCY.

We should endeavor to discover in the phenomena of dependency all the discoverable forces which tend to depress certain members of society and to hinder their progress. We leave to psychology and philosophy the important questions relating to the use of the word "cause" in relation to human conduct. In this connection we mean by "causes" all those physical and moral facts which observation shows to be uniformly followed by certain results in character, conduct and condition. While we believe and insist that there is a vast difference between physical and moral causation, between the force of gravity and the stress of motive, yet we must recognize the pressure of forces, internal and external, which tend to produce morbid conditions and vicious conduct. We shall consider these causes under three heads: those which spring from heredity, from environment, and from the personal reaction on heredity and environment.

1. **Hereditary Causes of Depression.** There is a struggle for existence on the earth among all vegetables and

animals, and among kinds and races. Space is limited, and also means of subsistence; but the power of propagation has no limits. In this struggle for existence the "fittest survive;" that is, those which are best adapted to the environment; not always the highest and best absolutely. All vegetables and animals produce offspring which resemble them. "Conformity to type." There is also a perpetual tendency to variation. This is caused partly by external changes in the environment, partly by internal changes, by the interaction of external and internal forces, and by causes yet unknown or vaguely known. This tendency to vary is caused or assisted by natural selection, sexual selection, and artificial selection by the conscious efforts of man. There is also a tendency to revert to ancestral type (atavism). This is a brief summary of some of the most important forces with which we must count in studying pauperism.

With special reference to the morbid conditions which issue in insanity and pauperism, the words of Mercier may be quoted, while his work cited will furnish many illustrations. "The stability or instability of a person's highest nervous arrangements depends primarily and chiefly upon inheritance." The laws of inheritance are two: the law of Inheritance and the law of Sanguinity.)

The law of Inheritance: the offspring tend to inherit every attribute of the parents. An attribute which appeared in the parent at a certain time of life tends to appear in the offspring at a corresponding time of life. When the same attribute appears in several generations, but is not congenital, it may appear at an earlier stage in each successive generation. Attributes pertaining to one parent (especially those appearing later in life, when the reproductive function is active), tend to be produced in the offspring of that sex only. Attributes peculiar to one parent may be most apparent at one period of the life of the offspring, and those of the other at another. From the possession by the offspring of one attribute peculiar to one parent, we may infer the possession of other attributes peculiar to the same parent. When an attribute exists in an individual, is absent in his offspring, and reappears in the third or some subsequent generation, it is said to be latent in those generations in which it does not appear, and the individual in whom at length it appears is said to "revert," in so far as that attribute is concerned, to the ancestor in whom it was present.

The second law of Heredity : Sanguinity. "There are certain limits, on the one hand of similarity, and on the other of dissimilarity, between two individuals, between which limits only can the union of those individuals be fertile, and, in proportion as these limits are approached, the offspring deteriorates."

The following are the most important tentative generalizations of Mr. Dugdale in "The Jukes," relating to pauperism. "Pauperism is an indication of weakness of some kind, either youth, disease, old age, or injury, or, for women, childbirth." It is divisible into hereditary and induced pauperism. Hereditary pauperism rests chiefly upon disease in some form, tends to terminate in extinction, and may be called the sociological aspect of physical degeneration. The debility and diseases which enter most largely in its production are the result of sexual licentiousness. Pauperism in old age, especially in the meridian of life, indicates a hereditary tendency which may or may not be modified by the environment. Pauperism follows men more frequently than women, indicating a decided tendency to hereditary pauperism. The different degrees of adult pauperism, from out-door relief to alms-house charity, indicate, in the main, different gradations of waning vitality. In this light the whole question is opened up, whether indolence, which the dogmatic aphorism says "is the root of all evil," is not, after all, a mark of under vitalization, and an effect which acts only as a secondary cause."

"Running alongside of licentiousness, and as inseparable from it as illegitimacy, are the diseases which are distinctive of it and which produce social phenomena which are the direct subjects of the present investigation. In the wake of disease follows pauperism, so in studying the one we must discuss the other. But disease treats of physiological states; it is a biological question; therefore, the social questions included in the consideration of pauperism rest, in large measure, upon the data furnished by the study of vital force. Lines of intermarriage between "Jukes" show a minimum of crime. Pauperism preponderates in the consanguineous lines." Since intermarriage of those who possess morbid states in common tends to increase those diseased conditions in the offspring, it follows that the marriage of "Jukes" would produce feeble paupers, while intermarriage with outside stock would furnish more vigorous offspring, who would enter crime careers. The weak members of a degenerate stock take to mendicancy, the stronger to crime.

The tendency to revert to past conditions must be noticed. The great historic fact of morals and spiritual life is that man has had to come up from a very lowly state. Theology may call it depravity and anthropology name it savage and barbarous culture. Both describe the same humble level above which, at great cost, man has been slowly

educated and lifted. Many writers of the eighteenth century, before the teachings of Darwinism dissipated the
dream, taught a different story. No anthropologist of our
day would write as did J. J. Rousseau : "The fundamental
principle of all morality, on which all the reasonings of my
writings are based . . . is that man is a being naturally
good, loving justice and order; that there is no original
perversity in the human heart, and that the first movements
of nature are always right."[1] Man has only by degrees
attained morality and become conscious of the ideal possibilities of his nature. It is the late conquest of these
ideals which gives promise of more rapid advance in the
future.

The question whether "acquired characteristics" are
inherited is in dispute among biologists, and therefore it
must be regarded as an open question among sociologists.
But no practical measure will be greatly affected by the controversy. Perhaps if Weissmann's theory comes to be
accepted, more stress will be laid upon environment than
upon heredity.

On the question whether acquired characteristics are
inherited see :

Weissman, "Essays on Heredity and Kindred Biological Sub-
jects." 2 vols.
Sully, "The Human Mind." Vol. I., p. 138.
Pflüger; "Ueber den Einfluss der Schwercraft," etc. Archiv. f.
Physiol. Bnd., xxxii, 1883 (referred to by Weissmann).
Strahan, "Marriage and Disease." Ch. iii.
J. Arthur Thomson, "The History and Theory of Heredity." 1889,
(with bibliography).
Neo - Darwinism and Neo - Lamarckism, by Lester F. Ward, 1891.
G. J. Romanes in *Con. Rev.* Vol. 57, 1890.
Many articles in *Amer. Naturalist* and other periodicals.

---

[1] Compare Le Play, *Economie Sociale*, ch. 1.

2. **Environment.** A second class of causes may be summed up under the head "*Environment.*"

A person not only inherits internal characteristics, but is born into a world of external forces, which act upon him from the beginning to the end. A member of a feeble stock generally enters upon the estate of the poor and suffers from their environment.

(*a*) Inorganic environment. Dependency is affected by the quality of soil and the nature of the climate. The "Jukes" did not own fat lands. The habits of mendicants in sunny southern lands are different from those in the rigorous northern countries. The northern winter season is the time when multitudes pass over the line which places a family among the suppliants of charity.

(*b*) Organic. Dependency is affected by the quantity and quality of the vegetable and animal products of the habitat. Dearth, famine, excessive rainfall, late and early frosts, floods, grasshoppers and other insect devastators, diseases among domestic animals, are all causes of temporary appeals for help. After great and general calamities many persons are found to trade upon sympathy who had heretofore supported themselves.

It must not be forgotten that while the earth modifies man it may also be modified by man.

On this subject one may read :

Buckle's "History of Civilization in England."
Malthus' "Essay on Population."
Bonar's "Malthus."
Criticism of Malthus, by H. George in "Progress and Poverty."
Guyot's "Earth and Man."
Marsh, "The Earth as Modified by Human Action."

On these causes see :

Ritchie, "Darwinism and Politics."
Mercier, "Sanity and Insanity."

A. G. Warner, "Statistical Determination of the Causes of Poverty"
in Am. Statistic. Ass. Rep., 1889, and Johns Hopkins Studies
No. 7, July, 1889.
Strahan, "Marriage and Disease."
Dugdale, "The Jukes."
Darwin's "Animals and Plants Under Domestication," "Origin of
Species," "Descent of Man."
H. Spencer, "Biology."
Th. Ribot, "Heredity."
Walter Bagehot, "Physics and Politics."
Oscar Schmidt, "The Theory of Darwinism and Descent."

ᕽ (*c*) The Social Environment. A bare analysis will suggest the essential facts : the works referred to will furnish
illustrations.

ᕽ *A*. Domestic.

The housing of the poor is a prolific source of beggary,
and it is a remediable evil.   Where the rooms are too few
and too small for cleanliness, health, vigor, privacy, we find
the nidus for hatching the egg of pauperism.

Riis, "How the Other Half Lives," closing chapters.
Jahrbücher für Nationalökonomie und Stat., March, 1892, p. 431.

Illegitimate children often inherit a diseased and enfeebled body, but their worst curse, if they survive infancy, is
the "environment of neglect."

> "We quarreled like brutes, and who wonders ?
> What self - respect could we keep,
> Worse housed than your hacks and your pointers,
> Worse fed than your hogs and your sheep ?
>
> Our daughters with base - born babies
> Have wandered away in their shame ;
> If your misses had slept, squire, where they did,
> Your misses might do the same."
> C. KINGSLEY'S "The Bad Squire."

Demoralized homes, misruled by contentious, drunken,
immoral parents, cast their children upon the world as beg-

gars or as plunderers. The family is the unit of society, and its conduct determines the conditions of the future race. The evil example of parents, their idleness, vice and crime, help to break down the barriers against the motives which tend to produce dependents. The divorce of parents frequently leaves a weak woman to carry the burden of the children. For generally it is the man who deserts the post of duty. The misfortunes of parents, as sickness, accident, and enfeebled old age, swell the volume of dependency. But society could easily care for all such cases if they stood alone — as they never do.

B. Educational defects are to be charged with a great part of the cost of pauperism.

In a country where common schools abound, mere illiteracy may soon become a very small factor. But the average child must be trained to work at some useful art or become an anti-social or extra-social being. Idleness means licentiousness, and this means feebleness. Inefficiency excludes from employment and produces the tramp class. The mere absence of kindergartens, kitchen gardens, sloyd, manual training, and technical schools is a source of social peril.

See works on Manual Training, by C. H. Ham and C. M. Woodward.

C. Industrial conditions favorable to the increase of dependency. Here must be considered the nature of the occupation and its tendency to increase sickness and mortality. Some callings expose their members to accident and disease. One of every twelve trainmen in the United States is injured each year. Dusty trades tend to produce lung diseases. In certain occupations periodical idleness is inevitable, and this acts upon the habits of industry and on the family income and domestic life.

Billings, "Vital and Medical Statistics."

11th Census, Bulletin 100.

Körösi, "Sterblichkeit der Stadt Budapest in den Jahren, 1876-1881, und deren Ursachen."

New Jersey Bureau of Labor Statistics, 1889, Part I, on "Health and Trade-Life of Workmen."

Travers Twiss, " Tests of a Thriving Population."

Dwight Porter, "A Sanitary Inspection of certain Tenement House Districts of Boston."

Chapin, " Preventable Causes of Poverty," *Forum*, June, 1889.

"Class-Mortality Statistics," Jour. Royal Stat. Soc., June, 1887.

Newsholme, " Elements of Vital Statistics."

Grimshaw, Reports as Registrar General of Ireland.

Prof. H. C. Adams, " The Slaughter of Railway Employés," *Forum*, June, 1892.

But industrial conditions may increase pauperism in less direct ways.

The principle is this: All economic disorder or loss, local and general, tends to increase dependency. At this point sociology waits on political economy to determine what those conditions are.

Here may be considered :

The excess of population as compared with the means of subsistence. Matthew Arnold says that children are not " sent," they are made.

See Malthus' "Essay," J. S. Mill, Cairnes, and other standard works on Political Economy; and the other side in Henry George's " Poverty and Progress."

The absence of organization among wage receivers. " Organized labor is now beyond the reach of poverty. Pauperism is recruited from the ranks of unorganized labor. The labor question touches pauperism only through the unemployed and unorganized." (Prof. Tucker).

The undue congestion of population in large communities, a result of the use of machinery, division of labor, and many other causes, the rhythmic alternations of demand for labor and of enforced idleness, changes in industry by improvement of machinery, by transfer of vast commercial and manufacturing concerns to other centers, by specialization of industries, by the employment of women and children in place of men are to be counted here.

D. Causes of Dependency arising from defects in Government and in social institutions sustained by law. While slavery has been abolished in America its effects linger. Customs and sentiments remain over from the age of slavery, together with economic disadvantages, which hold down many, white and black, in North and South, whose ancestors slavery cursed. The tendency of slavery is not only to rob the slave of his earnings and to debase him, but also to reduce the reward of free laborers to those of the level of slave labor, to discourage skill and invention, and to make useful toil disreputable.

While we have no standing army in the United States we are expending enough money on war expenses, in the form of debt, interest and pensions, in time of peace, to support a great standing army. This is not said by way of criticism, but to suggest one of the causes of dependency, since all expenses of government must ultimately be paid out of the product of painful industry. The war system of Europe sends its impoverished, crippled, pauperized victims to our shores for support. Unwise interference with freedom of trade has often brought on crises attended with great suffering and degradations. For an example see Manzoni's "I Promessi Sposi," ch. xxviii.

Where government has lowered the value of its coins, or dishonored its promises to pay real money, destitution has always followed. The failure of government to protect life, liberty, property and character has been attended by economic difficulties in which the weaker members of society suffer first and most. Capital is timid. Most laborers must work all the time in order to live. Enterprise is frightened and crippled by ignorant financial legislation. The effects strike deep into society. Unwise state subsidies to private charities increase pauperism directly and indirectly.

See Mrs. Lowell's "Report on the Care of Dependent Children in the State of New York and Elsewhere." 1890. Ward, Dynamic Sociology, Vol. I., p. 519.

It is manifest that any oppressive customs or laws relating to land tenure or taxation must reduce many to a condition of poverty and increase the liability to pauperism and crime. The actual effects of various social and industrial usages and laws on these points are subjects upon which economic science must speak the final word.

Professor Tucker gives these references to the subject :

Communal Land Tenure : Wallace's Russia, chapter on the " Mir."
Ashley's " Economic History," chapter on the Manor and Village Community.
Parliamentary reports on the English system of landlord and tenant.
On holding land under mortgage in the U. S. *Political Science Quar.* Sept. 1889.
And. Rev. Sept. 1890.
State Reports.
On Land Nationalization : H. George, " Progress and Poverty."
Rae, " Contemporary Socialism."
Laveleye, *Co. Rev.* Nov. 1881
G. Gunton, *Forum,* March, 1887.
W. T. Harris, *Forum,* July, 1887.
Herbert Spencer in " Justice " modifies his early views on the nationalization of land. See "A Perplexed Philosopher" for Mr. George's account of the phases of Mr. Spencer's doctrine.

E. Moral causes of dependency. All vicious and corrupting customs in society provide a depressing environ

ment. The luxury and vices of the rich tend to destroy
the hopes and morality of the less favored.   Adam Smith,
John S. Mill and Kingsley have shown the absurdity and
mischief of the maxim that the wastefulness of the rich is
the advantage of the poor.   The spendthrift who " causes
money to circulate," and gives employment to the poor in
ministering to his sensual delight or extravagant habits,
does harm, while the enlightened miser does good by putting his hoards to productive use.   The ostentatious children of luxury make the poor discontented with toil and
eager to " enjoy life."   We shall mention later those moral
causes which are personal rather than part of the environment.

> Adam Smith, " Wealth of Nations."
> J. S. Mill, Political Economy.
> C. Kingsley, " Alton Locke."

F. Corruptions in the Church aggravate the evils of
dependency.   An apathetic and formal church rays out
darkness instead of light.   Men stumble over a lamp that
is not lighted to direct their steps.   A selfish church, without enthusiasm for humanity, more intent on defending a
philosophy than on being a blessing to men, divided up
into classes, with sharp lines drawn to distinguish the strata
of culture and wealth, is sure to make it more hard for the
weak to rise in the world.   The hope of the worst lies in
loving contact with the best.   The church is rendered incompetent to deal with pauperism and kindred evils by its
sectarian divisions.   While there is a great and growing
unity of feeling and sentiment among Christians that is
truly hopeful, it has never as yet found adequate expression
in organized and effective action.   It is weak through its
division and lack of a common agency for centralizing its
forces.

See article on the " Municipal Church," by Washington Gladden, in *Review of Reviews*, October, 1892. One bane of church charity is its indiscriminate, emotional, unreasoning, unscientific almsgiving. Its benevolence is often maleficent rather than beneficent. Sectarian almsgiving, a sort of ecclesiastical (I refuse to say religious) bribery, is to blame for the pauperization of many a family in our cities. Missions vie with each other for the opportunity of destroying the self-respect and self-help of poor families, by distributing old clothes and fitful supplies of groceries, while they refuse persistently to coöperate through the Association of Charities in wise measures for exterminating the cursed disease of pauperism.

Mere ecclesiasticism, as distinguished from religious philanthropy, often multiplies institutions as monuments of their glory, to the detriment of the very classes they are honestly meant to help. The ministry, as natural leaders of social reforms on the side of charity, need what few educational institutions have until recently attempted to supply, a thorough training in the methods of social science. They who look at these subjects from a single point of view, as law, or ethics, or religion, or political science, or economics, must blunder by defect. All society must move together if these diseases of the social body are to be thoroughly healed.

G. Immigration adds to the volume of dependency in the United States.

Too great and rapid influx of foreigners, even of a good character, presses laboring men to the wall by direct competition. A gentle rain long continued will enrich a meadow, while a flood after a storm-burst will ruin the soil with gullies and sand. If laborers are imported in great numbers under contract to work at lower than current wages, these evils become insufferable. And if the immigrants are accustomed to a very low standard of living, competition with them in the labor market exercises its most destructive influence. Strikes follow. The families that had reached a moderate social condition are depressed, and their places are taken by a horde of people who supply our prisons and alms-houses with inmates, and who soon become themselves lawless and restless under government. The excessive importation of laborers " renders nugatory all the efforts of labor organizations to increase wages by strikes or combinations."

Statistics show the extent to which dependency and crime in this country are increased by the influx of undesirable elements, but they cannot reveal the suffering caused by the competition of industrious people with those accustomed to a lower standard of living, and by the struggles and fears of the effort to remain self-supporting.

Dr. M. B. Anderson (N. C. C., 1876) treated the subject of the ethical and political principles involved and the social effects of immigration in relation to the dependent and other unsocial classes.

" First. A nation is a moral organism which owes certain duties to its members, and to which its members owe certain duties in return. The bond between government and subject is a reciprocal one. Therefore, every citizen or subject is bound to maintain by his property, and defend by his life, the government, which extends to him its protection ; and, on the other hand, by the common practice of civilized peoples, the government assumes the care of its subjects when they are unable to care for themselves.

Second. This obligation of a nation towards its dependent classes cannot be transferred to another without that other's consent. Commercial nations recognize this principle in their provisions through the consular system for the care of shipwrecked, discharged or disabled seamen. The foreign consuls of civilized nations provide for their maintenance, and return them to their homes.

Third. It is clearly an offense against the comity of nations for any government, national or municipal, to throw the burden of caring for its dependent population upon any foreign country. But it has been proved beyond all question, that both foreign municipalities and foreign nations have provided, at the public expense, for the transportation of considerable numbers of their pauper class to the United States. It is beyond all question that paupers and criminals, in considerable numbers, have been sent to the United States by their relatives.

Fourth. A nation becomes bound to support a foreign-born pauper only through his naturalization. Naturalization involves a reciprocal contract. The naturalized party repudiates his allegiance to the country in which he was born, and takes upon himself all the obligations of a citizen. He becomes bound to pay taxes according to his ability, and, if necessary, to serve in the army or navy against domestic or foreign enemies; but an alien is free from a large measure of these obligations, and the state, on its part, comes under no obligation to maintain him, if he becomes dependent.

The American sailor or resident living in England, who becomes a pauper, appeals naturally and rightfully to his own consul for protection and aid. There is no reason in the nature of the case why we should maintain paupers who are subjects of Great Britain or Germany, who are landed upon our shores in a dependent condition, or in such a state of mental or bodily health that they must necessarily become dependent. We are no more bound, apart from the general law of humanity, to maintain such persons than we are to pay the interest on the English national debt, or furnish conscripts for the German army."

R. M. Smith, "Emigration and Immigration." Full bibliography at end.

N. C. C., from 1879, especially 1887, and 1891.

Dr. Dana's paper, Amer. Social Science Ass'n, 1888.

3. Personal Causes of Dependency.—This is not the place for a discussion on "freedom of will." That belongs to psychology and philosophy. It is sufficient for our present purpose to accept the statement of one who, contrary to the view held by the writer, teaches that "if the universe is the theater of law, freedom is a delusion." There is no such conflict between freedom and law, either in human government or in the general government of the moral universe. No advocate of freedom claims that one can choose outside of the alternatives offered in experience. "No mind is free till it becomes free. . . . Moral freedom, if possessed at all, is gained only after a certain psychical development has been gone through." (Ladd, Introduction to Philosophy, p. 298). Liberty of choice with us is not infinite but limited. Heredity and environment present the only objects of possible selection. But the choice of man counts for something in the preference of motives and the direction of attention. Even Mr. Ward, in his attack on the doctrine of freedom, says: "The will is an effect as well as a cause." We say the will is a cause as well as an effect. Compare Ward, "Dynamic Sociology, Vol. I, p. 50, with James Martineau, "Types of Ethical Theory." The question is of practical importance, because measures directed to the restoration of the dependents who have any power of initiative left must appeal to the sense of ability to start afresh and be self-determining.

The vices which cause pauperism are personal traits. The chief of such vices are indolence, fitfulness of industry, neglect of prudence and thrift, nomadic unsocial habits, intemperance, gluttony, sexual excesses and abuses, lawlessness in relation to rights of property and person. These characteristics are aggravated by hereditary and environing causes, and we may never be able to measure statistically the part of each element in a vice, but in all ordinary persons the element of personal responsibility must be regarded as real.

Conclusion.—All these causes are interwoven. Society is an organism in which each member is, reciprocally, means and end. A depressing physical environment, as an unhealthy tenement house, produces disease and weakness; this reduces earning power; and the lowering of wages means dependence. Low wages give inferior clothing and food, and defective house-room; close contact increases immorality; and all work together to destroy self-respect and self-help. The causes of destruction move in a vicious circle. The doctrine of I Corinthians, chapter xii, quoted on the title page of Schäffle's great work, is sound and necessary.

F. H. Wines, N. C. C., 1886, p. 206, and 1890, p. 68,

CHAPTER VII.

GENERAL PRINCIPLES RELATING TO THE TREATMENT OF DEPENDENCY.

1. **The social ideal** or purpose which should govern this treatment. The end determines the method. If the pur-

pose is not comprehensive and lofty the means will be
narrow and inadequate.   If we are to invent methods we
must keep before us the object of the invention.

> "I hold you will not compass your poor ends
> Of barley - feeding and material ease,
> Without a poet's individualism
> To work your universal.   It takes a soul
> To move a body; it takes a high - souled man
> To move the masses . . . . . even to a cleaner stye;
> It takes the ideal, to blow a hair's breath off
> The dust of the actual . . . . .
> Life develops from within."   MRS. BROWNING, "Aurora Leigh."

To merely feed and clothe the poor is to treat them as
animals and to treat ourselves as soulless things..   The
ideals of the "Kingdom of God," as presented in the
words and actions of Jesus, are coming to be regarded as
inclusive of all physical, intellectual, moral and eternal
good for all men.   The problems of caring for the poor
are simply parts of the great purpose which runs through
the ages.   Society as a whole cannot move forward while
the feeble members lag behind.   And society cannot cultivate the most refined nature while it witnesses without sympathy or rational effort to help the miseries of a great multitude of the less favored of its brotherhood.   To the ideal
aim of the Divine Kingdom of fraternity, all arts, all sciences
contribute.   Sociology is simply the name for the philosophy of the movement in that direction.

2. Comprehensiveness.   We must avoid riding hobbies to
the extent of forgetting the labors of others who toil in
different fields from our own.   All the causes of dependency must be studied and considered.   In the previous
chapter we have endeavored to analyze these causes.

All the remedial methods which promise good must be

thoughtfully considered, and a method found for securing unity, harmony, and efficiency of action.   Dr. Flint in his "Practice of Medicine" has an analysis of the remedial methods of the healing art : " Prophylactic, abortive, curative, palliative, sanitary, hygienic, sustaining." The titles are very suggestive for us.

3. Analysis. From time to time the students of Charity and Correction, and the public agents of aid and reformation, should carefully analyze the classes of dependents for whom relief is sought. These classes should be located and measured, and the extent and nature of need should be published for the information of citizens.   This is the end sought by the great charitable organizations, by the state and national boards and bureaus, and such agencies deserve the support and attention of all citizens of influence.

4. Order of discussion.   In considering the complex problems of charity we may adopt an order based on these classes who are in need, or on the kinds of social institutions provided for their care.   Convenience of discussion requires that we follow now one now the other of these plans.

CHAPTER VIII.

THE RATIONAL GROUNDS OF STATE CARE OF DEPENDENTS.

This is a question much debated by able men all over the civilized world.

1. Objections to state aid. There is the view of men who oppose aid to dependents by the state on theoretical and on practical grounds. It is said that the function of the state is to protect rights: that each social form has a special and peculiar function and does its best work when it does not attempt functions to which it is not adapted. It is also said that in practice state help is injurious. State charity is collected by taxation and is not a free gift. The tendency of the state system of helping the poor is to repress sympathy of individuals by removing occasion for its immediate exercise. Compulsory state aid interferes with the wholesome efforts of nature to weed out the inferior and incompetent in the struggle for existence. The official poor law prevents the weak from adapting themselves to social conditions through the discipline of hardship and effort. State charity does not diminish but increases the sum total of human suffering. "Out of a given population, the greater the number living on the bounty of others, the smaller must be the number living by labor; and the smaller the number living by labor, the smaller must be the production of food and other necessaries, the greater must be the distress."

There are others who would limit the state care to indoor relief while they would not deny other forms of help to the poor from a state treasury.

See Herbert Spencer, "Social Statics," and "Man vs. the State," ed. 1892, p. 144.

W. G. Sumner, "What Social Classes Owe to each Other."

Thomas Chalmers, "The Christian and Civic Economy of Large Towns."

Ratzinger, "Geschichte der kirchlichen Armenwesen," ed. 1884, S. 541.

Herzog, "Realencyclopædia," Art. "Armenpflege."

Naville, "De la Charité legale."

Emminghaus, "Das Armenwesen und die Armengesetzgebung in den Europaischen Staaten."

2. **Arguments in favor of state aid.** Those who favor state relief found their argument upon various considerations of interest and duty. It has been said that the state should provide for cases of extreme distress in order to avoid revolutions stirred by desperate men, and to diminish the petty and annoying attacks upon property which arise from distress. The moral ground of state help is sometimes stated in this way: "The hospitals (of Illinois) are entirely free; there is no charge to any individual; on the ground that when a taxpayer pays his tax to maintain the institution, he is entitled to the benefits of the institution if the occasion ever arises." (F. H. Wines, N. C. C. 1875, p. 22).

This assumes that the state is the organ of society for its own convenience, and that citizens generally support it and are entitled to its advantages. Others teach that the members of society are under obligations to assist each other in misfortune and misery; that the state is the only institution through which society can effectually manifest its sympathy and fostering care; and that on this ground state care is to be based. "Every society upon arriving at a certain stage of civilization finds it positively necessary for its own sake, that is to say, for the satisfaction of its own humanity, and for the due performance of the purposes for which societies exist, to provide that no person, no matter what has been his life, or what may be the consequences, shall perish for want of the bare necessaries of existence." Fowle, "The Poor Law," p. 10. J. S. Mill, "Political Economy:" "It will be admitted to be right that human beings should help one another, and the more so in proportion to the urgency of the need, and none need help so urgently as one who is starving."

"The claim to help, therefore, created by destitution is one of the strongest which can exist, and there is *prima facie* the amplest reason for making the relief of so extreme an exigency as certain to those who require it as by any arrangements of society it can be made."

It is sometimes said that state charity, since it is collected by taxation and enforced by government, is not charity. This is only in part true. Those who are unwilling to be taxed for this purpose of course have no claim to the title of benevolence. But there is a diffused sentiment of humanity in a society which votes taxes for these purposes. The humane institutions which are supported in consequence of popular votes are witnesses to the existence of such sentiments of sympathy and philanthropy. On the other hand, even personal gifts to the distressed and indigent are sometimes the result of selfish considerations rather than of genuine humanity.

3. Conclusion. Assuming that the members of society are under obligations to aid the unfortunate and feeble, it does not follow that this ought to be done through the state. All that follows is, that we should choose the most prudent and suitable method to effect the end. The state is not the only organ of society. It is necessary, therefore, to study inductively and deductively the results of past and present experience and to propose improvements after this study.

CHAPTER IX.

STATE CHARITIES : — OUTDOOR RELIEF.

"Indoor relief" is that which is administered in an institution, as in a poor house, while "outdoor relief" is administered in the homes of the indigent.

1. **Historical and Comparative.** It is not within the plan of this introduction to discuss the ancient forms of charity in the Roman, Greek, Hebrew, and early Christian states. As Mr. Sanborn illustrates in his article on Pauperism (Lalor's Cyclopædia), the problem is not new. The attempts to mitigate the miseries of extreme poverty have initiated all kinds of experiments.

In the Middle Ages were founded many church institutions for the care of the poor, many of which are still in existence. The monasteries were refuges of those in trouble. The Church was the chief almoner of mercy. The breaking up of the monasteries, and the ecclesiastical divisions of Protestantism, together with the new theories of rights of the laity, made it impossible for the Church to administer the charity of modern Europe. During the modern period each country has worked out its problem in its own way.

In Greece, with its mild climate and low standard of comfort for the laborer, pauperism is not a serious matter for society. "In Greece, with a population of more than 2,000,000, about as many as Massachusetts contains, there is, in fact, no public charity at all, or so little as to be practically of no account. . . . All that is done in this way comes from endowments of wealthy persons, or subscriptions yearly made by the benevolent, the national government occasionally giving a piece of land or remitting a tax for the benefit of these private charities, but granting no subsidy, and never appropriating a yearly sum for regular expenses of support and relief. There is a strong opposition, on the part of the endowed and private charities, to any action by the public authorities in the direction of voting public money or assuming the oversight of indoor and outdoor relief. It seems to be feared that political interference with the private charities would be the result of state action, and that the care of the poor would become a part of the political machinery, and be less wisely managed than now."

F. H. Sanborn, N. C. C., '90.

In Italy the tendency is different.   The government has for several years been assuming the control of all church and endowed charities.   It has determined to unify the work of beneficence, and to limit their abuses and to stop begging.   The systems of private and church charity in Italy have broken down, have failed to diminish suffering, have increased a shameless pauperism, and the state has been compelled to assume control.

Papers of Mr. F. H. Sanborn, N. C. C., 1890, '91.
Journal des Economistes Oct. 1889.   *Nuova Antologia*, May, 1891.

In Germany we see a system of state organized private charity.   Relief is furnished by the state and administered by the state, but private persons are required to give their time and service in caring for the peculiar wants of each case.   The "Elberfeld System" is the type of the German principle.

Forum, Dec. 1892.
Schönberg's Handbuch Pol. Ökonomie, Art.   "Armenwesen."
Emminghaus' "Das Armenwensen." N. C. C. 1891, p. 167.
Jahrbuch fur Gesetzgebung, 1892, p. 187.

The French system does not provide state funds for the poor to the extent that is done in Germany.   "No one can do anything except through state machinery.   Private charity supplies the funds, and the state machinery administers them.   Indoor relief is restricted as far as possible; families are encouraged to take care of their own poor."

D. O. Kellogg, *Atlantic Mag.*, May, 1883.
Maurice Block, "Dictionnaire Administrative Française."

We note one tendency common to Italy, France, and Germany — the assumption by the state of control over all private and ecclesiastical charities. History shows reasons for this tendency. Private charity may create a demand for help which burdens the state with the load of the demoralized products of conflicting, irregular, and indiscriminating almsgiving. From sheer necessity the modern states have been compelled to have oversight of personal charity.

A principle early adopted in various European countries was that the local parish is responsible for the poor of that district. Two regulations seemed to follow logically from this principle, and they were tried on a large scale: that no person liable to become dependent should be permitted to secure a residence in a new parish, and that no person should marry without giving the poor authorities proof that he was able to support his family. The first of these regulations prevented the free movement of labor: a poor man out of employment in one district could not go to a place where his labor was likely to be needed. This increased dependency. This rule worked hardship to indigent strangers who fell sick in a place; the duty of providing for him was avoided lest he gain a residence, and he was liable to be carried off, at risk of his life, to his own parish. The other rule tended to demoralize the family. The poor authorities might prevent the marriage of those whom they regarded as too poor to marry, but they could not prevent illegitimate births. Both regulations were abandoned or modified.

Art. "Armenwesen," Schönberg's Handbuch der Pol. Ökon.

The English poor laws are of great interest to Americans, because they have so largely influenced our legislation and customs. After the breaking up of the monasteries, where misery found an asylum, the people began to respond to the calls of distress. Then legislators gave attention to beggary, which had become defiant and impudent. During the past thousand years English history notices the attempt of law and custom to relieve or repress beggars. Many of the statutes were cruel beyond belief and as inefficient as they were harsh. The sturdy solicitors of alms were sometimes made bloody with the lash and sometimes enslaved. But in the sixteenth century milder laws were enacted. It was decreed during the reign of Elizabeth that the parish officers should "gently solicit" help for the poor, and if this did not secure the necessary amount, the parson should exhort and admonish, and if these measures failed the jail was opened for the froward and obstinate miser. Later legislation of the time of Elizabeth is the real foundation of the poor laws which are copied in America.

> Art. "Pauperism," Lalor's Cyclopædia.
> Fowle or Aschrott on the English Poor Law.
> Nicholl's History of the English Poor Law.
> Eden's State of the Poor.
> Loch, "Charity Organization."

The limits and scope of this work do not admit a historical sketch of ancient charities.

For the charities of the Christian Church the following works may be used:

> R. S. Storrs, "The Divine Origin of Christianity Indicated by its Historical Effects."
> C. L. Brace, "Gesta Christi."
> Pfleiderer, "Philosophy of History," Vol. 3.
> The Church Histories of Fisher, Neander, Schaff.
> Uhlhorn's "Christian Charity in the Ancient Church."
> Bingham's "Antiquities."
> Schmidt, "The Social Results of Early Christianity."
> "Teachings of the Twelve Apostles," Ch. I.

On Hebrew Charities, consult :

Ewald's "Antiquities."
Schürer's "The Jewish People in the Time of Jesus Christ."

On the Roman method of caring for the poor, consult:

Niebuhr, Arnold, Mommsen.
De Coulanges, "The Ancient City."

2. Outdoor Official Relief.—Arguments on both sides. No subject has caused more discussion and revealed wider differences of judgment among enlightened and benevolent persons.

a) The case stated in favor of outdoor public relief of dependent families and persons. It is argued that the duty of caring for the poor of the community is common to all, and that the burden should be shared by all. This is impossible unless the fund for charity is raised by taxation. Under this system each contributes according to his wealth. It is also claimed that the agency of the state can secure more thorough investigation and prevent imposition ; that the charities of the state, indoor and outdoor, ought to be included under one harmonious and complete system in order to secure efficiency and economy ; that great public misfortunes cannot be relieved by private charity ; that vagrant beggars cannot be controlled by private agencies, but must be under police supervision ; that in Europe Church and private charity, in both Catholic and Protestant countries, has broken down, and there the State has been compelled to take charge of measures of relief ; that we cannot as yet depend upon personal charities to care for all the poor at all times, benevolence being fitful, unsystematic and local ; that there would be much indiscriminate almsgiving if it was not known that the most desperate cases would surely be provided for by the state.

b) On the other hand it is claimed by those who would abolish outdoor public relief: that it is unnecessary, since private charity would meet all needs if it were known that taxation for this purpose could not be expected; that official relief is too costly, since those who administer it do not feel the sacrifice of giving; that the existence of a public fund invites political corruption; that the system separates the poor from the successful, and reduces the social bond to the single point where the pauper meets the paid officer of state charity; that the system extinguishes benevolence in the rich and gratitude in the poor; that it fosters communistic sentiments, and educates the poor to regard the state treasury as the natural source of their livelihood; that it tends to lower wages, since the assisted pauper can afford to work at a lower rate than his unassisted poor neighbor; that it tends to excite hostility against the state, since it awakens hopes which no government can meet; that it tends to make many citizens depend on the community more than on their own energy, foresight and economy, and so demoralizes and pauperizes them; and that by producing idleness it increases misery by reducing the sum of commodities which can be enjoyed.

c) Judgment of the case. We are obliged to deal with a relatively permanent fact, that outdoor official relief is a part of our social custom, side by side with voluntary beneficence. Both forms of relief are liable to abuses. Church and private charity in Italy and France produced increasing beggary, and the same evils grew to unbearable proportions under the poor law of England. The worst evils are due more to the character of the people, and to existing social forces and opportunities, than to any particular system of relief. At present it is a question of administration, and practical measures must be directed to the improvement of methods of administration. With a reformed poor law England was able to diminish its pauperism while continuing outdoor official relief.

See N. C. C. 1891 and 1890.

Mrs. C. R. Lowell on "The Economical and Moral Effects of Public Outdoor Relief."

Mr. Seth Low, N. C. C. 1879.

3. **Principles of administration** of outdoor official relief.

a) As to officials. These are either county or township or municipal. Very generally in the North the county commissioners control the expenditure, and township trustees act as almoners with considerable power and often little responsibility. The German experience should teach us that all boards of control should be unsalaried persons of repute in the community, appointed and not elected. Their agents should be appointed upon a fixed salary, and should continue in office during good behavior, since experience is of great value. All boards should be composed of persons of both parties, so as to be non-partisan. Local charities should be inspected by state agents of the central board. b) The modes of assessing, collecting, disbursing and auditing funds should be governed by general laws. c) Recipients should be residents. Help to non-residents, aided in time of exigency by local authorities, is to be charged to the county of residence or to the commonwealth. Immigration of paupers from one district to another by aid of authorities should be prevented by common agreement and legislation. d) The forms of application and regulations as to investigation and records are to be fixed by state laws. Aid should be given in articles of primary necessity, as food, fuel and clothing. Never is it safe to give money, and seldom general orders. In cities medical attendance and medicines are necessities to be furnished by the poor authorities if not otherwise provided. Often these are supplied by private institutions. It is seldom well to give money for rent, and never to set up in business or buy tools. "The fundamental principle with respect to the relief of the poor is, that the condition of the pauper ought to be, on the whole, less eligible than that of the independent laborer." The poorest independent laborer ought not to be worse off than the pauper he helps, and the pauper himself should not be rewarded for depending on the exertions of others. e) Repressive measures. It is necessary first of all to make the nearest relatives of a dependent person feel the responsibility of his care. The prospect of the poor house for those who are unwilling to work when able, and the manifestation of social reaction against unsocial pauperism are desirable in the limitation of dependency. But cure and not revenge must control repressive measures. State officials do well to coöperate with private charities and associated efforts to correct abuses. Benevolent societies often care for curable cases, and leave the hopeless paupers to the county authorities.

CHAPTER X.

MEDICAL CHARITIES.

These forms of philanthropic effort are very necessary, and they are as little abused as any. Sickness or accident may disable the most industrious and honorable person.

1. **Hospitals.** *a*) Mode of support. A hospital may be supported by the state or city, by corporations of benevolent persons, by endowments, by subsidies from the public

treasury to private institutions, and partly by fees received from those able to pay. All these methods are actually in use. It is a serious question whether a city should ever subsidize a private or church hospital. The danger of scandal is great. Hospitals may continue to exist which are not needed because the subsidy keeps them alive. For the Brooklyn experience see N. C. C., 1890, p. 177. *b*) Classification. In small communities hospitals are not so specialized as in cities. "General hospitals" receive all cases except contagious and infectious diseases. "Emergency hospitals" are provided for persons requiring immediate help. Special hospitals are often provided by public authorities for classes of cases demanding separation. "Pest houses" are usually erected for times of small-pox, cholera, yellow fever. They may be temporary or permanent structures. Special hospitals for the treatment of scarlet fever and diphtheria are not so common as they should be. In suppressing these plagues such institutions would afford valuable assistance. Almshouses have infirmary wards for the sick. Marine hospitals are supported partly by the government and partly by fees from sailors. In connection with efforts to suppress loathsome disease and the pauperism that accompanies it, it is urged that state hospitals for venereal diseases are needed, where persons afflicted with these dangerous maladies can be kept for two years or more until they are well, or as nearly sound as medical art can make them. N. C. C., 1889, p. 57.

c) Social interest in the internal arrangement and management of hospitals centers in the method of securing competent officers. Nowhere is it more important to have expert service. But visitors of ordinary intelligence can keep before them some principles of judgment. The public can know whether a hospital is clean and efficient according to reasonable standards. Friendly coöperation of citizens with the authorities may prevent abuses. N. C. C., 1891, "Hospital Cleanliness," 1890, p. 155; "Hospital government and its relation to the city." *d*) Where a hospital is supported by the public its government should be vested in a non-partisan board, appointed and not elected. These boards should be composed of men and women of first rank of intelligence and character, and from various professions. It is thought best to have a business man, not a physician, for superintendent. But the physicians in charge should be secured power corresponding to their responsibility. Principles of civil service reform should regulate admission and discharge of employés. *e*) Hospitals should avoid encouraging pauperism. "Physicians owe it to themselves to do less unpaid work among the poor. No profession and no class of men do so much without hope of reward. . . . . The hospital and out-patient department ought to relieve them of this unrequited toil. All patients who resort to hospitals, except the destitute and abject poor, ought to pay something for hospital care. . . . . Charity given indiscriminately is demoralizing. It begets thriftlessness and improvidence and leads to pauperization." (Dr. Hurd, N. C. C., 1890, p. 162.) In spite of the danger of pauperizing the dependent the hospital performs important social functions. It gives the poor the most important help; it promotes medical science; it trains students of the healing art; it trains capable nurses, whose character and services are of the highest order.

2. **Out-patients.** The medical staff of a hospital frequently render aid to the poor patients in their homes. This gives practice to young physicians under the direction of their instructors. The perils are, that other physicians

may be robbed of legitimate sources of income, the poor may be pauperized, and inefficient service may result in injury to the patients.

3. **Dispensaries** are connected with hospitals or may be separate. The danger of pauperizing dependents reappears here. Some persons will accept medicine who would refuse food or clothing. Physicians and benevolent persons should limit these abuses by the methods of inquiry used in the Association of Charities. Subsidies from a public treasury increase the danger of perversion.

4. **City and county physicians.** These are provided at public expense and generally are paid salaries. It is not to be expected that the highest ability can be thus secured, but it is important to the patients and the public that the office be awarded on grounds apart from political services for a party. It would appear wise to have city physicians appointed by Boards of Health, subject to discharge by them, with a report of reasons to the Mayor.

5. **Training Schools for Nurses.** No higher service is rendered to humanity than by this Agency. But nurses are often overworked. They should be protected by statute. The school should be under the control of the board governing the hospital, and should not be independent of it.

6. **Boards of Health, city and state.** The chief function of these bodies is to prevent disease. They should be appointed in every community. The relations of the local board to the state board need to be carefully defined in order to avoid collision in time of plague. These boards render valuable service to society in the inspection of immi-

grants at ports, and in watching conditions favorable to the increase of preventable diseases. By improving the conditions of life they make recovery more certain and rapid, and sickness less common. Thus they diminish dependency which often begins with a disabling sickness.

Of medical charity in general it may be said that "a large number of acute cases of disease would, but for their intervention, become chronic and permanently disabling." By the diffusion of knowledge on subjects of hygiene and sanitation the medical authorities may diminish social loss. (N. C. C. 1883, p. 433; 1875, p. 52; 1877, p. 31; 1891, p. 52; 1890, p. 110). Also other years of N. C. C.

CHAPTER XI.

THE COUNTY POOR HOUSE.

During the earlier history of our country, when population was scant and scattered, friendless and dependent persons were generally cared for by local officers through a system of boarding-out among farmers. Apparently we are slowly returning to an early custom when we adopt this method. As the communities came to be more complex it was found difficult to secure proper care of indigent persons who needed shelter. Dependent children were bound out and poor houses were erected for indoor relief. Into these receptacles flowed all sorts of rejected social material; the aged, the sick, the insane, the forsaken children, the inebriate, the blind, the deaf mute, the worn-out criminal, the epileptic, the demented and paralytic. And as the poor farm was the most unattractive place in the county, and as the inmates were friendless, the most abominable abuses grew up, and in many places still continue.

The English Almshouse as it existed early in this century was painted by Crabbe ("The Village," Book I).

"Thus groan the old, till by disease oppressed,
They taste a final woe, and then they rest.
Their's is yon House that holds the parish poor,
Whose walls of mud scarce bear the broken door;
There, where the putrid vapors, flagging, play,
And the dull wheel hums doleful through the day; —
There children dwell who know no parents' care;
Parents, who know no children's love, dwell there!
Heart-broken matrons on their joyless bed,
Forsaken wives, and mothers never wed,
Dejected widows with unheeded tears,
And crippled age with more than childhood fears;
The lame, the blind, and far the happiest they!
The moping idiot, and the madman gay.
　　Here, too, the sick their final doom receive,
Here brought, amid the scenes of grief, to grieve."

Our American poor houses are usually well built and are often almost palatial. They are not made of mud. But many still retain the mixed, unclassified and miserable population described above.

1. **Principles of Management.** — As a matter of fact, the poor house is governed nominally by county commissioners, and actually by some person appointed by them for political considerations. In spite of this vicious custom, many excellent appointments are made, and in consequence of this method multitudes of bad appointments are made or good superintendents are hampered. Employés should be appointed and continued under civil service rules, a doctrine entirely sound and usually ignored. The residents of the asylum should be required to work as far as

they are able, not only to earn their living, but to promote their health and happiness. Private and church charity can find a field for exercise in the poor house by furnishing religious services and music, by directing recreations for the old people, and by securing for them, especially for old women in winter, some work which they are competent to do. The visits of intelligent and benevolent persons at regular times would prevent the worst abuses and administer much comfort. (N. C. C., 1890, p. 107). Careful rules should govern the admission and departure of inmates. The poor house should not be a comfortable winter harbor for tramps and a sobering place for drunkards. It should not be used to foster vice by becoming a foundling asylum, "with no questions asked." The buildings should be substantial, but very plain and unadorned. They are sometimes so fine in appearance and appointments as to show marked contrast with the average homes of modest taxpayers who support them. The life should not be so attractive as to furnish a positive motive for men to desert honest industry for a residence in the county mansions.

2. **Classification.** — The tendency in our day is to specialize institutions. All are agreed that children should not be kept in county asylums with paupers, and Michigan and Massachusetts have led the way in this important reform. Dickens said: "Throw a child under a cart-horse's feet and a loaded wagon sooner than take him to an almshouse." State institutions are provided for the dependent blind and for deaf mutes. The actual criminals are, of course, furnished separate accommodations. But the crying evil still demands remedy that respectable and unfortunate persons, people who have worked honestly and hard all their lives, are forced to reside in their friendless and

unprotected old age with persons who in character and habit are still criminals in all except the power to execute criminal intentions. Still remains the wrong of compelling the same dependent to live in contact with demented persons whose filthy habits and strange manner are repulsive beyond description. It is manifest that the classification of the poor in the county house needs to be carried much further. Perhaps the time will come when most of the dependents will be scattered about and boarded in families, under state supervision, while those who require institutional treatment will be divided among a few special institutions adapted to their peculiar needs. The county poor ⌣ house, like the county jail, is a disgrace that we should wipe out.

See views of Mr. Sanborn and Bishop Gillespie (N. C. C., 1890, p. 79 and xxiii.) Letchworth's " Poor House Administration." Report Illinois Board, 1890, a detailed description of the state of poor houses in this state, as it applies to the country generally. (N. C. C., 1879, p. 96). Statutes of the various states show the form of early legislation, especially the statutes before 1850.

3. **Categories of inspection** for visitors to poor houses. — A person with ordinary standards of comfort and a healthy olfactory organ may study a poor house with advantage by observing facts relating to these points: First, physical conditions; site, drainage, light, accessibility, buildings; materials, form, style, cost, adaptation to classes relieved, sewage and drainage, disposal of night soil, ventilation, cleanliness of floors, walls, cellars, food, dietary and cooking; bathing, clothing, washing, ironing. Secondly, social and moral conditions; provision for the intellectual life, as reading matter, pictures, music, amusements; provision for the religious life, books, services, friendly visits; useful

industry ; classification, separation of sexes, absence of children, separation of insane and other defectives who are injurious in such a place. Thirdly, administration ; powers and duties of the commissioners in control ; local officers, titles, mode of appointment and tenure of office, duties ; woman attendants on the woman's side ; treatment of visitors and inmates ; discipline in work, hours of sleep and meals, conversation, recreation, punishments ; cost per capita, conditions of admission and discharge, and the judgment of the officers on all these points.

CHAPTER XII.

HOMELESS DEPENDENTS.

A distinction is sometimes made between tramps and vagrants ; the former having no legal settlement, while the latter may claim relief in a certain district. Both must be carefully distinguished from unemployed destitute persons who honestly travel in search of work. The problem of the unemployed is not new. The breaking up of the monasteries before and at the Reformation left thousands · of the homeless without resources. The people, knowing their need, gave them alms at their doors, sometimes urged by threats and sometimes induced by charity. The evils of beggary rose to alarming proportions. Then followed repressive measures and the poor laws of all European nations. Part of the criminal code has always touched these evils. The object of such statutes is to bring under police control all those persons who, without actually committing any trespass, are guilty of habits inconsistent with the good order of society.

The statistics on this subject are very unsatisfactory. In Massachusetts in 1887, out of 816,470 engaged in gainful occupations 29.59 per cent. were unemployed at their principal occupations. We may expect more full and accurate reports in the new census. The extent of enforced idleness varies not only with the years of prosperity and reverses, but with seasons and weather. Conclusions based on fragmentary statements of facts are of little value.

1. **Enforced Idleness** is caused by general and by personal conditions, industrial depression, strikes and lockouts, cessation of works for repairs, and also by physical weakness, mental infirmity, and, most of all, by absence of skill and special training. During times of enforced idleness the danger of acquiring pauper habits of thought and feeling is increased.) *Relief measures.* Employment bureaus in private hands are very liable to abuse, although the business is honorable.) Many of these agencies rank with pawnshops in the degree of injustice to the poor. (Employment bureaus in connection with churches, the Y. M. C. A., and other societies, are useful within a limited range) (The Association of Charities secures employment for many persons in cities. Few skilled workers ever apply to such bureaus. In Ohio the state legislature adopted a plan to promote the " mobilization " of labor. The Ohio reports of 1890 and afterward give plan and results. (The tradeunions help to diffuse information as to the places where work is most needed in special callings.) Probably a union of all these agencies, under the direction of a national bureau, would be the most efficient method of reducing this evil within narrow limits. But education in trades and arts would do more. We leave out of account the theories as to new schemes of taxation which to many seem promising.

It seems probable that, through agreements of employers and unions, a better distribution of time over the year might be made. National statistics of the condition of trade, published frequently and regularly, would aid those seeking to come together as employer and employed.

2. **The Tramp.**— The tramp is a vagrant beggar, in whom the roving disposition which characterizes defective natures is highly developed. He is a modern Bedouin. The tramp is a distinct social peril. He carries vermin and loathsome contagious diseases from place to place. In his person and habits syphilis finds a nidus. He communicates his disposition and disease to his children. He is a constant and ubiquitous menace to life and property. He is a venal voter in dense communities, and a corrupting element in politics. See Mr. J. J. McCook's articles in *Charities Review*, June, 1892. Tramps constitute a great part of the force of chronic offenders and drunkards who march in procession before city police judges and receive short sentences. Free soup houses only increase the plague. Work must ever accompany relief. Any remedy which helps tramps at the expense of the industrious poor, as by taking work away from the sober to give it to the drunkard, cannot fail to hurt society. In Europe various experiments are being tried which should be watched with interest. The German labor-colonies attempt to give a temporary resting place for wanderers, together with an opportunity to work and learn something useful. Their success has not been very great. The Dutch home-colonies aim to provide a permanent home for those whose weakness and inefficiency unfit them for competition in free society. General Booth and the Salvation Army have set on foot a scheme of gigantic proportions which is the object of

world - wide interest and discussion.) (See Part IV. on Preventive Measures).

In the United States many methods have been tried with varying success. (Severe repressive laws have, perhaps, driven these wanderers from a locality or state, without diminishing the evil at large.) The Associations of Charity in cities seek to arrest persistent beggars, to investigate the stories of all applicants, to offer work to all who are in extreme distress.) In the present state of things this method is the best known. (Tramps should be treated humanely, for they are human and many are capable of reformation.) Their sentiments that give promise of amendment are seen in the stories of Bret Harte. (The first effort should be to classify vagrants according to the causes and tendencies of their unsocial habit.) Confirmed inebriates should be segregated and given special employment. Those unfit for the struggle of city life might be colonized, and some would be rehabilitated and trained for useful service and happiness.

Willink, "Dutch Home Labor Colonies."

Booth's "In Darkest England," and the criticisms of Loch, Bosanquet and Dwyer.

Huxley's "Social Diseases and Worse Remedies."

Gadderbaum's "Die Arbeiter Kolonie."

"German Labor Colonies" (Peabody) *Forum*, February, 1892.

Warner, "Some Experiments on Behalf of the Unemployed;"
   Quarterly Journal of Economy, October, 1890, and July, 1892.

"History of Vagrants and Vagrancy," by Ribton-Turner.

G. Berthold, "Statistik der deutschen Arbeiter Kolonien."

Mills, "Poverty and the State," N. C. C. 1886, p. 188, and 1891, p. 168.

English Poor Law Report, 1834 (History of English Experience).

Schönberg's "Handbuch Pol. Ökon."

Luther's "Book of Beggars."

Rogers', "Six Centuries of Work and Wages."

Greene's "History of the English People."

CHAPTER XIII.

VOLUNTARY CHARITIES.

1. **Individual.**— In personal gifts the relation is most like that of family or neighborly service. Assistance rendered with the evident purpose of humiliating the recipient and exalting the patron is not of charity but of pride. The best help is that which is rendered as a social act between friends. Such giving requires tact and love. Indiscriminate alms-giving is a distinct social peril. The act of benevolence is private, but the effect is public, social. (Johns Hopkins University Studies, No. 2). The best private relief is that which prevents the needy person from becoming a public charge. Often a loan with counsel is better than a gift. The highest gift for the depressed is fellowship in thought, wisdom and sympathy. No citizen can afford to give to strangers without using the mediation of the Association of Charities, in large communities. Even in improving material conditions a poor person with intelligence and patience may often help a dependent family more than money could do. There is work for all. Large gifts are most useful in establishing and endowing institutions, as hospitals, schools, libraries, dispensaries. In experimental charity, preventive schemes and educational beneficence, private munificence finds its safest field. The state is slow to act on new ground. Large communities are not easily led to consider swiftly changing conditions and needs. During the initial stages of an enterprise vigorous and successful men may carry public service until all

are educated to appreciate it. Examples are numerous and increasing ; the Peabody Funds for housing the poor, and for educating the colored people ; the Slater Fund ; the Pratt, Drexel, Cooper and Armour Institutes. The societies for preventing cruelty to animals and children, the societies for aiding discharged prisoners, kindergartens, and manual training and trade schools must generally be started by individual givers.

Carnegie's "Gospel of Wealth," *And. Rev.*, June, 1891.

Nor. Am. Rev., April and May, 1891.

Nineteenth Cent., November and December, 1890, and March, 1891.

Articles by Gladstone, Manning, Felix Adler, Hughes, Gibbons, Potter, Phelps, Chamberlain.

2. **Benevolent Relief Societies.**—(*a*) Origin. State aid is not adequate to meet all needs. The amount and kind of aid determined by law and rule must be suited to an average case and cannot take account of special conditions. Many persons would suffer, even to starvation, rather than associate with paupers in a public office and have their names recorded in a public register. Self respect is social wealth, and should be preserved by delicate personal care. The resources of money and time of benevolent individuals are not adequate to meet all these cases, and must be combined. Out of these conditions arise relief societies. (*b*) Having already (Ch. ix.-xi.) shown the laws regulating outdoor relief by the state, it is not necessary to repeat those principles here. Voluntary societies must observe economical laws as well as the state, or distress is increased. (*c*) Perils attending these organizations. They may be unduly multiplied. There are too many philanthropists who get the credit for starting societies which others must afterwards support in order to save the credit of the community. They may overlap, several societies

covering the same ground, while other ground is neglected. Relatively less deserving societies often absorb the available charity resources of a community by their loud and persistent advertising. The expense of management is frequently out of proportion to the volume of work needed. The officers of a society may become a close corporation without responsibility, and abuses have often come from this cause. Pauperism is actually encouraged in order to show the public reason for the existence of the society. Depending, as they must, on impulsive benevolence, they may fail just when they are most needed. These evils have all been observed in this country and abroad. (*d*) Modes of raising funds. The only unobjectionable, and the most effective method, is to present all the facts to the public and ask for contributions. Questionable methods are those which appeal to mixed motives, and fail to educate the community in genuine charity. Such are all the ways resorted to of raising funds by spectacles, entertainments, plays, balls. A more refined age will see the shocking contrast between the occasion of sport and the miseries it is thought to relieve. Sorrow and shame should not be associated with splendor, extravagance and luxury. Let the occasion of mirth justify itself, but not make a pretext of heaven-born charity. The indirect methods are often very costly and the expenses swallow up the income. While something may be said for such questionable modes, absolutely nothing can be argued in favor of raising money by gambling, lotteries and kindred devices. Gambling habits are among the chief causes of pauperism and crime, and they need no stimulation from reputable people.

3. **Church Charities.**—Most churches take up collections for indigent members. Usually these are not very great in

amount nor very liable to abuse. Some churches have not made anything like adequate provision for their unfortunate members; but this is not common. The Society of St. Vincent of Paul is well worth the study of Protestants, and it is doing an excellent work in many Roman Catholic parishes. After what has been said it is not necessary to repeat the principles of relief. There is a great danger which Dr. Chalmers pointed out that the promise of material help may act as a cause of hypocrisy. A hungry person is greatly tempted to lie and profess any faith for food and drink. By coöperation through an association of charities these dangers are reduced to a minimum. The most hopeful church charities are educational. Alms seldom afford permanent relief, but one who knows how to live can take care of himself. Kindergartens, kitchen gardens, day nurseries, sewing schools, physical-culture classes, mothers' meetings (without bribes), penny-saving schemes, cheerful entertainments which instruct, musical and other artistic pleasures, friendly visits in homes on a basis of genuine fellowship, are some of the ways in which churches may best labor for the uplifting of the poor. The undeveloped resources of the poor themselves have never yet been measured.

4. Endowed Charities.—There are relatively permanent needs of communities which are best provided for by secure incomes. Certain classes of persons and certain districts are apt to be forgotten. But it is also true that endowments are often perverted. The original direction of the bequest may be unwise. The conditions may so change that the income of the fund is no longer required for the purpose designated. The fund may create a demand for it far beyond the power of society to meet. The right of the

" dead hand " to control forever the use of gifts must be limited by the commonwealth. The living world cannot be ruled from the grave. Respect for the dead and for public documents must not ruin the present generation. Endowments are presumably for the good of men : if they become evil the original purpose must be regarded. Endowments must be under the control of the state.

5. **The State,** in the last analysis, is the only organization which can control the whole field of charity. Individual charity is more tender and personal ; voluntary societies are more responsive to sudden calls and unexpected sufferings ; the church can employ a higher range of spiritual forces ; but the state alone is the organ of all members of society, and it alone has an acknowledged right to supervise and govern all institutions. The state should never subsidize private and church charities, and only in extreme and special cases employ such agencies and pay for definite services actually rendered. The state does not seem to be a proper agency for the distribution of private, social or church contributions, especially for outdoor relief, although it must be confessed that France and Germany have much to teach us on this point. On one point, however, there can be little question, when one has surveyed the history of charities : the state alone can inspect and control special benevolence, and this right to control is more and more necessary with the advance of civilization and the increasing number and complexity of social membership. It appears probable that in the future this kind of state action, with coöperation between public and private persons, will increase in the United States. Scandals connected with many private institutions already call for searching investigation and vigorous action.

See N. C. C., 1889, " Our Charities and our Churches," by Dr. A. G. Warner. " Parish Problems," by W. Gladden, and others.

CHAPTER XIV.

CHARITY ORGANIZATION.

Under this title we may discuss all those institutions whose purpose is to secure harmony and efficiency in benevolent efforts.

1. **Municipal and Town Organization.**—*a*) Principles and objects. These are carefully stated in the publications of the societies. The object which includes all is, the promotion of whatever tends to the permanent improvement of the condition of the poor. In particular, the object is to study the causes of pauperism and to reduce vagrancy and dependency ; to prevent indiscriminate and duplicate giving ; to secure the community from imposture ; to see that all deserving cases of destitution are properly relieved ; to make employment the basis of relief; to elevate the home life, health and habits of the poor ; to prevent children from growing up paupers. The New York Society proposes : (1) " To be a center of intercommunication between the various churches and charitable agencies in the city ; to foster harmonious coöperation between them, and to check the evils of the overlapping of relief : (2) To investigate thoroughly, and without charge, the cases of all applicants for relief which are referred to the society for inquiry, and to send the persons having a legitimate interest in such cases full reports of the results of investigation ;

and to provide visitors who shall personally attend cases needing counsel and advice : (3) To obtain from the proper charities and charitable individuals suitable and adequate relief for deserving cases : (4) To procure work for poor persons who are capable of being wholly or partially self-supporting : (5) To repress mendicity by the above means and by the prosecution of impostors : (6) To promote the general welfare of the poor by social and sanitary reforms, and by the inculcation of habits of providence and self-dependence."

A society claiming to do the work of charity on modern principles should provide distinctly for all these objects. In the degree to which they are carried out the society is successful. Methods must be adapted to the local conditions, although some elements are universally necessary, as the office for registration, the personal visitors, the gratuitous inquiry, the prompt response, the uniform system of records.

b) Organization. The membership is usually composed of all persons who contribute annually to the funds. Some local municipal officers, as mayor, officers of the poor, and delegates from churches and charitable societies, become members *ex officio*, or by designation. The usual officers are elected at the annual meeting, as president, vice-presidents, treasurer. The general secretary is the essential person, and he may be elected or appointed by the directors, and should be salaried in order to give his time to the work. Women have succeeded as secretaries. Special training is very desirable here. The office is beginning to command eminent service of college graduates.

In large cities a central council, with additional district councils, are organized for the consideration of general principles and for determining the treatment of particular cases.

In forming a new society it is desirable to have the personal visit of an expert.

c) Friendly visitors are persons who volunteer to befriend the poor. A society should not wait for these to offer their services. Incompetent visitors do harm. Busy people think they have no time. But if a particular family of dependents is assigned to a man he is more likely to accept the responsibility. In Germany citizens are obliged by law to accept such work, and persons of highest social position do not shirk. In the handbooks published by the societies hints will be found for all classes of cases. Thousands of persons have been encouraged and directed to self-support who, without such friendly interest, would have continued to be a public charge. In many cases, where a dependent person belongs to some church, or has an inclination for any, he is brought into the circle of that church.

It is necessary, however, that the ordinary visitors of the society should not use their position for any kind of proselyting. "Every department of this work shall be completely severed from all questions of religious belief, politics or nationality." Yet the society is at liberty to strengthen any natural bond of fellowship, whether of religious beliefs, family, or nationality, and this service is often all that is required.

d) Relief. On this point societies follow different policies. Probably the tendency of the most careful students of experience is toward the New York platform: "The society shall not directly dispense alms in any form." The reasons given are, that enough relief is already provided by many societies, if it were properly distributed; that if relief is given in material forms the primary and characteristic object,—to lift people above dependence,—may be lost out of sight; that a society for organizing all relief agencies should not compete with any of them, but should be the servant of all, while independent of each.

It is claimed, on the other hand, in some places, that the same officers can administer relief and keep the common records; that expenses of administration are thus diminished; and that equal efficiency can be secured. It is urged by friends of both methods that all the principal charities ought to have their central offices under one roof, so that action may be intelligent, prompt and harmonious.

In some cities the society does not give alms, but has associated with it a relief society to aid in case of material need. In other cities it is found sufficient to ask certain benevolent citizens to help as occasion arises. If a fund is known to be on hand applicants will flock in to claim their share as if they had a right to it. This embarrasses effort to prevent beggary.

e) In small communities it is quite as important to have charity organization as in cities. Each county, at least, should bring its benevolent forces into regiment. "Pauper families arise largely in small communities and ultimately drift to the larger ones. The large cities have enough to do in caring for the 56 per cent. of paupers who are foreign-born, for it is to them that the indigent alien first makes his way. The American pauper should be cared for where he originates." (Mr. Rosenau).

(N. C. C. 1887, and 1891, p. 31). Mrs. Lowell's paper on this subject is published in tract form.

A county or township conference might study the conditions which are unfavorable to vigorous, healthy, manly life, and which tend to increase pauperism and crime. It might study how to promote objects of advantage to all the community, as well as of special classes, as drainage, schools, public reading rooms, libraries, decent bathing places, clean and orderly streets, the preservation of peace and good morals, the enforcement of liquor laws. It might do much to educate public opinion on such subjects. It could confer with public officers to secure their coöperation. It could establish courses of lectures, promote suitable industrial education for adults, training schools for boys and girls, and the collection of small savings among those liable to grow up with improvident habits. It could bring music and pictures within the reach of the poorest ; and it could encourage the formation of clubs for study among those who have left school. In all ways it might cultivate a civic spirit of duty and fellowship through common interests of broad and noble purpose. Much of our national pauperism comes from the congestion of population in cities, and much of the drift to cities is caused by the awful monotony and vacuity of country and village life. Such a society, working in many places, would help arrest this tendency. It is true that church and lodge already work in this direction, but a society is needed to hold all the best elements together for mutual advantage, and to prevent the degradation of those in special peril. It is evident without argument that a society in a small community must be less special and more comprehensive than in a city.

f) Results. The usefulness of a relief society of the old type is popularly measured by the number of its clients and the amount of help given ; but the success of an organization society is measured by the decrease of dependents. Actual results of scientific methods have been shown in decrease of outdoor and indoor relief of appeals for aid, and of tramps ; in greater harmony between churches and societies for relief ; in increase of industrial, educational and

preventive charity; in the establishment of friendly relations between prosperous and indigent persons, with mutual
advantage; in the improvement of local government; in
the enforcement of neglected statutes relating to vice,
cruelty to animals and children, sanitation, tenement
houses, and in the promotion of provident and mutual
benefit schemes. The cost of organization is considerable,
and has been urged as an objection. In small cities it may
be from $3,000 to $4,000, in large cities it has been from
$5,000 to $15,000 in one year, while in smaller communities
it may not reach more than a few hundred dollars. On the
other hand the direct saving effected is enormous. In
Buffalo, it is claimed that the saving was about $48,000.
In Elberfield the tax upon each taxpayer fell from 4.45
francs to 2 francs. In London in 1869 there were 138,536
paupers, while in 1886 the number fell, largely, though not
entirely, through the organization society, to 89,926. Illustrations might be multiplied, but the best results cannot be
tabulated.

2. **State Boards of Charities and Correction.**—These
boards, under various titles, exist in some states, and should
be formed in all. They are of two types: those which
have power of control over state institutions, and those
which have only advisory powers. "The generally received
opinion is that it is better, all things considered, that each
institution should have its own trustees, entirely devoted to
its interests, and that the central supervising board should
possess as little executive authority or power as possible."
(F. H. Wines). One of the most important features of the
more recent English poor laws is the establishment of the
Local Government Board, since 1834. (Fowle's Poor Law,
ch. v. N. C. C., 1879–80, p. 26, and each year after). In

some respects this Board resembles our State Boards of Charities and Corrections.

3. **National Service** in relation to pauperism must be confined to the collection and diffusion of exact information. The reports on Labor, Agriculture, Temperance, Family, Education, and the consular reports of foreign conditions, are very helpful in securing harmony and intelligence. The census reports are of highest value, but they come out slowly, and are soon antiquated for many purposes. Mr. McCulloch suggested (N. C. C., 1891), that the National Conference should coöperate with local authorities in keeping the census reports of the dependents and allied classes revised for each year. Where legislation is involved, this is of great importance.

Out of a vast mass of material we may select a few writings of interest.

Loch, "Charity Organization."
Gurteen, "Hand Book of Charity Organization."
Mrs. J. S. Lowell, "Public Relief and Private Charity."
Mrs. Field, "How to Help the Poor." N. C. C., since 1879.
The *Forum*, December, 1892, articles by Professor Peabody and Mr. Riis on German and New York Charities.
Tracts published by the Boston, Baltimore, Philadelphia and Boston societies.
Essays by Octavia Hill. "Hand Book for Friendly Visitors among the Poor," (Putnams).

CHAPTER XV.

CARE OF DEPENDENT CHILDREN.

Children are, like old people, proper objects of charity, since they are helpless. This care is hopeful, since youth is plastic. Yet there are grave dangers in the removal of children from the care of those who are responsible for their nurture.

1. **Foundlings.** — The helplessness and misery of a deserted babe are conclusive arguments for pity. Foundling asylums have been provided to prevent infanticide. During all ages of Christianity, the church has sought to remove the strongest motive to commit that crime which in savage and even civilized nations has been so general. And yet, with the most careful management, it has seemed doubtful whether harlotry and child-murder have not been increased by this very care. Where the terms of admission have been lax, it is certain that the evils have been aggravated. The conditions of its birth and early exposure render the foundling's hold on life precarious. Institutions, if crowded, are deadly to deserted babes. In fact the loss of life is so great, that such institutions serve no end whatever. If the mother is not cared for with the infant, it dies, unless the offspring of shame is placed in a home. It is not possible to supply wet nurses for all foundlings. And while the mother is the natural protector, the misery and degradation of being linked to the visible sign of her sin, makes it often doubtful whether it is not better to separate them forever, and send the child where its origin will be hidden. Society must regard the influence of its treatment on the parents. If possible, both parents must be brought to assume the responsibility of the infant life. Many asylums refuse to encourage vice by receiving an unwedded mother with her second infant. To protect the morality of society it is imperative that deserted children, legitimate or illegitimate, should not be received secretly and without question, The laws punishing infanticide, though stern, are necessary and

must be enforced. The legal provisions for enforcing parental responsibility must be carried out.

Under the most careful system much injury is inevitable. Foundling asylums may mitigate, but cannot cure the wrongs which spring from personal and social immoralities. Educational and preventive efforts are far more promising than palliative measures. After long trial, the London asylum (Foundling Hospital) was compelled to adopt these rules ; the child must be illegitimate, under twelve years of age, the mother not a pauper in the almshouse, her previous character must be good, the father not forthcoming. But what is to be done with the others who are not here classified ? That is hard to say ! Society cannot undo a wrong once done. What is sown must be reaped. The inevitable consequence of misery must remain, despite all legal enactments and charitable anodynes, a permanent argument and plea against lawless self-indulgence.

2. **Children in the poor house.**—In the earlier history of our country there was no other place for orphans, and the evils were not so glaring because child-life was valuable for its labor, and homes were ready. But as the population increased in numbers, and the poor decreased in quality, the evil of having young persons in the poor house was slowly seen to be monstrous. The character of the residents of these institutions is demoralizing, for they are so often indolent, coarse and immoral. The pauper record injures the prospects of the child. The authorities of the county asylum are not able, even if competent, to oversee apprenticed and adopted orphans during their minority. And yet, as late as 1888, Mr. Randall said all but four of the states had some children in these miserable places.

3. **Child Saving Institutions.**—The next step generally taken, and that often by private enterprise, was to transfer dependent children to asylums and orphanages. (*a*) There are three types of these institutiöns. The congregate or "barrack" system has been most common. It is claimed for the large building that it is less costly to provide, especially in crowded cities, and that its government is more unified. It is believed that such large buildings are more liable to destructive fires and more exposed to disease, and that the crowding of many together is unnatural. For the congregate plan a substitute is offered in the "cottage system," in which only a moderate number are kept under one roof, in a way more nearly resembling family life. If the numbers are large, this method is inconvenient and costly. In the Coldwater, Michigan, School, both methods are combined; a central building contains offices, school, shops, dining hall, residence of superintendent and assistants and all that is common. The sleeping and study rooms are in separate houses, which accommodate about fifty children with the house mother. The Rose Orphanage, at Terre Haute, Indiana, is an excellent example of this system.

b) These institutions serve a necessary purpose. They are rescue stations for the perishing and abused waifs of misfortune and of criminal parentage. They are needed to train dependent and ill-bred children for decent homes. Many rescued children are physically and morally in need of quarantine until they are fit to offer to suitable families for adoption. And the period of detention should be long enough to accomplish the purpose.

The usefulness of the best orphange is limited. Sickness and mortality result from crowding. Certain grave vices are often learned from vicious children. In the best institutions, if the person is retained too long he becomes accustomed to the forms and spirit of a rigid establishment, and so unfit for the personal responsibility of family life. The young require for their best development the care of foster-parents, if they have lost their own, and the most gentle of superintendents cannot father and mother too large a brood. Another grave consideration is the cost of keeping children in an asylum. Every institution by a law of its being is impelled to preserve its place and power. Officers have a natural pride in ruling over large numbers. Salaries are generally given according to the visible magnitude of the work. It is easier to run in a groove than move out with energy to adjust the wards to new circumstances. Attachments spring up for the best children. Sometimes we must add the influence of a conscientious but injurious ecclesiasticism, which loses sight of the interest of the child and holds him in the asylum rather than let him go to a good home where a slightly different creed may be taught. If the institution is partly supported by city subsidies, these evils are increased. And thus it happens very often that such asylums are crowded at great cost of money to the patrons and of character to the child.

c) Modes of support. Such institutions may be supported by the state, by churches and other corporations, or by endowments. It is not wise to give public support to church charities. All such retreats should be under the care of the state, since it alone can protect the rights of the child and the interests of all.

4. **The Placing-out system.**—The best place for a child is a good home. The placing-out system has been practiced for a long time. The Michigan method may be taken as an example of a highly developed form of state action. The law prohibits the authorities to send children to poor

houses. A general state public school is provided for a
temporary home. When approved homes have been found
the wards are sent to them. In each county a local agent
is appointed to watch over the interests of these minors.
A general agent travels over the state in the common interest
of school and children. All these factors work efficiently
and harmoniously together. In connection with many
private asylums this system is carried out. But a general
organization is needed to secure economy and thorough
watchcare. Perhaps many orphanages might unite in
employing agents to secure homes and guard the interests
of children. With this provision private institutions seem
desirable for superior classes of dependents, and for that variety and competition which are so necessary to prevent stag-
nation and routine. The placing-out system has its perils.
See Mr. L. P. Alden's "Shady-side of the Placing-out
System." Premature release from the quarantine stage,
hasty selection of unfit homes, neglect of oversight, inter-
state migration of defective and criminal children are
among the perils or abuses of this good method. In some
communities it is found difficult to secure the adoption of
all dependent children, and in such cases they are boarded
at the expense of the state or corporation caring for them.
Grave objections are urged against this plan, but it seems to
have worked, on the whole, better than the strict asylum
method. N. C. C. 1890, p. 194.

Valuable discussion of the points raised in this chapter
may be found in the N. C. C.   •

"Kindergartens and Social Reforms," 1888, p. 247.
"The Influence of Manual Training on Character, by F. Adler,
1888, p. 272.
N. C. C., 1891, articles by Messrs. Finley, Folks, Dudley, Kellogg.
The Michigan and Massachusetts plans for placing out, N. C. C.
1888, and 1889.

"The Care of Dependent Children," by Mrs. Lowell.
"Children of the State," by Miss Florence D. Hill.
E. C. Wines "Prisons and Child-saving Institutions."
Lallemand, "Histoire des Enfants Abandonées et Delaissés."

Maxims.— Dr. Wichern, of the Rauhe Haus, being asked
by what means he was able to produce such wonderful
changes in the conduct of children under his care, said:
" By the Word of God and music."

Dr. E. C. Wines : "The normal place of education for
such children, is the fields in the country, entirely discon-
nected from institutions for the treatment of pauperism and
crime."

The state is the guardian of rights. All children have
rights to physical care and education. The primary duty
lies with the parents. If it be possible to enforce this obligation, that should be done. Most of the evils of society
arise from demoralized homes. The family is the unit of
society. But if the family fail, through misfortune, vice or
death, then a new home is necessary. As long as possible,
the state should help hold up the family and coöperate
with it. But when the family is recreant and abdicates its
functions, the state must secure as nearly normal conditions
as may be in its power. The asylum is only a temporary
station on the way from the ruined home to the permanent
home with foster parents.

Seventeen Propositions on Child-Saving.— Presented by
Hon. W. P. Letchworth to the *Fifteenth National Conference
of Charities and Correction* during the debate on the Report
of the Committee on the Care and Disposal of Dependent
Children.

First. There should be a proper classification primarily into the
following divisions : (*a*) Children thrown upon the public for support by

misfortune or poverty of parents. (*b*) Truants from school subject to the compulsory-education laws. (*c*) Children homeless, or with bad associations who are in danger of falling, and who need home-like care and training, rather than reformatory treatment. (*d*) Incorrigibles, felons, those experienced in crime and the fallen needing reformation.

Second. Provision should be made for girls, except the younger class, in institutions separate from boys.

Third. The institution should be home-like in character, and its administration as nearly as possible that of family life. ˙

Fourth. Small institutions on the open or cottage plan should be provided for boys, upon farms in the country, where agriculture and gardening may be combined with a thorough indoor and common-school system.

Fifth. The labor of children should, under no circumstances, be hired to contractors.

Sixth. Government supervision should be exercised over all institutions for children, and frequent examinations made as to sanitary and other conditions, annual approval by the Government being requisite to the continuance of the work.

Seventh. Power should be lodged in a central authority to transfer inmates from one institution to another, in order to perfect and maintain classifications; also to remove juvenile offenders from institutions and place them in family care during good conduct; also to remove from institutional care and to place permanently in homes all children suited to family life.

Eighth. There should be provided a governmental agency to act in the interest of juvenile offenders when on trial. The agency should be vested with power, with the approval of the judge, to take the delinquent into custody under suspended sentence and place him on probation in a family.

Ninth. Disinterested benevolence should control and direct work as far as practicable, the state or local government contributing, if need be, but not to an extent sufficient to meet the whole expense.

Tenth. The coöperation of women of elevated character should be considered essential to the attainment of the highest success.

Eleventh. Parents able to do so, should be made to contribute to the support of their children while under reformatory treatment.

Twelfth. When debased parents have demonstrated their inability or unwillingness to support their children, and the latter in consequence have become a charge upon the public, the interest of the child should be regarded as paramount, and the rights of the parents should cease, the state assuming control.

Thirteenth. Children who in their home life had been environed by vicious associations and adverse influences, should on their release from institutional custody, be transplanted to new and, perhaps, distant homes with good surroundings.

Fourteenth. A study of the child's character and a knowledge of its antecedents should be considered essential to successful work.

Fifteenth. The delinquent child should be regarded as morally diseased, and a correct diagnosis of its moral condition should be made and carefully considered in applying remedies for the cure. This having been done, the strengthening of character by awakening hope, building up self-respect, and inculcating moral and religious principles will be more easily effected.

Sixteenth. In the process of restoration, homes in good families should be made available to the utmost extent possible.

Seventeenth. Technological training should be given in juvenile reformatories where practicable.

"Despair of humanity is distrust of God."—GOETHE.

"Let others admire witches and magicians as much as they will, who can by their art bring them their lost precious things and jewels: I honor and admire a good physician much more who can (as God's instrument) by the knowledge of nature, bring a man to his right wits again when he has lost them."—CASAUBON; quoted by Maudesley.

CHAPTER XVI.

THE INSANE.

(Defectives are, in a special sense, dependents, and require a separate treatment.) We do not attempt in this study to instruct experts, but to arrange the judgments of experts for social uses. Mercier gives good reasons for diffusing information about the insane among the laity. It may tend to diminish the absurd and unreasoning horror with which insane people are regarded; may prevent well-meaning persons from making idiots of themselves by talking of insane persons in their presence; may render the services of magistrates, lawyers and jurors in trials involving the insane more valuable; and may sometimes bring those liable to become insane under timely treatment. Where all institutions depend upon popular suffrage it is essential that the people be instructed.

1. **Definitions.**—No satisfactory definition of insanity has been made, since the phases of disease are so complex and varied. Examples of attempts at definition may

be given. "A disease of a person by which his power of self-determination is taken away." (Schüle). "A seriously impaired condition of the mental functions, involving the intellect, emotions or will, or one or more of these faculties, exclusive of temporary states produced by or accompanying acute intoxications or acute febrile diseases. From the denotation of the word are also usually excluded mental defects resulting from arrested development and idiocy, and such conditions as simple trance, ecstasy, catalepsy and often senile dementia."

2. **Statistics of Insanity.** — These are found in the United States census and in the reports of the boards of various states. (Chapter III.) Apparently the insane have increased more rapidly than the population in the United States. But statistics must be used with caution, because more humane care and accurate methods may bring many to notice who before were not enumerated, while the same humane care lengthens the average life of the insane, and so accumulates them in asylums.

3. **Causes of Insanity.** — Much that was said about the causes of Dependency is applicable here, and need not be repeated. (Chapter VI.) There may be a hereditary predisposition to insanity, and this is aggravated by intermarriage with persons with the same tendency. The physical environment may produce insanity by offering an insufficient supply of food, by indications of danger suddenly presented, by actual strokes upon the greater nerve-centers, by any cause which produces inflammation, as excessive heat, by poisons in air, water, food, and generally by any external influence which seriously impairs the physical health.

As the immediate environment of the mind is the body, we may regard the brain as itself part of the environment, and "direct stress" as an immediate cause of insanity. Pressure, lesions, degeneration of tissue, inflammation are interior causes of mental alienation. Indirect stress includes the mental changes occurring at puberty and the menopause, abnormal activity of the reproductive functions, excesses, child-bearing, and fevers. External and internal conditions act together. The social circumstances are influential. All that affects the livelihood, as exhausting employment, fluctuations in business, precariousness; unfavorable conditions in the family, as quarrels, disgrace, fear, neglect, jealousy; disturbances in society, state and industry; changes in the political world, as in the excitement, suspense and reactions of campaigns; morbid excitement attending religious revivals; are all conditions which increase the danger of insanity among those exposed to this danger.

4. Forms of Insanity. — We must determine these in order to fix upon appropriate social treatment. But the subject is difficult and obscure, and demands the best expert talent. The kinds of mental disturbance shade off into each other, the same person manifests disease of the brain in different ways during the progress of the malady. Dr. W. A. Hammond uses Esquirol's classification in "Insanity in its Medico-legal Relations." 1) Melancholia. Perversion of the understanding in regard to one object or a limited number of objects, with the predominance of sadness or depression of mind. 2) Monomania. Perversion of understanding limited to a single object or small number of objects, with predominance of mental excitement. 3) Mania. Perversion embraces all kinds of objects, and is accompanied with mental excitement. 4) Dementia. Incapacity for reasoning, from the fact that the organs of thought have lost their energy and the force necessary for performing their functions. 5) Imbecility or idiocy. The organs have never been sufficiently well conformed to permit those afflicted to reason correctly.

See Krafft - Ebing's classification in Century Dictionary, and Schüle's in Ziemssen. An American committee of alienists proposed this classification : Mania, acute, re - current, chronic, puerperal ; Melancholia ; Primary Delusional Insanity ; Dementia, primary, secondary, senile, organic ; General Paralysis ; Epilepsy ; Toxic Insanity ; Congenital Mental Deficiency, idiocy, imbecility and cretinism.

Some of the more important works on this subject are :

Bucknill and Tuke, "Psychological Medicine."
Blandford, "Insanity and Its Treatment."
Maudsley, "The Pathology of the Mind." *Journal of Medical Science*. Works of Pinel and Esquirol, Krafft-Ebing, Schüle (in Ziemssen's Handbuch), Wharton and Stillé, "Treatise of Medical Jurisprudence."
E. C. Mann, "Manual of Psychological Medicine."
W. P. Letchworth, "The Insane in Foreign Countries."
Mercier, "Sanity and Insanity" (brief and popular).
D. H. Tuke, "The Insane in the United States and Canada."
Discussions in N. C. C.
Ireland, "Idiocy and Imbecility."
Paul Sollier, "The Idiot and the Imbecile."
Classic English, loaded with learning and curious quotation, "The Anatomy of Melancholy," by Burton.
Spitzka's "Manual of Insanity."
Clouston, "Mental Diseases."
Gower's, "Diseases of the Nervous System."
Charcot, "Maladies du Système Nerveux."
H. C. Burdett, "Hospitals and Asylums."
Ray, "Medical Jurisprudence."
Taylor's "Medical Jurisprudence."

5. Administration of Relief. — *a*) There are many technical aspects of the subject not to be discussed here, such as medicinal and surgical treatment, and the symptoms of various forms of mental disease. All that general society can do is to set in motion political machinery for selecting and retaining the most competent alienists and nurses of aliens. A more definite judgment can be formed by the public on the forms of buildings required and the system of care which fixes these forms. One principle generally accepted is, that the buildings and grounds should be arranged to secure classification, room for varied interests and occupations, and air. The specialization of treatment has advanced very far in the century since criminals, debtors and madmen were promiscuously crowded into the same halls, and that without regard to sex or personal conditions. And this change could not be wrought without some growth of general intelligence on the subject. The expert alienists can achieve no great progress without popular consent, and for this reason the learned must take the public into their confidence.

b) For many years a controversy has been raging over the question whether the chronic pauper insane should be held in state asylums or in local county asylums. No one favors the commitment of acute and probably curable cases to local care, but many think the dependent insane who are thought to be incurable can be more economically and even comfortably cared for in county asylums. The N. C. C. discussions often recur to this matter. The county plan is presented and favored by Mr. H. H. Giles, of Wisconsin, (N. C. C., 1891, p. 78). The essential features of the "Wisconsin plan" are : The chronic pauper insane, who are harmless, are kept in county institutions, and all acute cases remain in state hospitals. If a county has no asylum it may board its patients in another county. Each asylum is under state supervision, so that the system is really not purely local. There is no resident physician. On behalf of this method it is claimed that it is more economical for the taxpayers; that it is more humane, in that it permits many of the insane to reside nearer their friends, and secures more variety of occupation than can be had in the great state institutions. It is claimed there is less need of irksome restraint. It is universally agreed that county care without rigid state supervision is intolerable. The abuses of the helpless insane in county poor houses all over the country are flagrant, notorious and horrible. An example may be found in the Illinois Reports for 1890. The county jail and the county poor house are twin blots on our honor as a nation.

In favor of exclusively state care of the insane, read the summary of argument by Mr. O. Craig (N. C. C., 1891, p. 85). Mr. Craig declares that the medical supervision of state authorities is necessary; that the more beautiful surroundings of state institutions are favorable to cure; that the small county asylums cannot furnish facilities for classification, and for changes according to the changes of patients; that labor in state institutions is more apt to be for the benefit of the patient; that the county asylum brings the stigma of pauperism on the indigent insane; that adequate state supervision can be given to a few large institutions, but not to many scattered small ones; that the state care is quite as economical as the county plan; that the insane are, legally, wards of the state and not of the county.

Mr. W. P. Letchworth, accepting county care in certain cases as a fact to be practically dealt with, lays down the conditions of proper treatment of chronic pauper insane:

"They should be placed under independent management, the members of which should be appointed by the courts for long terms, and should be unsalaried. These boards should be governed, as near as may be, by the same rules that govern boards of managers of state asylums. Accommodation entirely separate from that for sane paupers should be provided on considerable tracts of good land, conveniently accessible by rail or water. The financial and other transactions should be kept separate from those relating to the relief of ordinary paupers. The standard of care should be such as to meet the approval of state authorities."

c) Private insane asylums are sometimes provided in order to secure the separation of insane friends of families able to support them without state aid. They can afford superior comforts and luxuries, and, in some cases, superior medical assistance and nursing. The competition of private with public institutions is wholesome, and variety of methods is a condition of progress. The scientific methods of caring for the mentally unsound are the same for all institutions. There is, however, special need that private asylums should not pass from public inspection and control. The danger of using the asylum for a private person is a real danger, although it has been sometimes grossly exaggerated. Honest and capable management will always welcome fair and careful investigation.

d) The Colony plan of caring for the harmless insane. At Gheel, in Belgium, is a community whose principal business it is to keep insane persons as boarders. A central building for special cases and for administration purposes is the only plant provided by the state, and the cost of this was only $150,000. Set in contrast with this expensive structures like those of the United States, as the

Willard Asylum, which cost $1,600,000, the interest on which sum is a great addition to current expenses. This colony plan has all the advantages of centralized supervision, classification and low cost, while the degree of freedom enjoyed is a marked feature. Of course, only a certain class of the insane can be treated in this way, but this class is large. (N. C. C., 1891, p. 173). Letchworth's "Insane in Foreign Countries."

The Scotch method of caring for harmless insane persons is to board them out among selected families. It has been tried in Massachusetts with encouraging success. (Mr. F. B. Sanborn, N. C. C., 1886. Letchworth, p. 352). Carefully selected demented persons may be better provided for in private families without detriment to the community and with comfort and content to themselves. Many are thus made self-supporting by their labor who would otherwise be a lifelong burden to the state. In Belgium, Scotland and Massachusetts it is not found difficult to secure proper families for their care.

6. **The Popular View of Insanity** is to be considered because it determines the treatment of these unfortunate persons when they are abroad, when they are before the law and in asylums. Experts can do little more than average intelligence or superstitions permit them to do. As words are fossilized history, they carry with them the philosophy of the past and sometimes influence thought. "Lunatic" reminds us of the days when the insane were supposed to be affected by the heavenly bodies. "Epileptic," "possessed," "demonized," suggest the ancient explanation of insanity as the product of malign spiritual influences. "Bedlam" was a corruption of "Bethlehem Hospital," a monastic institution converted by Henry VIII into

an asylum or rather dungeon-house for furious lunatics. Shakespeare uses the term in application to "Bedlam beggars" who "sometimes with lunatic bans, sometimes with prayers, enforce their charity." Letchworth, Ch. I. D. R. Tuke, "History of the Insane in the British Isles." To such notions are due the horrible, illogical and cruel treatment of the insane up to recent years. Consistency cannot be expected in superstition, and these wanderers have been sometimes the objects of religious awe, and often of fiendish cruelty. Even to this day we can with difficulty rid the popular mind of the thought that insanity is something more than the result of physical disorder. While this is not the place to discuss the interesting question of the relation of the Bible to insanity, it may be worth while to call attention to the fact that the Founder of Christianity never treated those called "possessed" with anything but kindness; he never upbraided nor tormented, but always healed them, treating them as he treated other sick folk. Many of his disciples have overlooked this fact.

7. The Insane before the Law. — Mr. F. H. Wines has discussed this question with reference to our conditions in the International Record and in the Illinois reports, fifth to eleventh. Compare Letchworth, Wharton and Stillé and E. C. Mann.

We are able to indicate only a few points for study. *a)* How Mental unsoundness is detected. The main social principle here is that experts must be secured and trusted. In no situation is trained talent more essential. If the symptoms of threatening insanity were more generally taught many could be cured, and much suffering and injustice could be avoided. In a country where insanity is so

common it would seem wise to employ the University
Extension methods on this subject. *b*) Mental unsoundness affects civil rights. The general principle is that
"contracts or wills of idiots or lunatics will not be enforced."
"Fraud itself vitiates a contract, and in this the contracting
party's intellect becomes an essential item for consideration.
Acts and contracts of persons of weak understanding will
be held void when such persons have been imposed upon
by cunning or undue influence." Weakness of intellect
from extreme old age works disability. But great caution
is needed, for the object of law is to protect old age, not
to render it more defenceless. The right to manage one's
own estate comes under the same principles. The unsound
in mind are the wards of the commonwealth, and their
property is held in trust for them.

d) Responsibility for crime. The deciding principle
here is that "medical science is part of the common
law of the land." Idiocy and imbecility may render
a person incapable of distinguishing between right
and wrong in the particular act. One may be suffering
under a delusion as to circumstances which, if true, would
relieve the act from responsibility. The act may be the
natural consequence of the delusion. One may be under
a morbid and uncontrollable impulse to commit the particular act. The doctrine of homicidal mania is recognized
by the courts. As to states of intoxication: "Insanity
produced by *delirum tremens* affects responsibility in the
same way as insanity produced by any other cause. Insanity immediately produced by intoxication does not destroy
responsibility when the patient, when sane and responsible,
voluntarily made himself intoxicated. While intoxication
is, *per se*, no defense to the fact of guilt, yet when the
question of intent or premeditation is concerned, it is

material for the purpose of determining the precise degree."

e) Admission to an asylum or hospital. It seems to be generally agreed that provisions should be made for voluntary self-commitment by those who are aware of their need of treatment. N. C. C. 1891. In emergency cases, where the insane patient is liable to injure himself or others, the violently insane should be committed on the certificate of one reputable physician, pending judicial proceedings. They should not be detained in prisons or jails, but in special "receptacles" provided for this purpose. It is wrong to connect crime and insanity in the popular mind. Judicial commitments should be upon the findings of physicians. These physicians may be empowered to act directly or may be summoned by court or jury. In doubtful cases alienist experts should be consulted. This commitment should be final, so far as admission to the hospital is concerned, and not to be reviewed by the superintendent until he has had time to examine the case. (Dr. W. B. Fletcher). Patients are not to be taken to a hospital by deception. Women patients should be attended to the institution by women. The admission should be as free as possible from the appearance of criminal process, and as near as possible to the forms of admission to any hospital. (Wines). The examination should never be in open court, but the patient should be attended before the court by a few trusted friends, a physician and a legal adviser. Some of our laws on the subject bear the marks of obsolete views of the nature of insanity, as kindred to crime.

f. The power to discharge is not properly vested in the superintendent, because in such a case the patients will regard him as their enemy when they are restrained. This power should be known to be vested in a state board of lunacy, and should be exercised upon the certificate of two medical expert alienists who have examined the case. Probationary discharges are recommended in many cases that gradual trials of liberty may be made. *g*) The rights of the insane, as to person and property and means of happiness, are not to be unreasonably limited. Letters to the state authorities should be forwarded unopened, but those addressed to private persons should come under the eye of the officers of the institution. They are often unfit to go further. *h*) Post - mortem examinations should always be made, with the consent of the relatives, in the interest of justice and of science.

On the methods of commitment to asylums in the United States see N. C. C. 1892, papers by Drs. S. Smith and R. Dewey.

8. The Criminal Insane. (*a*) Characteristics. Persons of this class have violated the laws which protect persons, property, and peace, but they are pronounced irresponsible. Many of these were originally "imbeciles." Others have become insane, with dangerous tendencies. (*b*) Treatment. These patients should not be admitted to the ordinary hospitals for the insane. Insanity is a misfortune, and it is wrong and cruel to wound the feelings of the patients and their friends by compelling them to live in an institution with persons who have been marked as murderers. "A charitable institution is not equipped either in its construction or its administration, to take care of dangerous criminals. The ordinary reputable insane and their friends object to the enforced contact with such associates. The 'insanity dodge' is constantly practiced by convicts in the prison and by criminals on trial, as a means of escape from the consequences of their crimes, and many do so escape. The presence of these criminals is dangerous and demoralizing in the hospitals, and their frequent escapes result in serious injury to the community." (Dr. Dewey Rep. Kankakee Hospital, 1890).

"The danger of relapse after a cure is very great, and a shrewd lunatic may very readily deceive those about him into the belief that he is cured, when, in fact, he is only planning his escape from durance." "There ought to be penitentiary asylums, in which insane criminals should be placed, and in which they may be under scientific treatment." Dr. W. A. Hammond, "Insanity and its Relations to Crime." Whether we regard retribution, prevention, example, or reform, the insane criminals are to be isolated from other persons of diseased nervous systems. In the later chapters on Imbeciles and Criminals we shall see that we touch here the border-land between insanity and crime, and the resemblances may modify essentially the social and legal treatment of some criminals.

9. The Insane Drunkard. Many inebriates live on the borderland between insanity and crime, and manifest the morbid traits of both conditions. The present general policy is to let them alone, or to fine them and imprison them for a short term. This policy is an utter failure in every respect. It does not reform nor cure the inebriate; it does not protect his family and society; and it does not prevent the propagation of an enfeebled and vicious stock. Confirmed inebriates should not be placed in insane asylums, because these institutions are not adapted to repress, confine and correct them. They should not be imprisoned for short terms, because this does not affect hardened offenders, and it breaks the spirit of curable inebriates.

They cannot be successfully treated in voluntary private inebriate asylums, because as soon as they are sobered up they desire to leave before the treatment can afford a permanent cure. (The new methods of the various "gold cures" are left out of account because they are, to the writer, a mystery, and materials for a judgment are not to be obtained).

Confirmed inebriates should be confined, on the basis of an inquest similar to that appropriate for the insane, in special state institutions, and for terms of at least two or three years. In these institutions they should be obliged to work for the benefit of themselves, their families and of society. Such powers of detention ought never to be conferred by the state on any private or church institution. The working of the Massachusetts asylum will be watched with eager interest. (Boston Association Charities Report, 1892, p. 29.) Dr. J. C. Bucknill ("Habitual Drunkenness") would treat the confirmed inebriate as a criminal. Since drunkards usually violate the criminal code they should be apprehended and subjected to cumulative sentences until they win their right to freedom by reform, or manifest their incorrigibility and become permanent residents of penal institutions. On the "Keeley Cure in relation to Insanity and Drunkenness," see paper by Dr. R. Dewey, N. C. C. 1892.

CHAPTER XVII.

THE FEEBLE MINDED.

"Gather up the fragments, that nothing be lost." We have come to the lowest stratum of human life. Yet our hearts respond to the noble words of Dr. G. H. Knight: "Inside these walls we have no imbeciles, no idiots, no fools. They are always in our thoughts and speech, in every condition and age, simply 'the children'; and the best we have and can do is none too good for them."

1. **Statistics.** Dr. A. G. Warner estimates that there are about 30,000 of this class in the United States, of whom 5000 are in special institutions. "About one-fifth come from the well-to-do classes; about one-fifth from the pauper classes; and the remainder from the laboring classes." Dr. C. T. Wilbur, on the basis of Michigan facts, thinks they are as numerous as the insane, and that there are 90,000 in the United States. Dr. W. B. Fish thinks there are over 38,000 "custodial cases of idiocy." Rev. O. McCulloch estimated 77,000. Rev. F. H. Wines expresses the belief that the feeble minded equal the insane in numbers. We must wait for the census returns. (N. C. C. 1890 and 1891.) It is difficult to get accurate reports, because parents hide the facts through shame and affection, and because in the popular intelligence insanity and idiocy are not distinguished.

2. **Characteristics.** —The feeble-minded should be distinguished from the insane. "Insanity is a derangement of

the mind from a diseased condition of the brain. Idiocy is an arrested development of mind. *An idiot may also be insane, as an acute or chronic disease of the brain may affect the mind, but, ordinarily, idiocy is an undeveloped condition of the mind, due to the want of normal development of the brain." Dementia is a condition resembling idiocy, and is caused by brain disease or by senile weakness. The peculiarities of the feeble-minded are shown in the degree of the power of attention, and in the character of the impulses to action.

Paul Sollier makes a sharp distinction between two classes of the feeble-minded, idiots and imbeciles. "The idiot is a being incapable of acting and thinking, an imperfectly developed individual. The imbecile is an abnormal, irregularly developed individual, who possesses the faculties of thinking and acting; but these are necessarily abnormal like the brain which produces them. The idiot can continuously show a good disposition; the imbecile is an egotist, often malicious, even toward those who mean well to him. (With the idiot one accomplishes most with mildness; with the imbecile most by fear.) The idiot is bashful, the imbecile usurping; the former industrious, the latter obstinately indolent; the one is kind, the other ugly. With the idiot the judgment is weak: with the imbecile, false; with the former will is weak, with the latter unreliable. The idiot is scarcely influenced by suggestion; the imbecile is affected by it." There are many exceptions, and all lines are crossed in nature. Speaking broadly the idiot is extra-social, the imbecile is anti-social. It is interesting and instructive to compare Sollier's studies of the imbecile with Lombroso's famous analyses of the "criminal born."

Dr. I. N. Kerlin (N. C. C. 1890, p 244) gives a description of the "moral imbecile" drawn from American clinical experience : "Derangement of the moral perceptions or emotional nature rather than in the intellectual life, which not infrequently is precocious. Unaccountable and unreasonable frenzies, long periods of sulks, and comfort in sulking ; motiveless and persistent lying ; thieving, generally without acquisitiveness ; a blind and headlong impulse toward arson ; delight in cruelty, first toward domestic pets, and later toward helpless or young companions ; self-inflicted violence, even to pain and the drawing of blood ; occasionally, delight in the sight of blood ; habitual wilfulness and defiance, even in the face of certain punishment ; a singular tolerance to surgical pain, and hebetude or insensibility under disciplinary inflictions." Dr. J. D. Scouller (N. C. C. 1884) gives a similar description of a certain class of boys sent to the reform school.

The causes of idiocy and imbecility are various and complex. The parents are not always depraved or diseased. Epilepsy, insanity, inebriety and sexual excesses and disorders in parents are congenital causes. Some great shock to the mother during pregnancy may result in arrested or perverted development of the child. Postnatal causes are fevers, meningitis, frights, shocks, changes at puberty, and precocious development.

3. **Classification.**—For social treatment idiots and imbeciles come into one class, although they are of all grades of weakness and derangement. For certain practical ends many epileptics may be treated with imbeciles, and many demented cases with profound idiots.

In this matter, as elsewhere, we see the truth that sociology must base its descriptions of classes, its estimates of social factors, its prediction of results, and its recommendations to legislators upon biology and psychology, normal and pathological (cf. De Greef, Les Lois Sociologiques).

4. The Method of Care.—N. C. C. 1888 (Dr. Kerlin, quoted N. C. C., 1891 p. 104, by Dr. Fish): "American institutions for the feeble-minded having already been in existence thirty years, it may be asserted that the experimental period has passed, and that when states shall proceed to' legislate for their defectives, it will be done on a permanent basis.

The grades of specific idiocy and imbecility presuppose a wide classification, and at the commencement this should be planned for somewhat as follows:

· First, central buildings for the school and industrial departments. Near at hand should be located the shops.

Second, separate buildings for the care of cases of paralysis and profound idiocy, with such special arrangement of dormitory and day rooms as the infirm character of the inmates may require.

Third, other remote buildings for the custodial and epileptic department, with accessories for both care and training.

Fourth, provision should continually be made for *colonizing* lads as they grow into manhood in properly arranged houses as farmers, gardeners, dairy help, etc."

Special state institutions for the feeble-minded should be provided for the sake of those unfortunate persons themselves. In such institutions, apart from the competitions of society with which they are incompetent to cope, they can live a comparatively happy life. Many of them feel keenly the open or covert criticism of their ways, and they do not suffer from the contrast in the society of their equals. The families to which they belong are entitled to be protected from the damage and danger to which they are exposed from this source. As taxpayers, all families have the right to the use of such schools for their children, since the public schools are not available. The waste of time and productive energy can be greatly reduced by the sequestration of the feeble - minded. Family life is demoralized and crippled by the presence of one of this class. Society must protect itself in this way. "Margaret the mother of criminals," whose progeny cost the state of New York at least $1,250,000, was a feeble - minded person. It is intolerable to permit such creatures to become parents, and so multiply and perpetuate pauperism, idiocy and crime.

5. **Results.**—"Of the feeble - minded who are received and trained in institutions ten to twenty per cent are so improved as to be able to enter life as bread - winners; from thirty to forty per cent are returned to their families so improved as to be self - helpful, or at least much less burdensome to their people ; and further, and of greater importance, one - half the whole number will need custodial care so long as they live." (N. C. C. 1888).

But this view needs the larger outlook suggested by Rev. F. H. Wines : "I think we are apt to be too much discouraged in all charitable work in consequence of our not seeing immediate results. There is a close connection between charitable work of every sort and the belief in the immortality of the soul. . . . How do you know what may be the ultimate result, in a future state, of efforts made in the present life ? How can you estimate the value of an effort to illumine the darkened mind of an idiot ? Nothing is ever lost in the way of benevolent endeavor ; it always tells somewhere."

Special works on the feeble - minded :

Schüle in Ziemmsen.
Ireland on "Idiocy."
Paul Sollier, "The Idiot and the Imbecile."
S. G. Howe, "Causes and Prevention of Idiocy."
Papers in N. N. C., 1892, and earlier.

CHAPTER XVIII.

EPILEPTICS, DEMENTS AND PARALYTICS.

Here we bring together three general classes of patients who require, in some respects, similar social treatment. Looking at the extreme forms of chronic cases, we may regard them all as helpless and unfit to remain in the family and other normal social conditions. Imbeciles are, in some points, akin to epileptics. But imbecility is more distinctly congenital and due to perverted development without disease. Epilepsy usually appears later, as at puberty, is the result of a diseased brain, and moves forward toward dementia. In egoistic impulses they are much alike, the embecile all the time, the epileptic periodically.

1. **Epileptics.**—While "some of the most distinguished men, from Julius Cæsar down, have been epileptics" (Dr. Walker), the epileptic is often an object of dread. Schüle says of him, "Egoism in developed cases is very marked. The epileptic lives for himself and loses the feeling for other men. Nothing can disturb the pedantic regulation of his needs. In the slightest opposition or restriction, he at once sees an enemy's hindrance, which he seeks without scruple to put out of the way. What others wish is

indifferent to him, so far as it does not touch his wishes. Epilepsy takes many forms; it may show itself from early childhood in convulsions; or in imbecility with epileptic tendency; or the early life may be quite sound, and epilepsy appear in youth with convulsions. It tends to terminate in dementia."

Dr. R. Gundry (N. C. C. 1890, p. 263): "They (epileptics) are a disturbing element in every asylum. However mild their forms of insanity generally, however amiable their character, they are liable to explosive paroxysms of fury; and their attacks are shocking to witness. It can be no question that their frequent fits exercise a very unfavorable influence upon other patients of an impressionable nature. For this reason, doubtless, many who should be under hospital care are refused admittance, and drift into various nooks and corners. Many find their way to the poor houses. Among these men are sometimes found excellent, reliable workers during the intervals, long or short, between their paroxysms.

Treatment.—Dr. Gundry advises a separate department of the Insane Hospital for epileptics. Others consider it wiser to have a special institution for them, or a farm colony, where they may labor in lucid intervals. Others favor placing them near the feeble minded and demented, to give their strength in providing for the more helpless charges. The medicinal and surgical treatment and nursing belong to the healing art. There are few institutions for these unfortunate persons in this country.

It is estimated that there are 100,000 epileptics in the United States. Dr. John Norris says that a cure is effected, under hospital methods, in 6½ per cent. of cases, and improvement is nearly all. It is economy to care for them in institutions.

2. Dements.—Many incurable patients of various kinds of insanity pass into this state. We have already spoken of their proper custody and care under the head of state and county care of the chronic insane.

3. Helpless paralytics are frequently reduced to the condition of infants or of the feeble-minded, and need similar care. Except under the most vigorous state inspection and control it is inhuman to trust these to county care. For those whose wealth is sufficient, it is not difficult to furnish nursing and retired rooms; but for the great majority of people the public care is the only adequate and humane provision.

CHAPTER XIX.

THE BLIND AND THE DEAF MUTES.

Persons of both these classes should be regarded as entitled to education at the expense of the state as much as other persons, and on the same grounds. The institutions which the state provides for them are not hospitals, asylums nor reformatories, but simply schools. These infirmities make it necessary to provide schools of forms distinct from other public schools. The pupils are not special objects of charity, unless provision for their board and clothing, in addition to education, may be so considered. It is on this social doctrine that such institutions rest; they are provided to fit special classes for their place and duty as citizens.

According to the census of 1880 there were of the blind in the United States 954 males and 1,112 females in 1,000,000 of population, not far from the European average.

It seems undesirable to hold the blind apart from society and treat them as a dependent class. Their defect is not analogous to that of the insane and helpless. They can be taught many of the arts of life, and can learn to support themselves. As many of them are friendless and exposed to peculiar trials, it is desirable to have some voluntary organization to study and guard their interests, to protect them from designing and unscrupulous persons, to secure them employment, and to advance their means of industrial and social progress. But they should not have permanent provision for support in adult life at public expense, nor in any other way be treated as paupers, so as to break down their self-respect and destroy their character and happiness.

N. C. C. 1888, p. 113; 1886, p. 233.

It is a grave question whether by frequent intermarriages of the blind the infirmity tends to become permanent in certain families.

The same principles apply to the deaf mutes. The state provides schools for them as for other members of the commonwealth. The aim of these schools is to teach them sign language, finger speech, writing, oral speech, and useful arts, so that they may not be kept out of social life, or may enter it on something like equal terms. The progress of educational methods for deaf mutes is a marvel of science and humanity, and the pedagogical results have enriched all school systems.

It is declared that in these institutions, as in so many other places, one serious impediment is "politics." Appointments which should be made on grounds of science and fitness are forced on grounds of political service. "The people have not established these institutions, and do not now support them at heavy cost, with a view to providing temporary homes for intriguing or starving partisans. The people do not build them to be converted into party ambulances."

It is at such points we discover the grand law of social science that society is an organism, a "body" whose organs are reciprocally related as means and ends. When one member suffers, all suffer with it.

PART III.—CRIME AND ITS SOCIAL TREATMENT.

> "Ah, little think the gay, ...
> Whom pleasure, power and affluence surround,
> How many pine in want, and dungeon-glooms;
> Shut from the common air."— *Thomson.*

> "Parum Est
> Coercere Improbos
> Poena,
> Nisi Probos Efficias
> Disciplina."

Quoted by JOHN HOWARD, in "The State of the Prisons," 1784, from the Reformatory of St. Michael at Rome.

Social Interest in Criminals. — In every large city there exist throngs of true barbarians — nay, savages. . . . They make the great bulk of the pauper, beggar and criminal classes of every country. The total cost of supporting, punishing and guarding against them constitutes half the charge of all legitimate government.

Every assault of savagery upon so complicated and extensive organization costs society an immense sacrifice.

There is even a worse consequence. So long as society has this burden on its shoulders, it cannot progress in refinement. It must cling to a large part of its old crudeness, as a protection against its unassimilated membership. It must be perpetually hampered by a heavy coat of mail in consequence of the perpetual dangers that beset it." — WARD, Dynamic Sociology, Vol. II, p. 594.

"Next to the free goodness and mercy of the Author of my being, temperance and cleanliness are my preservation. Trusting in Divine Providence, and believing myself in the way of duty, I visit the most noxious cells, and while thus employed, 'I fear no evil.' I never enter an hospital or prison before breakfast, and in an offensive room 1 seldom draw my breath deeply."— (JOHN HOWARD.)

"Our literature abounds in studies of social topics which are of little use, even when they are not positively misleading, because they do not approach their subjects from the sociological point of view. And it is out of the second and third rate followers of this class of writers that we are getting a deal of social quackery and cranks. A lot of social material and information is a poor substitute for sociological training."

SAMUEL W. DYKE.

CHAPTER XX.

CLASSIFICATION.

Morality and Law.— The classification of law - breakers depends on the moral distinctions and legal regulations made by a given society. "The criminal law is that part of the law which relates to the definition and punishment of acts and omissions which are punished as being (1) attacks upon the public order, internal or external; or (2) abuses or obstructions of the public authority; or (3) acts injurious to the public in general; or (4) attacks upon the persons of individuals, or upon rights annexed to their persons; or (5) attacks upon the property of individuals or rights connected with, and similar to, rights of property."

> J. F. Stephen. History of the Criminal Law in England, ch. I. Cf. Pike, History of Crime, vol. 2, p. 489.

Morality and law do not cover precisely the same field, though they ought to support each other, and usually do so. The law is the definite expression of the moral judgment and of the collective will of society in respect to acts or omissions regarded as injurious. It follows that society will treat as anti - social all those who are better or worse than the average, and this in varying degrees as the eccentric person makes society more or less uncomfortable. As society develops altruism it will not merely react against its unsocial members, but will see in them moral and spiritual possibilities which demand education. In primitive society little is thought of except revenge and protection. But even in the most humane stages of civilization the ele· ment of "resentment" will continue.

Morals cover the region, not only of actions, but also of thoughts, feelings and motives. Religion takes account of immoral acts and inward states, and calls them "sins." Law is limited to "definite overt acts or omissions capable of being distinctly proved. The sentence of the law is to the moral sentiment of the public in relation to the offence what a seal is to hot wax. It converts into a permanent final judgment what might otherwise be a transient sentiment. This close alliance between criminal law and moral sentiment is in all ways healthy and advantageous to the community. I think it highly desirable that criminals should be hated, that the punishments inflicted upon them should be so contrived as to give expression to that hatred, and to justify it so far as the public provision of means for expressing and gratifying a healthy natural sentiment can justify and encourage it." (Stephen). Compare the discussion of "Resentment" by Bishop Butler, in his "Sermons." Cf. Pike, His. of Crime, Vol. 2, Ch. xxii.

On the basis of these definitions of crime we may form our classification.

1. **The Political Criminal.**—In personal character the individuals of this class differ from "criminals" of the habitual and instinctive type, but in the fact of antagonism to law and public sentiment they are found

together. In savage society innovators of all kinds are promptly suppressed. When priests and chiefs become invested with governmental and divine honors, the whole force of the tribe is directed to the destruction of heretics. As state and church are not differentiated in early societies an offence against religious codes becomes an attack upon the state,—a crime. Dissent is treason. This union of church and state continues still in most countries of the world, even in Christendom.

It was under the Mosiac code, though wrongly interpreted and applied, that Jesus met his death as a "criminal." It was under the law of his country that Socrates was compelled to drink the deadly hemlock. When Roman emperors were deified by law Jews and Christians were capitally punished as "atheists" for refusing to pay divine honors to the head of the state. The history of European countries in our own time could show abundant examples of the infliction of degrading penalties on multitudes of the most conscientious and peaceable citizens. The history of America before the constitution would reveal similar examples of persecution according to law.

Stephen, History of Crim. Law, ch. xxv.
Bancroft, History of the United States.

When a reformer attacks anti-social laws and customs, especially in a backward community, he must expect to be treated as a criminal; and it is only in the light of subsequent events and discussions that we can even understand a case like that of John Brown the anti-slavery agitator. During the period of ferment about 1848, many of the best spirits of Germany were practically exiled for their political opinions.

It must, however, be noted that many who sincerely believe they are serving a humane cause are so anti-social in speech and action as to endanger all the products of past progress. The moral sentiments of the country generally supported the judicial findings against the anarchists of Chicago. So far as society is wrong in its sentiments and laws the only remedy is advance in culture of all kinds.

2. **Criminals by Passion.**—Men sometimes break the law under stress of sudden temptation, and the act is exceptional in their conduct. The motive may be one worthy of all honor, as where a man smites one who insults his wife or daughter. His usual instincts and habits are in harmony with public order. But society cannot permit even such a citizen to revert to the savage method of resenting insults and protecting rights. The duel, lynch-law and street brawls are "survivals" of primeval culture, or are examples of "arrested development" of moral culture. The duel has become a crime since about 1848, through a previous change in public sentiment crystallized into a statute in consequence of a tragedy.

3. **The Occasional Criminal** is a person of feeble will and moral fibre. If he is not tempted sorely, and if outward circumstances are favorable he may pass through life with a clean record. But if he is surrounded by evil companions, is not trained to regular habits of productive industry, and has no help from refining spiritual influences he may become a thief, a forger, a burglar or embezzler, according to his ability and his opportunity.

4. **The Habitual Criminal** has linked lawless acts into a chain of habit. The occasional criminal under favoring circumstances becomes a habitual criminal. The development may be slow or rapid, but when the vicious acts have

been often repeated and with impunity, the slavery is difficult to break.

5. **The Professional Criminal** is one who lives by lawless acts. He is a human parasite. There are many crime trades, and in each trade there are apprentices, journeymen and capitalists, as in legitimate and productive industries. Many of these are described in Byrnes' " Professional Criminals of America," and their photographs are given. The "Rogues' Gallery" in city police offices will furnish abundant illustrations, and the officers can relate many biographies.

It is interesting to note that there are social ranks and castes among professional criminals. Your absconding bank cashier will not associate in Montreal with common porch thieves. Bank burglars have no dealings with pickpockets. Gamblers travel along the great rivers and railroads with a distinct air of aristocracy, and not rarely advertise themselves as philanthropists.

"Professional criminals may be classed as exceptional incorrigibles, for the number of professional criminals in American prisons is not so great as is usually supposed. Probably not more than ten per cent. of state prisoners in New York can be of this class. Professional criminals develop out of all the other classes of criminals." Z. R. Brockway.

6. **The Instinctive Criminal.**—It is of this class that the "criminal anthropologists" more specially write. Lombroso calls them the "criminal born," which term assumes that the decisive conditions of the lawless career are congenital. The word "instinctive" is to be preferred because it includes not only hereditary but also all social and per-

sonal causes. Our description of "Imbeciles" and the
"Moral Insane" (in Part II), has already brought out one
phase of this subject. It is not difficult to assign many
law-breakers to this class. The causes may be ante-natal
or post-natal; it is the resulting condition which here concerns us. The ordinary legal view may be expressed in
these sentences from Stephen : "Our leading principle is
. . . . . that judges when directing juries have to do exclusively with this question,—Is this person responsible, in the
sense of being liable, by the law of England as it is, to be
punished for the act which he has done . . . . . If it is
true, as I think it is, that the law of England on this subject is unsufficiently expressed, it is no less true that medical knowledge relating to insanity is fragmentary, not well
arranged, and, to say the very least, quite as incomplete as
the law . . . . . No act is a crime if the person who does
it is, at the time where it is done, prevented either by defective mental power or by disease affecting his mind (a)
from knowing the nature and quality of his act, or (b) from
knowing the act is wrong, or (c) from controlling his own
conduct, unless the absence of the power of control has
been produced by his own default. . . . . . But an act
may be a crime (although the mind of the person who does
it is affected by disease) if the disease does not in fact produce upon his mind one or other of the effects above mentioned in reference to that act." And against the tendency
in some quarters to shield law-breakers from punishment
on the ground of a vicious nature : "My own experience
certainly is, that people who commit great crimes are
usually abominably wicked, and particularly murderers. I
have the very worst opinion of them . . . . . If I had not
had that experience, I should not have imagined that a
crime, which may be the result of a transient outbreak of

passion indicated such abominable heartless ferocity, and such depths of falsehood as are, in my experience, usually found in them. This peculiarity appears to me to be a reason not for sparing them, but for putting them to death. . . . . If the morally insane man is as able to abstain from crime as a sane bad man, and has the same reason—namely, fear of punishment—for abstaining from crime, why should not he be punished if he gives way to temptation?" We shall see how far this view agrees with that of the "anthropologists." Stephen is at least free from the "theological" prejudice. In the later chapters we shall indicate the marks of the Instinctive Criminal, physical and psychical.

Mr. Dugdale, "The Jukes," pp. 110–111, makes a minute classification of criminals who had come under his observation.

Typical classes of Criminals.—"The large proportion of habitual criminals raises the question: How shall their number be decreased? This requires the citing of typical cases which suggest reflections on the manner in which the law and the prison now deal with them. (1) Of those who are essentially not criminal, who are of sound mind and body, honest and industrious, and of good stock, there are, among state prison convicts, from one to two per cent. They are usually committed for crimes against the person, and belong to that class of men who are benefited by imprisonment, if the term of sentence is not too long. What they need is protection from the after recognition of habitual criminals, from contamination by loss of self-respect, and opportunity for mental culture. (2) First offenders who fall because they are vain, self-indulgent, and in the toils of lewd women. They abuse trusts by embezzlement, and represent a class who are quite too numerous in our midst.

When detected they often escape prosecution altogether for the sake of their parents, and because they are personally liked. The type is that of a descending family, in which the misuse of good faculties and the abuse of opportunities conspire to lead astray, but the good teachings of youth and the dear associations of home make reformation easy. (3) First offenders who have been led off into crime by bad associates. They are children of honest parents who, from indulgence or want of capacity, have not brought them up judiciously. In the foregoing we have what may be called types of sporadic crime, in which the primary element of disorder is only a movement of momentary passion kindled partly by feelings of self-respect, or educational neglect, uncomplicated by insane or criminal hereditary tendencies, and in which the criminal habit has not become fixed. (4) Convicts of low vitality, born of pauper parents, who have left them orphans in childhood so that they have drifted into habitual crime. (5) Illegitimate children born of intemperate, vicious and criminal parents, who have trained them to crime. These types have, in addition to parental neglect, a hereditary tendency to crime, pauperism or premature death. Many are, however, reformable, and, if such treatment is to be applied, the prerequisite is a knowledge of the ancestral defects, because the heredity is the main factor in their lives. (6) Contrivers of crime who look upon crime as a legitimate business, who "don't do no light things," but "go in for big money," and are irreclaimable. (7) Active executors of crime, who have passed their thirty-fifth year and are casting about to abandon the field as executors of crime, to enter that of crime capitalists. (8) Panderers to the vices of criminals, themselves the active abettors in facilitating crime. In this series, whatever may have been the road which each has traveled, whether forecast by hereditary transmission or induced by miseducated childhood, these men, past reform, dangerous and desperate, are of service to the state only as examples of the austerity of her justice. (9) Men who have acquired epilepsy or insanity, and whose crimes are, probably, the results of perverted minds. (10) Unfortunates who have inherited nervous and brain diseases which destroy the moral sense. (11) Persons who have forms of nervous disease which destroy the will power over the voluntary motions, and do acts of impulse which result in murders, attempts to kill and rape."

CHAPTER XXI.

CRIME CAUSES.

In Part I. the causes of pauperism and of organic defect have been indicated. Those same forces tend to produce criminals, whether they be from inheritance, environment or personal conduct. Setting aside extreme forms of imbecility and moral insanity, we discover in ordinary criminals the same elemental forces which move ordinary persons. There is nothing unintelligible in their conduct. The organic appetites which in all men tend to preserve the individual life and to maintain the species, and the derivative impulses which seek shelter, warmth, covering, and the intellectual, moral and spiritual impulses which result in higher culture, are all found in ordinary criminals. In the depraved classes the lower forces are dominant; the person is egoistic; the nobler nature is dwarfed, perverted or merely rudimentary. But the wildest freaks of the criminal may be understood by patient and sympathetic study. Theft is an evil direction of the universal desire for the means of satisfying physical and other wants.   Erotic vices are exaggerations of sins not unknown in polite society. Tattooing is an expression of nascent æsthetic tastes. Sentimentalism is deformed sentiment.   The brigands' superstition is the seamy side of the religious faculty.

Ellis gives a summary of crime causes under the head "cosmic, biological, and social."

1. Cosmic Causes.—Morrison has given the results of investigations of the effect of, *a*) *climate* on the production of crime and the determination of its forms.   There can be no question that climate has some influence on conduct and character ; but the phenomena of climate are so intermingled with those of history, race, and social customs that hitherto few definite conclusions have been reached. Apparently crimes against the person are more common in the South of Europe while crimes against property are more common in the North of Europe.

Quetelet says, " the number or crimes against *property* relatively to the number of crimes against the *person* increases considerably as we advance toward the *north*." (Tarde agrees with him).

Enrico Ferri arrives at the conclusion " that a maximum of crimes against the person is reached in the hot months, while, on the other hand, crimes against property come to a climax in the winter."

b) The effect of the *seasons* on crime is more distinctly marked.   The criminal within and without the prison is liable to attacks of irrational lawless impulses, and these attacks increase in the summer.   Throughout Europe the greater number of suicides happen in the two warm seasons.

"The prevalence of suicide rises and falls with the sun.
In London there are many more suicides in the sunny
month of June than in the gloomy month of November."
The influence of temperature on other forms of crime,
though not so great as with suicides, is very distinctly
shown in statistics. "Between six and eight per cent. of
the crime committed in England, may with reasonable
certainty be attributed to the direct action of temperature."
(Morrison). "In the Italian prisons, in the four hottest
months, there are the greatest number of offences against
prison discipline." (This judgment of Marro is questioned
by Colajanni).

2. **The Biological Factor.**— It is assumed that the psychical character and conduct are affected by the physical
condition, especially of the brain and nervous system. All
admit this to be true when the nervous derangement is
manifest. Deviations from the normal condition may
have their origin in eccentric variations from the family
type (atypic), or in reversion to former states (atavism),
or in morbid degeneration and deformity,— congenital or
post-natal. Lombroso's work emphasizes the conviction
that as we are all descended from savages, criminals are to
be regarded as examples of reversion to primitive character.
He does not deny other factors but makes much of atavism.
But Lombroso's views are by no means universally accepted
as final, nor are they claimed to be so by himself. His
writings cannot be ignored, and they mark an epoch in
the study of crime causes.

"A great portion of the crimes of modern days are but
our inheritance from a past state of barbarism. Naturalists
of the modern school point out primitive organisms which
still survive in their primitive form, though new species

have been developed out of them.   In the same manner there are still savages living in our midst, of the same blood and origin as ourselves, and yet unlike us in all except our common ancestry." (Pike).   On the "Criminal" Traits of Savages see Fiske, Discovery of America, Vol. 1, p. 49.

"The transmission of an improvement of natural capacity, mental as well as bodily, by exercise and training, is not only a reality but a chief determining factor in the evolution of the race. . . . This theory of mental heredity, manifestly tends to support the conclusion that the child brings with it into the world an outfit of instinctive tendencies or dispositions constituting the natural basis of the civilized and moralized man.   These tendencies, being comparatively late in their acquirement by the race, are necessarily inferior in strength to the deeper-seated and earlier-acquired impulses of the nature-man or savage." Sully.   "The Human Mind," Vol. I, p. 139.   He notices the objections of Weissman, but does not consider them conclusive.

3. The Social Factor.— In Part I. these elements have been noticed,— defects in domestic, industrial, governmental, educational, ecclesiastical, social and international relations.   The analyis there made need not be repeated here.   The Degenerate Stock has three main branches, organically united,— Dependents, Defectives and Delinquents.   They are one blood, and they tend to congregate in one social environment.

A few illustrations may be added.

Educational defects as cause of crime.   "The Federal Bureau of Education, from statistics applying to twenty states, has recently formulated these conclusions: (1) That about one-sixth of all the crime in the country is committed by persons wholly illiterate. (2) That about one-third of it is committed by persons practically illiterate. (3) That the proportion of criminals among the illiterates is about ten times as great as among those who have been instructed in the elements of a common school education or beyond." We must be our own guard, however, against overestimating the value of mere instruction without moral training and power to gain a livelihood by skilled labor.

See Pike, History of Crime, near close of Volume II.

Mr. C. E. Felton (N. P. A., 1891, p. 113), has thus summarized the chief social factors which cause crime: "The ease with which habitual criminals avoid arrest, and thereby or otherwise escape punishment for their offences; the lightness of sentences if convicted; the laxity of discipline in our prisons; the present senseless views of the public and the acts of the legislatures as to systems of prison labor, and its ease to the prisoner; the abundance and variety of the food received; the comfortable quarters in which prisoners are housed; the easy access of friends by visitation; and the readiness with which a sensational press and a sympathetic public accepts as true the complaints of prisoners, thereby making the prison officer the recognized servant of the prisoners through the public. . . . The lack of police surveillance over the discharged criminal also increases the temptation to renew crime life."

Mr. C. F. Coffin, after a visit to England, expresses these judgments: (1) The judges (in England) have got in the habit of passing shorter sentences. (This tends to diminish the prison population). (2) Fines have been largely substituted for imprisonment. (Same effect). (3) Emigration has sent out many criminals. We receive those sent out, and thus, while crime seems to decrease in England, it increases with us. (Census Bulletin 31). Our county jails and prisons mingle the young with old adepts and form schools of crime. The effects of slavery in the South and of unsocial economic conditions everywhere, low wages, extravagance, class strife and hatred, are to be counted among social causes of lawlessness.

Cf. Hon. R. B. Hayes and Judge Wayland, N. P. A., 1891, p. 17 and p. 39.

Economic Causes of Crime.—" If love is, as the poet says, the tyrant of gods and of men, it is certainly much less so than hunger. Misery is a worse counsellor than amorous passions. To cite only one proof, the statistics of France, from 1836 to 1880, established the fact that after physical suffering and cerebral maladies, misery, reverses of fortune and drunkenness, are the worst general determining motions of suicide. Family disgraces, lust, jealousy, and debauch fall into the third grade. And it must be admitted that in case of cerebral disorders and family disgrace, the loss of money, or an unhappy situation, are very important considerations." (De Greef.)   Cf. Marshall's " Principles of Economics," pp. 1-3.

"Criminals are men who, in a great degree, are moved and directed by the impulses around them; their characters are formed by the civilization in which they move. They are, in many respects, the representative men of the country. It is a hard thing to draw an indictment against a criminal which is not, in some respects, an indictment of the community in which he has lived." Governor Seymour. N. P. A., 1890, p. 71.

> "Yet why, you ask, these humble crimes relate,
> Why make the Poor as guilty as the Great ?

To show the great, those mightier sons of pride,
How near in vice the lowest are allied ;
Such are their natures and their passions such,
But these disguise too little, those too much :
So shall the man of power and pleasure see
In his own slave as vile a wretch as he ;
In his luxurious lord the servant find
His own low pleasures and degenerate mind :
And each in all the kindred vices trace,
Of a poor, blind, bewilder'd, erring race,
Who, a short time in varied fortune past,
Die, and are equal in the dust at last."
                    CRABBE, "The Village."

            "Tremble thou wretch,
    That has within thee undivulged crimes
    Unwhipped of justice."   SHAKSPEARE, "Lear," III. 2.

4. **The Personal Will** counts for something as a cause of criminal conduct.   Men choose to do evil deeds, and thus, through habit, set up evil dispositions, and such dispositions become, in turn, the fountain of other evil deeds.   Crimes not only come to people but come from people.   It is on this fact of freedom to choose or refuse that we base our social judgments and our appeals for moral reformation. At any rate Judge Wayland is right in saying to those who plead the bondage of will: "'The less the criminal's will is free, ·the more his body should be held fast."   Stephen says : "Each individual man is an unknown something,—as such he is other and more than a combination of the parts which we can see and touch,—and his conduct depends upon the quality of the unknown something which he is."   This is a rather vague way of admitting freedom of will.   The power to refuse and choose is no more "unknown" than the power to see or hear or judge.

The necessity for avoiding hasty and narrow generaliza-tions is happily put by Rev. F. H. Wines in the Census

Bulletin 182: "Ignorance is a cause of crime. Nevertheless 66.57 per cent. of all prisoners charged with homicide have received the rudiments of an education, in English or in their own tongue, and 3.44 per cent have received a higher education. Ignorance of a trade is a cause of crime. But 19.35 per cent are returned as mechanics or apprentices, and a much larger number have the necessary skill to follow mechanical pursuits. Idleness is a cause of crime. But 82.21 per cent. were employed at the time of their arrest. Intemperance is a cause of crime, though a less active and immediate cause than is popularly supposed. But 20.10 per cent. were total abstainers, and only 19.87 per cent. are returned as drunkards. The root of crime is not in circumstances, but in character. The saying of the Great Teacher will forever remain true: 'Out of the heart proceed evil thoughts, murders.' Science confirms the moral teaching of religion."

On the Causes of Crime, see Lombroso "Criminal Man," early chapters, and the introduction by Letourneau.

Morrison, "Crime and Its Causes."

G. Rylands, "Crime, Its Causes and Remedy."

Dugdale's "The Jukes."

MacDonald's "Criminology."

Letourneau, "Evolution Juridique."

CHAPTER XXII.

CRIMINAL ANTHROPOLOGY—PHYSICAL.

"There are no crimes; there are only criminals!"—LACASSAGNE.

"It is well that the problem of the science of criminal anthropology has been attacked from its most important

side, that of the type.....This point is scarcely recognized,
even by the most respectable savants.   The reasons for this
are many: above all, there are the criminals by occasion or
by passion, who do not belong to the type, and should not."
(Lombroso.)

It should be understood that the marks here given are
those which belong to the "criminal type."   The books of
H. Ellis and A. MacDonald supply to English readers the
established results and the tentative generalizations of the
European investigations.   We shall briefly indicate these as
suggesting the principles of social treatment.   It must be
said that very eminent students regard the evidence as
inconclusive and very contradictory.

1. **The Skull and Brain.**—It is understood that we are
here dealing with a special and limited class of law-breakers,
the "Instinctive Criminals."   Among all the persons actually
charged with crime, comparatively few can be distinguished
from normal men by physical characteristics.   It is none
the less important to secure reliable means of distinguishing even a small class of law-breakers.   The following statements indicate the present state of knowledge, but they
must be received with caution, as open to modification by
further study.   "The average size of criminal's heads is
probably about the same as that of ordinary people's
heads ; but both small and large heads are found in greater
proportion, the medium-sized heads being deficient."
Thieves more frequently have small heads; the large heads
are usually found among murderers." (Ellis.) The peculiarities of the skull are apparently exaggerated.   If the criminal belongs to a race with long skulls that characteristic is
apt to be marked.   So in the broad-headed races.   The
pointed top is often found among criminals.   In a "com-

plete criminal" one may expect "a feeble cranial capacity, a heavy and developed lower jaw, a large orbital capacity, and jutting eye arches.   The skull is often abnormal and asymmetrical." (Letourneau.)   A receding forehead is found among persons of unusual mental power, but, taken together with other defects, is one mark of inferior organization.

The study of the brains of criminals, in comparison with those of normal persons, has reached certain tentative generalizations.   Topinard finds an inferiority of some 30 grammes in the average weights.   But the shape, quality, development and conditions of the brain are more important than the size.   "What the brains of criminals present, not characteristically, but in common with those of other individuals badly endowed, though by no means criminals, is a frequent totality of defective conditions from the point of view of their regular functions, and which renders them inferior."   (Hervé, quoted by Ellis).

Various diseased conditions have been found in the brains of criminals beyond the average of men, as "pigmentation, degenerating capillaries, cysts, thickened and adhering membranes, the vestiges of old hyperæmia and hæmorrhages."   Meningitis is common.   In the fœtus and developing child the brain affects the skull, and in later years it seems probable that the abnormal forms and precocious closing of the skull affect the brain.   They seem to have mutual influence on each other.   But which is primary we cannot yet determine.   In the same way while the abnormal brain affects character and habits, the indulgence of vices or bad habits of any kind, in consequence of defective training, helps to shape the brain and determine its condition and structure.   The food, drink, home training, temper, conduct may leave deep marks on the brain which were not congenital.

2. The Face.—Assuming provisionally that congenital criminals are examples of reversion to inferior ancestral character, or are instances of arrested and perverted development, we should expect points of resemblance to savages, imbeciles, and the insane. Some of these marks are pointed out · by criminologists, but the ground is too new for dogmatic generalizations about physiognomy. MacDonald's conclusion is a model of scientific caution : "Physiognomy, though uncertain, gives us valuable hints sometimes." Prisoners with hair clipped, beard two days old, eager to escape, balked in plans, look much more like savages than the same men dressed in citizens' garb and walking on the street. It is thought by many experts that the following facial marks characterize a large number of instinctive criminals. "The criminal, as to æsthetic physiognomy, differs little from the ordinary man, except in the case of women criminals, who are almost always homely, if not repulsive." "The beard is scant or absent, but the hair abundant. The ears project. Very often the nose is twisted or flat. The countenance is often feminine with the man, virile with the woman. The Mongoloid projection of the zygomatic arches is not rare." "The intellectual physiognomy shows an inferiority in criminals, and when in an exceptional way there is superiority, it is rather of the nature of cunning and shrewdness. The inferiority is marked by vulgarity, by meager cranial dimensions, small forehead, dull eyes. The moral physiognomy is marked in its lowest form with a sort of unresponsiveness ; there is sometimes the debauched, haggard visage." The different kinds of criminals have characteristic features. "Those guilty of rape (if not cretins) almost always have a projecting eye, delicate physiognomy, large lips and eye-lids ; the most of them are slender, blond, rachitic. The pederasts often have a feminine elegance, long and curly hair, and, even in prison garb, a certain feminine figure, a delicate skin, childish look, and abundance of glossy hair, parted in the middle. Murderers, and thieves who break open houses, have woolly hair, are deformed in the cranium, have powerful jaws, enormous zygomæ. Habitual homicides have a glassy, cold, immobile, sometimes bloody, and dejected look ; often an aquiline nose, or, better, a hooked one, like a bird of prey, always large ; the jaws are also large, ears long, hair woolly, abundant and rich (dark) ; beard rare ; canine teeth, very large ; the lips are thin. A large number of forgers and swindlers have an artlessness, and something clerical in their manner, which gives confidence to their victims ; some have a haggard look, very small eyes, crooked nose, and face of an old woman."— (MacDonald). Many persons having these marks have never become criminals, but when many elements of inferiority are combined, the liability to yield to temptation is increased. Lombroso quotes proverbs which prove that these signs of facial expression have produced a popular impression which agrees with that made upon the minds of careful observers. The pallid skin, the scant beard, the masculine voice, and bearded face of woman, the smiling countenance averted, the small and twinkling eyes, are all noted in these sayings of the nations. The statues of Nero, Tiberius, and Caligula show the reflection of their biographies. Sensitive women, ignorant of the seamy side of life, shrink instinctively from the presence of the criminal. While police judges and officers may be unable to analyze their impressions, they can usually discriminate members of the lawless classes from others with a fair degree of accuracy. But the marks by which they judge are, perhaps, more often the signs of vicious habits than of congenital defect and monstrosity.

The Teeth.—Since dental anomalies are supposed to mark reversion, the teeth of criminals are being studied. "A fourth molar, found generally among the platyrhine apes, is occasionally found in man." They may be looked for in criminals. Peculiarities of size and defect in the canines have been observed. In idiots the teeth and palate are frequently deformed. No generalized conclusions seem to be reached.

The Ears.—It is thought that the "criminal type" shows in an unusual number of examples voluminous, projecting, handle - shaped ears ; pointed projection in the outer margin of the ear ("Darwinian tubercle"), the doubling of the posterior branch of the fork of the antihelix, a conical tragus, and absence of lobule.

The Nose.—Ottolenghi thinks the "criminal nose in general is rectilinear, more rarely undulating, with horizontal base, of medium length, rather large, and deviating to one side."

Wrinkles are frequent, even in young criminals, and give to them the appearance of age. The expression of lower impulses, as shown in the marks about the nose and mouth, is more pronounced than that of the eyes. Intelligence and geniality are seldom manifested in the habitual lines of the face.

3. **The Hair.** — Beards are thought to be usually scant and hair abundant and dark. Baldness is rare. Nothing decisive is asserted as to color.

4. **The Bony Structure,** muscular system, and internal organs. — The points most frequently observed are the

unusual length of the extended arms, the feeble muscular energy, grave deficiency in the lungs and chest, stooping shoulders, excessive number of cases of heart disease, abnormal and diseased sexual organs.   These defects go with all others which show the criminal type to be degraded and defective.   Some of the peculiarities noticed in criminals are common with epileptics and imbeciles.   But the relation of insanity to crime is a matter of grave controversy, and the boundary lines are not fixed in medical or legal science.

5. **Insensibility.**—In persons of the criminal type physical insensibility is noticeable, while they are peculiarly sensitive to meteoric changes.   We have seen that crimes increase with hot weather and that prison discipline is more difficult in summer and just before electrical storms.   Many criminals are very agile and quick in their movements, but they have low powers of endurance.   The average of the color-blind is high.   The number of left-handed criminals is above the normal.   As with the lower races and idiots, so among criminals, we find a general incapacity for blushing.   The smygmograph reveals feeble vascular reaction.   The pulse shows a change by the plethysmograph when objects are presented which excite fear, lust, and most of all, vanity.

The average eyesight of criminals is good.   The sense of hearing is often obtuse.   The olfactory sense is defective.   The sense of taste is more developed in the normal man than in the criminal, and more developed in the occasional criminal than in the instinctive criminal.

Of special interest is the insensibility to pain which is shown very generally by criminals.   This they share in common with the lower races of mankind and imbeciles, a fact which suggests either degeneration, arrested development or atavism, or all of these.   Many illustrations are given by Lombroso, Ellis and MacDonald.   Criminals recover rapidly from wounds, unless alcohol or some specific poison aggravates the sore.

These facts of physical insensibility are closely connected with the moral obtuseness of criminals which is so plainly marked, and may be regarded as both cause and effect of crimes which are selfish and cruel.

CHAPTER XXIII.

CRIMINAL ANTHROPOLOGY—PSYCHICAL.

Holding steadily in mind the fact that we are now considering only one class of those named "criminals" before the law, the "instinctive" criminals, we may sum up the chief characteristics. We refer to Lombroso, Ellis, MacDonald and others for illustrations.

1. **Intellectual Power and Intelligence.**—Lombroso gives as a result of his investigations, his judgment that if we could establish an average of mental ability with the precision possible in the case of observations on skulls, it would be found that the average is lower than the normal, with exaggerations of superiority and inferiority. The intellectual life of instinctive criminals is affected by their physical condition and moral peculiarities. They are lazy and incapable of continuous application. In consequence of this fact they are poor scholars, slow and uncertain in their progress. They are "thoughtless," in the

sense that they are frivolous and wanting in forecast. Their wit turns to making light of their offenses, and in ridicule of all things precious and sacred. Lombroso doubts a somewhat popular belief that if criminals would apply their talents to useful industry they would excel. Seldom can remarkable talent be found among them. They are impostors, but not skillful. Their combinations, more or less ingenious, lack coherence and · logic. The skill they show is due chiefly to constant repetition of a narrow range of actions. Lombroso's theory that genius is akin to crime and insanity requires further examination and is much disputed, although cases of genius with congenital tendencies of a morbid nature have been found.

The men of science furnish a small ratio of criminals, while the excitable and less balanced artistic temperament tends more frequently to anti-social habits.

Language reveals intellectual traits as well as moral character and social tendencies. The peculiarity of the language of criminals is found in their slang (argot). The syntax and idioms of the ordinary language are not changed, but a new vocabulary is invented. The most general feature, and that which reminds us of primitive languages, consists in indicating an object by one of its attributes. Death is called " the cruel," " the certain." Slang reveals the hidden workings of the criminal mind. Shame is " the bloody ;" hour, " the rapid ;" the prison, " la petite sainte ;" preaching, " the wearisome ;" the moon, " the spy."

Slang may be used to conceal one's meaning from listeners, in which case the word is lengthened or transformed, but by fixed rules understood in the choice circle of thieves. Words are borrowed from foreign tongues. The German thieves borrow Hebrew words; those of Italy enrich their vocabulary from German and French sources. Archaic forms, long since disused, are preserved in this slang. English robbers are the most obstinate conservators of Anglo-Saxon terms; as "frow" for girl, and "mems" for month. These forms rise and die, succeeding each other with rapidity. This corresponds to the fickle, volatile nature of the inventors. The slang of thieves belongs to the whole country, and runs even over political divisions as in Italy before the union of states. And some phrases, as "tick" for watch, are common in several nations. The lawless are vagabonds, and call themselves in German slang "strohmer," or running water. Among the causes of thieves' slang are the desire to conceal one's purposes from the public and from officers; the inclination common to each social community and profession to use phrases peculiar to its mode of life; the caprice and hunger for fresh sensations; love of irony and coarse pleasantry; a propensity to look for the ridiculous side of events, common among vagabonds and idlers; and tradition, which binds century to century. Lombroso insists that atavism appears here a cause: "They speak as savages because they are savages in the midst of a brilliant European civilization."

Cf. Lombroso, Ellis, MacDonald. Avé-Lallemant (Ueber die Gaunerthum) quoted by Schäffle, "Bau and Leben," Bud. I.

Prison inscriptions, hieroglyphs and signs.—"The tramps in the United States have a regular system of marking doors and gates with chalk, which any one can observe in cities. Mischievous boys occasionally imitate these signs. They have been observed in all European countries. They are sign-posts for the confraternity. There is a hieroglyphic for theft, for a theft completed, for the direction a thief has taken in flight, for a benevolent resident, a

severe domestic, or a dangerous dog.   Is it not curious
that these 'savages in the midst of civilization' should
recur to the earliest forms of written language?"   The
style of writing has been studied carefully, and some have
thought it resembled that of the insane.   But this is uncertain, and the matter requires further investigation.   The
inscriptions found on the walls of cells are full of interest
as frank revelations of the mental traits and culture of
criminals.   These inscriptions manifest the shallow wit,
the sentimentalism, the volatile emotion, the gross obscenity,
the narrow mental range, and the lawless, egoistic impulses
of this class.   It is worth while to gather and preserve them,
under careful watch and ward, in order to enter into the
criminal mode of thought.   Many prisons will furnish
materials for the study.

Literature.—Lombroso gives a chapter to this subject,
and cites a considerable bibliography.   Prose and poetry
have been written by criminals and for criminals.   Thieves
eagerly devour such intellectual food, and their evil tendencies are aggravated by such means.   The prison life has
produced expressions of the pent-up passions and perverted impulses of their inhabitants.   One celebrates in verse
his pillaging of the merchant on the road, his murder of the
noble in his castle, his debauches, and loves to be honored
as a king by the world.   The weariness and terror, the
loneliness and revenge of the life of prison are themes for
their pens and songs.   Very few criminals have been capable of producing anything that could be called literature.
The world could spare every line without serious loss.   The
"realism" which reproduces their life, though it be in the
powerful hand of such men as Balzac, Hugo, Dumas and
Zola, cannot be an enduring element in literature.   True
art cannot live except in pure and serene regions, and all

the more does it seek such an atmosphere when it feels the sad contrasts in the world.   (Lombroso.)

The writings of criminals are still human, and bear the marks of the redeeming instincts of humanity.   As when one composes a poem, in which he sees in the darkness of his Italian cell the "little hands of his mother signalling her love to him, and the tears streaming from both her eyes," and tells her "we are in this hell, condemned, and you, dear mother, breathe in vain your prayers."   But the glorification of lust, revenge and cruelty is more common, and has no rational use save to reveal the real character of this miserable class.

Philosophy.—Prison inscriptions and poems reveal the ethical system of criminals.   "He is unworthy of our esteem, who repents and proposes in the future to observe the laws.   True men are rare who in the prison know how to laugh and play the fool."   The great Italian writer quotes this sentence : "I will tear his face who speaks ill of the Vicaria (prison at Palermo).   He who says that the prison corrects, oh! how he deceives himself!   There we learn to take without being taken!"   He adds : "They who believe in the reforming force of punishment have only to read this."   Mr. Ellis says : "In considering the problems of crime, and the way to deal with them, it is of no little importance to have a clear conception of the social justification for crime from the criminal's point of view.   Not only is he free from remorse ; he either denies his crime or justifies it as a duty, at all events as a trifle."   He is a citizen of a different world from ours.   He judges himself by the standards of his tribe.   Among savages it is a merit to kill a member of a tribe with which a man's tribe is at war, and criminals are at war with us all.   Many criminals on reflection are fatalists. "If God has given to us the instinct to steal, He has given to others the instinct to imprison us; the world is an amusing theatre." Browning's "Caliban on Setebos" reasons much like those criminals who are capable of speculation, for that great poet in this poem entered into the very soul of savages and of criminals. Cynical inscriptions are often found. Judges are all corrupt; wealth buys liberty; rich men are rascals, who are free through bribery; women are not to be trusted. A Milanese thief said: "I do not rob; I merely take from the rich their superfluities; and, besides, do not advocates and merchants rob?"

Gamblers sincerely regard their occupation as justifiable speculation. They cannot see the difference between their trade and any other. It is thus that the worst men keep their self-respect. "I may be a thief; but, thank God, I am a respectable man." In the philosophy of criminals hunger brings back original communistic rights. So completely are ordinary reasonings reversed in this social Inferno, that one man, cited by Ellis, soberly maintained that "thieving was an honorable pursuit," and that religion, law, patriotism, and bodily disease were the real and only enemies of humanity.

2. **Æsthetic Marks.**— The manifestations of artistic impulses in criminals show the same low average of dullness, incapacity, coarseness and eccentricity which we meet in their intellectual life. Tattooing is common among the lowest grade of criminals in all countries although it is by no means confined to them. Many persons of defective taste are fond of having pictures on their arms and breasts, even if they cause much pain. As tattooing is general among savages, the school of Lombroso

regard the modern use of it by law-breakers as an additional proof of atavism. There is an additional motive in the gregarious and imitative instincts of this class, and in the proof of physical endurance of which these persons are so vain. "The greater number of tattooed criminals are found among recidivists and instinctive criminals, especially those having committed crimes against the person. The fewest are found among swindlers and forgers, the most intelligent class of criminals. Criminals frequently refrain from tattooing themselves because they know these marks form an easy method of recognition in the hands of the police." (Ellis.) Erotic passion, religious sentimentalism, vengeance, social ties all find expression in tattooing. The poetry of criminals proves at once that the æsthetic feeling is not extinguished by a life of crime, and that in such an atmosphere it can produce few perfect flowers. Such soil and climate are unfavorable to the growth of beautiful works. Cf. Tylor, Anthropology, p. 237.

3. **Emotional and Moral Characteristics.**—Instability is one of the most common traits of the instinctive criminal. Like savages, spoiled children and some of the insane, they are impetuous, fickle, changeful. Love may be intense to-day and to-morrow turn to murderous hate. Dickens has portrayed in Bill Sykes and his paramour this moral feature. Cf. Ribot, " Diseases of the Will."

Sentimentalism.—The forger may be a model husband and father. The cruel murderer may be fond of a pet cat. There is in the most hardened men a tender spot somewhere ; and it is on this side of their nature that efforts at reformation must begin.

Vanity is thought to be almost universal. To indulge it men will take great risks in theft and with officers of justice. They will boast of their deeds even when they thereby expose themselves to more severe punishment. With them moral order is wrong side out. The bottom is at the top. Assassins are proud of murder. Among thieves it is a real disgrace not to steal. A showy dress bought with the gains of crime is all the more attractive for its history. Hardened men will kill others or commit suicide in order to be sure of getting their names in the newspapers. There is a morbid hunger for notoriety which the sensational daily feeds and stimulates. In prison the greatest rascal is the envy of all, just as, among savage Indians, all the lads are eager to imitate the most bloody brave in adorning their belts with scalps taken by craft and murder. In the social treatment of crime this vanity must be considered.

Moral Insensibility.—Closely connected with the physical insensibility already mentioned is the moral insensibility of criminals. One who does not suffer pain and who is dull in imagination is apt to be quite indifferent to the pain of others. It is probable that a slight lapse from truth will give a morally healthy person more bitter pangs of remorse than a murder accompanied by torture gives to most murderers. In their cells criminals enjoy dreamless sleep and excellent appetite. They are not haunted by any fear from the moral authorities of the universe, nor disturbed by any shame. The only shame they feel among their comrades arises when the police have outwitted them.

4. The Religious Ideas and Feelings of instinctive criminals are dwarfed and distorted in common with the entire psychical developments. They are affected by the creed of their country and of their associates. "The criminal's God of peace and justice is a benevolent guardian and an accomplice." (McDonald). As the religious impulse enforces the moral judgments derived from all sources, it will, of course, seem to stimulate or excuse the anti-social acts which are approved in the ethical code of criminal society. But much of this evil direction of the highest nature must be due to the evil example, instruction and training of ecclesiastics. When the emphasis is laid on creed and ritual, rather than on righteousness, we must expect to find crime affected by this fact. It is easy to excite the religious feelings in our American prisons, and these emotions are not necessarily insincere. They simply lack depth and stability, and they are not supported by moral habits. It seems possible that many even of the lower kind of criminals could maintain a certain degree of moral and religious life so long as the prison walls act as substitute for personal will and character. In this view life-long imprisonment of incorrigibles may be an advantage to the criminals themselves. Of the assertion made that the Italian criminals are generally religious Morrison says: "Such a sentiment may be common among offenders in Italy; it is certainly rare among the same class in Great Britain."

It must be understood that many able students of criminals seriously question the conclusions of Lombroso. Topinard, an anthropologist of highest distinction, finds no certain marks on a criminal skull. Marro thinks a retreating forehead is not peculiar to this class. The conclusions in respect to the ear are not universally accepted. M. Joly thinks criminals are not particularly insensible to pain. The physiognomy of criminals is sometimes explained by their situation and habits rather than by heredity. The objections are stated by Morrison, ch. vii.: "It cannot be proved that the criminal has any distinct physical conformation, whether anatomical or morphological; and it cannot be proved that there is any inevitable alliance between anomalies of physical structure and a criminal mode of life. But it can be shown that criminals, taken as a whole, exhibit a higher proportion of physical anomalies, and a higher percentage of physical degeneracy than the rest of the community. With respect to the mental condition of criminals, it cannot be established that it is, on the whole, a condition of insanity, or even verging on insanity. But it can be established that the bulk of the criminal classes are of a humbly developed organization. Whether we call this low state of mental development, atavism, or degeneracy is, to a large extent, a matter of words; the fact of its widespread existence among criminals is the important point." Degeneracy is sometimes inherited, and sometimes acquired. There is a close connection between madness and crimes of blood.

Morrison presents objections to the conclusions of Lombroso. "Summing up our inquiries respecting the criminal type, we arrive, in the first place, at the general conclusion, that so far as it has a real existence it is not born with a man, but originates either in the *prison*, and is then merely a *prison* type, or in criminal *habits* of life, and is then a truly criminal type. As a matter of fact, the two types are in most cases cases blended together, the prison type with its hard, impassive rigidity of posture being superadded to the gait, gesture and demeanor of the habitual criminal. In combination these two types form a professional type, and constitute what Dr. Bruce Thompson has called 'a physique distinctly characteristic of the criminal class.' It is not, however, a type which admits of accurate description, and its practical utility is impaired by the fact that certain of its features are sometimes visible in men who have never been convicted of crime."

The view of the anthropologists of Italy (Lombroso and others) that the "criminel-nè" has certain anomalies of skull, brain convolutions, retreating forehead, projecting and deformed ears, distorted nose, insensibility to pain, tattooing, slang (argot) etc., is questioned by Morrison.

·   Letourneau, ("Evolution juridique," p. 509) says: "The 'born criminal' exists, and when he unites in himself the larger number of the traits ascribed to him (by Lombroso and his school) he is hardly corrigible. But what is the proportion of these degraded beings in the criminal population? We have not as yet exact information. Probably much less than 'criminal anthropologists' believe, since certain systems of graduated penalties, with individual and intelligent treatment, reduce the ratio of recidivists to ten per cent. or even to 2.68 per cent. In France it is 40, and in Belgium 70. The majority of criminals are criminals of occasion, whom a good education, better conditions of existence, and even a penitentiary correction of a more intelligent and humane sort would be sufficient to save and regenerate. The 'criminals born,' truly incorrigible, those whom it is the social interest to keep confined, as the insane, are a small number. And these, it is proper to recognize, are created, as Quetelet says, in large measure, by the vices of our social organization. They will become more rare when the profound reforms which the future promises shall have been accomplished, and society learns to treat them with humanity."

CHAPTER XXIV.

CRIMINAL ANTHROPOLOGY :—SOCIAL ELEMENTS.

Having considered certain characteristics of the members of the class of instructive criminals, we may here take into account several elements which aggravate or modify the tendencies to crime.

1. **Sex** has an important influence upon crime careers. "According to the judicial statistics of all civilized peoples, women are less addicted to crime than men, and boys are more addicted to crime than girls. Among most European people between five and six males are tried for offenses against the law to every one female." (Morrison.)

It is natural that women should more frequently be guilty of the crimes of infanticide and abortion. Owing to their feebleness, they must choose poison as their favorite method of committing murder. If women become criminals at all, they are hard, cruel and incorrigible. A larger average number of them are recidivists. Shame once broken down, they are desperate. As women compete with men in industry and public life they furnish an increasing number of law-breakers, as in England and Scotland, and the Baltic provinces. The opening of new industries for women may be an economic necessity of our times, but it is certainly accompanied by alarming increase of crime among women. The only wonder is that there are still so few criminal women.

See C. D. Wright's Report, Commissioner of Labor, 1888. Pike, vol. 2, p. 528. De Greef, Les Lois Sociologiques, 35–40. Letourneau, Evolution Juridique, p. 505.

2. Relation of Crime to Vice.—We have noted the fact that the various extra-social classes are confluent. The vices of drunkenness, indolence, vagabondage, and prostitution lead directly into overt acts of an anti-social nature. The vices produce the crimes, and there is no distinct line of demarcation between them.

3. Crime as a Profession.— In the part of population called "criminal" there are various strata or groups, each of which has distinguishing features. Men of certain endowments and defects drift toward the group to which they are most nearly allied ; and their circumstances act in the same direction. In every vocation, as is shown in caricatures and higher art, there are physical traits and common marks of dress, gesture and speech, which betray the nature of the calling. With instinctive criminals we must add the more serious deformities which mark them as abnormal.

There are, however, swindlers, sharpers, confidence men, gamblers, and speculators in crime who constitute a sort of crime aristocracy, and show few of the signs noted in the instinctive criminals. In looking over Byrne's photographs there seem to be few faces which present anything unusual, although a few are really attractive.

4. The Relations of Criminals to the Insane.—It is not necessary to repeat here what has been said in Part II., on the Insane, and especially on the Imbecile. "The group of instinctive criminals stands fairly apart among the other groups of criminals, approximating, but not

fusing with, these various morbid and atypical groups. . . .
It is much to be able to see, even so clearly as we do to-
day, the human classes of arrested or perverted development who lie in the dark pool at the foot of our social
ascent. Even our present knowledge is sufficient to serve
as the justification for a certain amount of social action."
Social justice can never be complete until it considers the
entire nature and antecedents of the criminal. The illegal
action must not be judged apart from the man who commits
it. And while much remains to be done by anthropologists,
what they have given us is the only solid ground for social
judgments and treatment.

5. **The Influence of Association.**—All human beings are
affected by the tendency to imitate, and this is especially
true of the young and the untaught. Hence the power of
the immediate social environment. To these universal
impulses are due several phenomena of criminal life of
supreme social interest.

(*a*) Societies of the anti-social classes. Very famous
are the "Camorra" and Mafia of Italy. But others are
known in America. The "White Caps" of Indiana seem
to have been associations of men to carry out lawless deeds.
Bands of horse-thieves were once common in the West.
Illicit distillers in the mountain regions of the South are
described in current fiction. The police of our cities are
constantly making discoveries of small groups of lawless
men, and even boys, bound together for a common purpose. Gambling clubs are everywhere. The saloons furnish the resort, parlor and banking-place for associated
criminals.

Where there is a form of government the legislation of
these associations is exceedingly severe. The death penalty

is the usual mode of enforcing discipline. The instinct of primitive communism is shown in the requirement that stolen property must be divided. The revelation of a crime is, in this social circle, treated as a grave crime.

(b) The public opinion of a criminal association is a curious and important study. It has an ethical code of its own. What is honorable elsewhere is shameful here. Ridicule and bodily harm are penalties for what we call morality.

(c) It is on the principle of social sympathy and imitation of associated persons that we can explain the outbursts of mob violence and the contagion or epidemics of crime which occasionally mark local or general history. In the French Revolution large masses of the population of Paris seemed to be insane with savage fury. In American cities, when some flagrant injury has stirred the people, many of them, especially if they come together, seem to be possessed by demons. Men who at other times manifest the disposition of a civilized race, in an hour of association with those who are seeking revenge, lose the marks of centuries of Christianity and turn savages. The culture is like the crust over the fires of a volcano, and in a few minutes the primitive state of society reigns supreme. Many strikes issue in such scenes, not because those who engage in them are worse than other men, but because they have the same origin as other men. Consider what must follow when men of low instincts, perverse appetites and passions, and feeble social sympathies, are acted upon by powerful social currents toward lawlessness.

(d) Here we may note the influence of the representations of crime and vice in painted or pictured form, in newspapers and cheap books. We do not have to travel to Italy for frequent illustrations. Every county jail in America will supply them. Boys read the details of highway robbery and piracy, and set about organizing bands for similar depredations. The finer sensibilities of delicate minds are hardened by constant reading of details of cruel and unclean actions. Those who are already feeble in purpose and idle are more strongly influenced. The daily newspapers are sometimes direct stimulants of crime, while the vile stuff misnamed obscene "literature," the illustrated papers and books so frequently found in barber shops, saloons and other places of resort, are chargeable with the suggestion and provocation of all the impulses which lead to rape, theft, arson, robbery and murder. Publication of facts and names probably is deterrent, while publication of disgusting and brutal details tends to harden the good and augment the ranks of the human animals of prey.

(e) In this connection Hypnotism finds a place. The instinctive criminal, in this respect as in others, is closely related to the Moral Imbecile who, as we have seen in Part II. is subject to the influence of suggestion. The employment of hypnotism in detecting, and even curing crime, has been suggested for experiment. Hypnotic states have been simulated by criminals for purposes of blackmail. These obscure phenomena promise to throw some light on the criminal nature, but the subject is too new to furnish fixed results of general value.

Lombroso recommends the following men and works as his coadjutors :

Lacassagne, *Archives d'anthropologie criminelle.*
Liszt, *Zeitschrift für gesammte Strafsrecht.*
Reggio, *Rivista sperimentale di freniatria.*
Mierzejewski, *Messager de psychiatrie ; Bulletin de la société d'anthropologie* (Bruxelles); *Revue philosophique* (Paris); and *Revue scientifique.*
Kowalewski, *Archives psychiatriques et legales.*

Morselli, *Rivista di filisofia scientifica; Archivio di psichiatria*, etc. (Turin).

Of books he names :

Garofalo, *Criminologia.*
Ferri, *Omicidio* and *Nuovi orizzonti di diritto penale.*
Balestrini, *Sull' aborto ed infanticidio.*
Lacassagne, *Le tatouage.*
Tarde, *Criminalité comparée.*
Ribot, *Maladies de la volonté.*
Espinas, *Sociétés animales.*
Flesch, Benedikt, Sommer and Knecht (on anatomy).
Drill and Roussel (on young criminals).
Guyau, Fouillée and Letourneau (on morals).

I have mentioned many of the most valuable accessible works in connection with each topic. The "Reader's Guide" (Putnams) will give other titles. An exhaustive bibliography may be found in McDonald's "Criminology," at the end.

CHAPTER XXV.

SOCIAL TREATMENT OF THE CRIMINAL—HISTORICAL.

The origin of law and order.

> "Cum prorepserunt primis animalia terris,
> Mutum et turpe pecus, glandem atque cubilia propter
> Unguibus et pugnis, dein fustibus, atque ita porro
> Pugnabant armis, quae post fabricaverat usus:
> Donec verba, quibus voces sensusque notarent,
> Nominaque invenere : dehinc absistere belfo,
> Oppida cœperunt munire, et ponere leges,
> Ne quis fur esset, neu latro, neu quis adulter."
> HORACE, Sat. I, iii, 99, quoted by Morgan, "Ancient Society."

In order to understand the criminal and social reaction against him, we need to study the unsocial acts and con-

duct in relation to the growth of the structures and functions of the social body.

We shall in the main follow here the analysis of Morgan, Maine, Spencer, Tylor and Letourneau. Not that
they are altogether in agreement, or that they have reached
fixed conclusions, but that we may find in their writings an
orderly arrangement of phenomena on which we may at
least direct criticism. It is not even necessary to accept
the extreme statements in regard to the antiquity of man
or the absolute beginnings of man on earth. Leaving these
questions quite open we can study the actual evils of human
society as revealed in the history of the past and the conditions of various races now existing. The subject is instructive to us, because we are certainly descendants of the
savage and barbarous tribes of Scandinavian and Teutonic
origin.

We may be obliged, by our system of interpreting the
Scriptures, to regard the savage and barbarous stages of culture as conditions of degradation from a previous higher
social state. But even then we must practically regard the
immediate ancestors of existing races, all who appear in
historical records and monuments, as ascending from low
level by slow and irregular progress. Practically we can
make no account of a primitive society of high moral and
intellectual culture, and of such race no traces have been
left ; certainly if anywhere not in the book of Genesis,
where the moral and social level is indicated by pictures of
passions, polygamy and anarchy.

"Mankind is passing from the age of *unconscious* to
that of *conscious* progress . . . . . The study of man and
civilization is not only a matter of scientific interest, but
at once passes into the practical business of life. We trace
in it the means of understanding our own lives and our

place in the world, vaguely and imperfectly it is true, but at any rate more clearly than any former generation. The knowledge of man's course of life, from the remote past to the present, will not only help us to forecast the future, but may guide us in our duty of leaving the world better than we found it." Tylor, Anthropology, p. 439-440.

The penal codes which have the greatest interest for us, are those of the American Indians, the Hebrew, the Roman, and the Teutonic. All these have affected our history and our modes of thinking and legislating.

1. The Social Treatment of Crime by the American Indians.—The Savage Ethnic Period. By this we do not mean a certain period in time, but a social condition. While it is supposed that all human beings were primitively savages, it is also true that some savages linger in our own times. Morgan ("Ancient Society") describes three stages, the Lower Status, Middle Status and Upper Status.

"The Lower Status of savagery was that wholly prehistoric stage, when man lived in their original restricted habitat and subsisted on fruit and nuts. To this period must be assigned the beginning of articulate speech. All existing races of men had passed beyond it at an unknown antiquity." (Fiske.)

The Middle Status of Savagery begins with the catching of fish and the use of fire. Then men could spread over the earth, at first following coasts and streams. "The natives of Australia are still in the Middle Status of Savagery." See Lumholz, "Among Cannibals."

The Upper Status of Savagery marks its beginning by the invention of the bow and arrow. This improved the methods of warfare between tribes, and also enabled those who used the invention to kill wild game and increase their food supply. "The lowest tribes in America, such as those upon the Columbia River, the Athabaskans of Hudson's Bay, the Fuegians and some other South American tribes, are in the upper status of savagery." "During the periods of savagery, hatchets and spearheads were made of rudely chipped stones." They were prowlers, and had no village life. Barbarism likewise, according to Morgan, has three stages. The beginning of the lower status of barbarism was marked by the invention of pottery. Spear-heads and edged tools were more carefully chipped, then polished.

The transition from the Lower Status to the Middle Status of barbarism is shown in the Old World by the domestication of horses, asses, oxen, sheep, goats, pigs and other animals. "Along with this goes considerable development of agriculture, thus enabling a small territory to support many people." In America these animals were unknown within historic times until they were brought over by the Spaniards. But the New World had maize, a nutritious and easily grown vegetable food. The potato was used in Peru. "The regular employment of tillage with irrigation" belongs at the early stage of the Middle Status of barbarism. Adobe-brick and stone for buildings belong in this period of culture. "Tools were greatly multiplied, improved polishing gave sharp and accurate points and edges, and at last metals began to be used as materials preferable to stone." In America copper was used, in the Old World "bronze." The Zuñis, the Aztecs, the Mayas and the Peruvians, at the discovery of America, had reached this stage.

"The custom of human sacrifice seems to have been a characteristic of the middle period of barbarism, and to have survived, with diminishing frequency, into the upper period." (Fiske, p. 119).

In the Old World the outward signs of culture were tents and herds, but at the same level in America were seen "strange and imposing edifices of stone."

The Upper Status of barbarism is marked, in the Old World, by the smelting of iron. But in America no tribe had learned this art. The Homeric poems show that the Greeks of that age knew the use of iron. The Germans in the time of Cæsar had gone so far.

See Tylor, Anthropology, p. 279. The Works of Schliemann furnish illustrations.

Fenton's Early Hebrew Life. Spencer, Prin. Soc. I. 724 – 737.

Mr. Fiske thus sums up the normal conditions of social life among the savages and barbarians of America. "Intertribal warfare was perpetual, save now and then for truces of brief duration. Warfare was attended by wholesale massacre. As many prisoners as could be managed were taken home by their captors; in some cases they were adopted into the tribe of the latter as a means of increasing its fighting strength, otherwise they were put to death with lingering torments. There was nothing which afforded the red man such exquisite delight as the spectacle of live human flesh lacerated with stone knives or hissing under the touch of firebrands, and for elaborate ingenuity in devising tortures they have never been equalled. Cannibalism was quite commonly practised. The scalps of slain enemies were always taken, and until they had attained such trophies the young men were not likely to find favor in the eyes of women. The Indian's notions of morality were those that belong to that state of society in which the tribe is the largest well-established political aggregate. Murder without the tribe was meritorious unless it entailed risk of war at an obvious disadvantage ; murder within the tribe was either revenged by blood - feud, or compounded by a present given to the victim's kinsmen."

While no private property exists, and marriage relations are very lax,—according to modern notions,—and murder without the tribe is meritorious, it might seem that "crime" would be impossible.   In reality primitive societies are exceedingly strict and rigid in enforcing the accepted social and ecclesiastical creed.

If the law of domestic life, for example, was that a man should take his wife from another clan, his own clan would find a way to enforce this law.   It might be legal for a woman to have several husbands (polyandry), or for several brothers to have their wives in common, or for a man to lend his wife to a stranger.   But if he transgressed the actual regulations of his clan he would be made to experience the severest rigors of the law of his people.

In industrial relations, while all lands and houses were possessed in common, each man might be required to furnish his share of the game or fish, or to cultivate the garden-plot assigned to him, for the common benefit.   In case of neglect a severe penalty was enforced.   Among the Mexicans "the delinquent member was deprived, not only of his right of user, but of all his rights as a clansman, and the only way to escape starvation was to work on some other lot, either in his own or some other clan, and be paid in such pittance from its produce as the occupant might choose to give him. "   This is hardly different from slavery, and the outcast, if lazy, could be made to wear a wooden collar, and in the last resort he became a sacrifice of priests to the gods.

The Aztecs lived in exogamous clans, and counted descent in the male line.   The family, as we understand it, was vaguely distinguished from the clan, but there were penalties for sexual irregularities. The husband owned his wife and the clan protected his rights. All were obliged to marry. The penalty for the crime of resisting the custom of the clan was expulsion. As the number of articles of personal property increased, even while lands and houses were still owned in common, theft was possible within the clan, and a method of punishment had to be devised. Probably this was at first the fist-right known among boys at our own schools ; but the individual would be supported by his clan chief, who was also judge. If crime, as defined by Stephen, is obstruction to the public authority, injury to the public order, to persons and to property, then within the clans of savages and barbarians crime was recognized and punished. Many of the details are lost beyond recovery, but the illustrations given serve to show the parallels and differences between primitive and modern codes.

These additional illustrations of savage and barbarian codes may be given :

" The ancient practice of blood revenge, which has prevailed so widely in the tribes of mankind, had its birthplace in the gens. It rested with this body to avenge the murder of one of its members. *Tribunals for the trial of criminals* and *laws prescribing their punishment, came late into existence in gentile society;* but they made their appearance before the institution of political society. The crime of murder is as old as human society, and its punishment by the revenge of kinsmen is as old as the crime itself." (Morgan, Ancient Society, p. 77).

Morgan quotes Adair's History American Indians :

" Their hearts burn violently day and night without intermission till they have shed blood for blood. They transmit from father to son the memory of the loss of their relations, or one of their own tribe, or family, though it was an old woman. "

But before revenge the members of the two gentes met in council, and an adjustment was sought by means of *compensation* to the relatives of the slain.

"The *property* of savages was inconsiderable. Their ideas concerning its value, its desirability and its inheritance were feeble. Rude weapons, fabrics, utensils, apparel, implements of flint, stone and bone, and personal ornaments represent the chief items of property in savage life. " Morgan, Ancient Society, p 529.

In such a condition of industrial society, "theft" within the clan would be almost unknown, and when it occurred the individual would protect himself if he could.

2. **The Hebrew Social Treatment of Crime.**—*Pre - Egyptian Period*, to about 1550 B. C. General Social facts. Property consisted in flocks, herds, precious metals, utensils and to some extent, lands ; slaves were part of the family ; polygamy was known, but not common ; concubinage was general. The head of the tribal family was military leader, judge, priest and ruler, the government being patriarchal. Lewdness, incest and unnatural lust were abhorred. Gen. xxxviii. 24. Revenge and lying were common, as shown in Jacob and Esau. Murder was punished by blood revenge. All the kinsmen of the slain person were bound to avenge his death, and the penalty might fall on any member of the family of the murderer as well as upon himself.

The punishment of theft was capital. Wars were not very bloody, and spoils were their chief object.

Egyptian Period. The Hebrews in Egypt increased their knowledge of industries ; polygamy continues ; national

life takes form ; " Elders " represent the people in councils.
In Egypt the Hebrews came into contact with a highly
developed code of laws which had religious sanctions, and
they were partly under its rule.   Hanging was a customary
mode of capital punishment (Gen. xl. 22); and the criminals
were kept 'bound' in prison (Gen. xxxix. 20) till their
fate was decided ; whether it depended on the will of the
sovereign, or the decision of the judges ; and these places
of confinement were under the immediate superintendence,
and within the house, of the chief of the police (Gen. xi. 3).
(Wilkinson).   " Executions were made as a rule by the
sword or the stick. . . . . The Court sitting to judge the
dead might prohibit the burial of sinners. " (Ebers). "The
bastinado was inflicted on both sexes. "

The time of the Wandering, under Moses, is ignored by
many of the Old Testament critics, on the ground that the
Pentateuch was written at a much later date, and that none
of it belongs to this period.   This is not the place for the
discussion ; but the main points can be mentioned under
the next head.

Period of the Judges and the Monarchy. The people
gradually pass from nomadic and pastoral occupations to
agriculture.   Manufactures are known.   Slavery affects the
forms of industry.   Polygamy is a sign of social pre-
eminence.   Instances of concubinage are given.   Fathers
have power of life and death over their children.   Laws are
regarded as divine, without reference to their subjects.
(Exodus xxi.-xxiii).   Capital crimes were : reviling God,
cursing the ruler, father or mother, killing a man with
murderous intent, smiting parents, witchcraft, man-stealing.
The custom of blood revenge is legally recognized.   In
case of manslaughter a refuge is opened.   Private revenge
is regulated by the law of taliation.   In one case a fine is

substituted. "If no mischief follow" the offender is to cause the damaged man to be thoroughly healed, and to pay for his loss of time. An ox goring a man to death, to be stoned ; the negligent owner to be killed if not ransomed. The law of adultery, rape, trial of the bride is found in Deut. xxii, 22, 23, 24, 25, 27. Robbery and theft, Deut. xxiv. 7. Prov. vi, 30, 31. False evidence and taliation, Deut. xix. 16.

If a slave is killed at once his owner is to be punished ; if seriously wounded, he is to be freed in compensation. A seducer is to marry the maid, or, if refused, to give her a dowry. Theft is to be punished by two - fold (stuff), four - fold (sheep), five - fold (oxen) restitution. No blood revenge admissible if a thief is killed in the act of breaking in at night - time. The " elders " of the tribes were rulers, and they were gradually superseded by the rising royal authority under Saul. The rules and laws, unwritten and written, are regarded as divine commands. "*Jus* and *fas*, which words with the Romans from the eldest period clearly distinguished secular and ecclesiastical law, with the Israelites were combined in the one term Thora." (L. Auerbach).

Examples :

Sins treated as crimes: Deut. xiii. 1–18, 20, 22 : xvii. 2–7, 12.
Cities of refuge for manslayers : Deut. xix. 2–13 : xxiv. 16 ; 2 Kings xiv. 6.
Responsibility of a society for a killing : Deut. xxi. 1–9.

The popular form of capital punishment was stoning ; under the kings the sword. Criminals were put to death in fetters (2 Sam. iii. 34). Capital punishment was made more deterring by the addition of burning the remains (Josh. vii. 25), hanging the corpse (Josh. viii. 29), exposing the head (2 Kings x. 8) or limbs (2 Sam. iv. 12) in public, and heaping stones on the grave (Josh. x. 27). "Imprisoning was not a regular punishment, but the kings had prisons in their own or their officials' houses. The food is described as particularly objectionable (1 Kings xxii. 27). The prisoners' feet were forced into the holes of a block" (Job xiii. 21).

Period of the Two Kingdoms.— The division of labor becomes more complex; new industries are opened; articles of luxury are imported or manufactured; commercial relations are extended into Asia, Europe and Africa. Slavery continues. The kings exact labor from the people for public works. While polygamy is known among the great, and the kings show their splendor in large harems, the custom of having several wives is not common. Concubinage is only too well known. Adultery of a betrothed or married wife is punished with death. The power of life and death is withdrawn from the father and transferred to the congregation. Parents and children are not longer legally answerable for each other. This marks the development of a political government and the disappearance of patriarchal institutions.

The centralized royal power becomes almost absolute, and the king is held sacred. The tribal organization is continued, though it decreased in importance by the evolution of royal rule and of town life. The heads of tribes and of sub-tribes become an aristocracy of the realm. In the northern kingdom the local administration of justice seems to have remained more or less in the hands of the "elders." King Jehoshaphat set judges through all the cities of Judah. More difficult cases were to be sent before the central court at Jerusalem.

The priests sometimes, as under Jehoshaphat, gained a share in the administration of justice.

Theories and sentiments associated with the law are:

Sin is regarded as a rebellion against the Divine King; early death, sickness, barrenness, are punishments of sin; long life and multitude of descendants are rewards of virtue. The guilt of a sinner may be visited on his children or his people, but individual responsibility is set by the side of social and organic responsibility. With the growth of wealth and luxury the prophets warn the great men against deceit and oppression of the poor.

Exilic Period, 598 B. C.— Poverty and other influences seem to check polygamy. Locally justice was administered, according to the ancient laws of the Hebrews, with a political head over the exiles.

Persian Period, 538 B. C.— Upon the return the courts of justice were reëstablished. The high priest becomes the highest authority, and priests and scribes, as keepers of the law are supreme judges.

Greek Period, 332 B. C.— Slavery continues, but treatment of slaves grows more lenient. Polygamy hardly general. Divorce is easy. The high priest is regarded as the chief political authority, and by the foreign rulers is placed near their representatives. Rulers and judges are appointed for districts. Greek towns with armed garrisons are planted.

Period of Independence, 167 B. C.— The Asmoneans came to be regarded as royal. The Sanhedrim is the highest legislative, administrative and judicial board. Owing to contests with foreigners the law becomes, with all its minute details, most scrupulously observed, and disobedience is crime.

Roman Period, 64 B. C.— By a law of Herod housebreakers might be sold into foreign slavery. Slavery for debt and theft continued. Polygamy legal, but not common. Divorce for men more easy. In 7 A. D. the right of executing capital punishment was withdrawn from the Jews. Money compensation is now the rule instead of taliation for bodily harm. A thief shall restore four-fold or be sold into home slavery. Robbers were treated as enemies. Debtors are imprisoned. After Herod the priestship is separated from princeship. The Sanhedrim has judicial powers, under permission of Roman rulers. Local justice was administered by courts of seven judges. Additional references : See Schürer's "The Jewish People in the Time of Jesus Christ." Ewald, "Jewish Antiquities."

Transition from Barbarism to Civilization.— The transition from ancient to modern laws, institutions, sentiments and theories of society in relation to crime is described and explained by Sir H. Maine, Ancient Law, ch. x.; H. Spencer, Principles of Sociology, Vol. II., pp. 229–643, Political Institutions. The details are shown more fully in the various volumes of "Descriptive Sociology," Pike's "History of Crime in England," Guizot's History of Civilization, Green, Short History of the English People.

Laws.— Mr. Spencer illustrates the development of four sources of *law;* inherited usages, special injunctions of deceased leaders, regulations given by predominant men, public will and opinion. In primitive times these are confused, and only in lapse of time are differentiated. Secular and sacred laws and regulations mingle in one code, in the laws of Moses and of Manu, for example. " To the injunctions of the undistinguished dead, which, qualified by the public opinion of the living in cases not prescribed for, constitute the code of conduct before any political organization has arisen, there come to be added the injunctions of the distinguished dead, when there have arisen chiefs who, in some measure, feared and obeyed in life, after death give origin to ghosts still more feared and

obeyed. And when, during that compounding of societies effected by war, such chiefs develop into kings, their
remembered commands and the commands supposed to be
given by their ghosts, become a sacred code of conduct,
partly embodying and partly adding to the code pre-
established by custom. The living ruler, able to legislate
only in respect of matters unprovided for, is bound by
these transmitted commands of the unknown and the
known who have passed away; save only in cases where
the living ruler is himself regarded as divine, in which
case his injunctions become laws having a like sacredness.
Hence the trait common to societies in early stages, that
the prescribed rules of conduct of whatever kind have a
religious sanction. Sacrificial observances, public duties,
moral injunctions, social ceremonies, habits of life, industrial regulations, and even modes of dressing, stand on the
same footing." Disobedience to the public authority is
both treason and irreligion, and hence the worst crime.
The regulation broken may be foolish or trivial: disobedience is crime. In process of time, on the field where the
divine powers or ancestors have not delivered opinions, the
ruler may give his own judgments. If he wishes to pass a
sentence which conflicts with the religious code, he does it
by means of a " legal fiction ;" he " interprets " the ancestral law out of existence and substitutes one of his own.
So secular laws grow.

Procedure.—The courts and forms of procedure have a
parallel development, from the council of the gens, phratry
or tribe, through kings who combine military and ecclesiastical authority in their absolute persons, down to the time
when, once more, through delegated political bodies, the
people speak their will in law. The court of primitive
times is also legislative and executive in enforcing its de-

crees. The same body which determines peace and war decides the compensation or penalty due in case of murder or theft. When a king rules absolutely he gives both law and decision. If an oligarchy rule, its votes are both laws and decrees of sentence in individual cases. But after a time kings find it necessary to set up courts to divide their judicial duties, and those, in time, become independent of him. With the growth of an intelligent industrial class the people assert their right to be judged by impartial courts. Thus, in brief, we come to have three coördinate branches of government, each subdivided and specialized, legislative, judicial and executive.

Differentiation of Civil and Criminal Laws.—Another important change appears in respect to the law of crime. In the earlier codes "the civil part of the law has trifling dimensions as compared with the criminal . . . . *The older codes are fuller and minuter in penal legislation."*

"Nine-tenths of the civil part of the law practiced by civilized societies are made up of the Law of Persons, of the Law of Property and of Inheritance, and of the Law of Contract. But it is plain that all these provinces of jurisprudence must shrink within narrow boundaries, the nearer we make our approaches to the infancy of social brotherhood. The Law of Persons, which is nothing else but the Law of Status, will be restricted to the scantiest limits as long as all forms of status are merged in common subjection to Paternal Power, as long as the Wife has no rights against her Husband, the Son none against his Father, and the Infant Ward none against the Agnates who are his Guardians. Similarly, the rules relating to Property and Succession can never be plentiful, so long as land and goods devolve within the family, and, if distributed at all, are distributed inside its circle." (Maine). *Contract* has

no place in ancient Codes. But Criminal Law of early
civilization is developed. Not, however, exactly in our
sense of crime—an offense against the state. The offenses
punished were treated as wrongs done to individuals, for
which compensation was required, and sins for which an
equalizing punishment was to be made to please the Deity."
" The primitive history of criminal law divides itself, therefore, into four stages. Understanding that the conception
of *Crime*, as distinguished from that of Wrong or Tort and
from that of *Sin*, involves the idea of injury to the state or
collective community, we first find that the commonwealth,
in literal conformity with the conception, itself interposed
directly, and by isolated acts, to avenge itself on the author
of the evil which it had suffered. This is the point from
which we start ; each indictment is now a bill of pains and
penalties, a special law naming the criminal and prescribing his punishment. A second step is accomplished when
the multiplicity of crimes compels the legislature to dele-
gate its powers to particular Quæstiones or Commissions,
each of which is deputed to investigate a particular accusation, and if it be proved, to punish the particular offender.
Yet *another* movement is made when the legislature, instead
of waiting for the alleged commission of a crime as the
occasion of appointing a Quæstio, periodically nominates
commissioners like the Quæstores Parricidii and the Duum-
viri Perduellionis, on the chance of certain classes of crimes
being committed, and in the expectation that they *will* be
perpetrated. The *last* stage is reached when the Quæstiones, from being periodical or occasional, become permanent Benches or chambers—where the judges, instead of
being named in the particular law nominating the commission, are directed to be chosen through all future time in a
particular way and from a particular class—and when cer-

tain acts are described in general language and declared to
be crimes, to be visited, in the event of their perpetration,
with specified penalties appropriated to each description."
(Maine, An. Law, pp. 372-3.)

3. The Roman Penal Code.—Since the Roman Criminal
Law extends over into the Christian Era, and carries with it,
in its final forms Italian, Hebrew, Greek and Christian elements, and combines them in the Justinian codes, I shall
treat the subject as furnishing a bridge from pre - Christian
to mediæval times.

We may take up the *Codes of Justinian* as a point of
review and prospect. In these laws we discover elements
derived from Roman, Greek and Hebrew-Christian sources.
A full account of this famous legislation would include a
summary of the legal and moral history of the Roman,
Greek, Hebrew and Christian peoples up to the time when
the barbarians of Northern Europe interrupted the progress of civilization in Southern Europe. But these codes
have more than a mere historic interest, for they have
help to form modern legislation and judicial procedure,
and are living and acting social forces at this hour.

· Authorities: Friedländer, "Sittengeschichte Roms."
· Gibbon, "Decline and Fall of the Roman Empire," ch
Histories of Rome by Duruy, Merivale.
Mommsen, "History of Rome."
Thierry, "Tableau de l'Empire Romain."
Stephen, "History of English Criminal Law," vol. I.
Letourneau, "Evolution Juridique."
Cf. Grote, "History of Greece."

The first literary monuments of Rome reveal the earlier
forms of government in the gens and the family. The
power, authority and responsibility of the father are the
central elements of social control. The *pater familias* holds

in his own person all rights over the persons and goods in his domicile, even over life and death. All the "patres" constitute one Roman people. Strangers have no rights, no law, no tribunal. The most conspicuous embodiment of the Roman criminal code is the Law of the Twelve Tables. Their character has been drawn by Gibbon.

The Twelve Tables "approve the inhuman and unequal principle of retaliation; and the forfeit of an eye for an eye, a tooth for a tooth, a limb for a limb, is rigorously exacted, unless the offender can redeem his pardon by a price of 300 pounds of copper. The decemvirs distributed with much liberality the slightest chastisement of flagellation and servitude; and *nine crimes* of a very different complexion are adjudged worthy of death. Any act of *treason* against the state, or of correspondence with the public enemy. The mode of execution was painful and ignominious; the head of the degenerate Roman was shrouded in a veil, his hands were tied behind his back, and after he had been scourged by the lictor, he was suspended in the midst of the forum on a cross, or inauspicious tree. *Nocturnal meetings in the city;* whatever might be the pretense, of pleasure, or religion, or the public good. The murder of a citizen; for which the common feelings of mankind demand the blood of the murderer. Poison is still more odious than the sword or dagger; and we are surprised to discover, in two flagitious events, how early such subtle wickedness had infected the simplicity of the republic, and the chaste virtues of the Roman matrons. The parricide who violated the duties of nature and gratitude, was cast into the river, or the sea, enclosed in a sack; and a cock, a viper, a dog, and a monkey, were successively added as the most suitable companions. The malice of an *incendiary*. After the previous ceremony of whipping, he himself was delivered to the flames; and in this example alone our reason is tempted to approve the justice of retaliation. *Judicial perjury*. The corrupt or malicious witness was thrown headlong from the Tarpeian rock to expiate his falsehood, which was rendered still more fatal by the severity of the penal laws, and the deficiency of written evidence. The corruption of a judge, who accepted bribes to pronounce an iniquitous sentence. Libels and satires, whose rude strains sometimes disturbed the peace of an illiterate city. The author was beaten with clubs, a worthy chastisement, but it is not certain that he was left to expire under the blows of the executioner. The nocturnal mischief of damaging or destroying a neighbor's corn. Magical incantations." (Gibbon). The *debtor's* body, as we see elsewhere, might be divided among the creditors. But, as Gibbon says, "As the manners of Rome were insensibly polished, the criminal code of the decemvirs was abolished by the humanity of accusers, witnesses, and judges; and impunity became the consequence of immoderate rigor."

Gradually the plebeians are admitted to legal rights and even to office. In 266 B. C. a prætorship for strangers is erected. The "law of nations" grows out of intercourse with the conquered world that had to be governed and held in order. Greek philosophy widens the scope and enlarges the principles of the Roman Law. The despotism of the Emperors becomes the unconscious instrument of forming general laws capable of application to many nations. The growth of human sentiment and the rise of Christianity modify the severity and harshness of the ancient legislation. The right to expose his infant or slay his son is taken from the father.

It was only under Christian influences that the act of

infanticide was made a crime. "The exposition of children was the prevailing and stubborn vice of antiquity : it was sometimes prescribed, often permitted, almost always practiced with impunity, by the nations who never entertained the Roman ideas of paternal power." (Gibbon).

It is in this state that the Roman law has come down to us, and that it has furnished the basis for modern nations which broke off from the Roman society. It holds then an immense place ; and this place will increase in the ratio that the feudal barbarism disappears and civilization extends. Bossuet (Discours sur l'histoire universelle, III. 6.) : "The Roman laws have appeared so holy that their majesty endures spite of the ruin of the Empire, and this is because good sense, which is the master of human life, reigns throughout, and that one sees nowhere a more beautiful application of the principles of natural equity."

Stephen (His. Cr. Law Eng., vol. I, p. 9, ch. ii.) gives extracts from the Justinian Codes.

"The Roman Lawyers in the days of Justinian divided crimes into these classes, Publica Judicia, Extraordinaria Crimina, and Privata Delicta."

Publica Judicia related to crimes which were specifically forbidden by particular laws under defined penalties, capital (death or exile) or not. The Lex Julia Majestatis was aimed at crimes against public authority, as treason and related offences. The Lex Julia de Adulteriis punished sexual crimes. . . . The punishment of adultery was exile, the woman losing half her dower and a third of her goods, and the man half his goods. The Lex Julia de Vi Publica et Privata related to crimes of violence. The punishment of Vis Publica was exile, and in some cases death ; the punishment of Vis Privata confiscation of the third of the offender's property and loss of certain civil rights. The

Lex Cornelia de Sicariis et Veneficiis has homicide for its main subject. The Lex Pompeia de Parricidiis defines parricide as killing any relative nearer than or in the degree of a first cousin. The Lex Cornelia de Falsis refers to forging and counterfeiting. The punishment of 'falsum' was, under the Antonines, in the case of a person of low rank, imprisonment in the mines; in the case of a person of higher rank, forfeiture of goods, and relegation to an island. The Lex Julia Repetendarum punished official extortion, the penalty being death or fourfold damages, according to the crime. The Lex Julia de Amnona was like modern laws against forestalling and regrating. The Lex Julia Peculatus, etc., punished peculation with service in the mines, exile and forfeiture of property, the rank of the offender being taken into account. The Lex Fabia punished selling a free man as a slave, at first with fine, but afterwards with the mines or death. The Extraordinaria Crimina were offences for which no specific law or punishment was provided. Here belong the attempt to seduce, corrupting of youth, the introduction of a new religion, engrossing, abortion, vagabondage, plundering tombs, extortion, some kinds of theft, receivers of robbers, fraud, unlawful associations. Privata Delicta were offences for which a special action was set apart involving a definite result for the injured party ; as theft, injuries to property, insults and wrongs done to reputation.

Procedure under the later Roman Law.—The Empire was divided in the time of Constantine into four Prætorian præfects. There were two forms of prosecution, Public and Private. The public procedure was as follows : The miles stationarius, or his inferior officer, arrests. The Eirenarcha holds a preliminary investigation (probably with the aid of torture) and commits for trial to the prison of the Civitas.

The trial took place before the præses, who had before him the report of the Eirenarcha.

In the case of a Private Prosecution the accuser cited the accused before the Præses, and obtained leave of the Præses to prosecute. The parties appeared before the judge. The accuser took an oath that his accusation was not calumnious, and he was liable to fine if his cause was proved false. A day was fixed for the trial, and the judges or præses heard the case and pronounced a verdict.

Stephen says of the relation of Roman and English codes : " It is natural to suppose that the system described above obtained here (in Britain) as well as elsewhere (before 409 A. D.) Whether any part of it escaped the German conquest, and so influenced the earlier and ultimately the existing English law is a question of purely antiquarian interest. The important influence of Roman upon English law was exercised through the founders of the English common law long after the Norman conquest. It had little or no influence on the modes of procedure. These were derived from other sources." We shall now indicate some of these other sources.

English History of Crime in these Periods.—The dominant theories, sentiments and laws of our age contain elements desired from the theories, sentiments and laws of our ancestors, and *especially* of our English ancestors.

The most important of these elements are : (a) *Barbarian,* derived from the original British tribes, and the later Teutonic tribes which came in after the Romans retreated from the island ; *Roman,* derived from the Roman occupation age, from the Normans, and from the influence of Roman legislation on more modern thought.

(b) As we have seen, the Roman code itself was a product of Roman, Greek, Hebrew and Christian influences.

(c) The development of the English people under influences economic, domestic, moral, social, political, religious.

Authorities for the History of Crime in England :
Green, Short History of the English People.
Pike, History of Crime in England.
Stephen, History of Criminal Law in England.
Letourneau, Evolution Juridique.
H. Spencer, Descriptive Sociology—English.

We have already studied the principles of the social treatment of crime among savages and barbarians.

Remembering that at the time of the Roman conquest, just before the Christian Era, the British Isles were populated by barbarians, we might here repeat the essential elements of the Criminal Codes of that time. The former discussion has prepared us for this study.

The British Period to 78 A. D.—It is known that they had towns, centers of trade, and even foreign commerce, with rings of bronze and iron for money ; some manufactures of cloth, weapons ; and certain rights of property were recognized and protected. The *lex talionis* was common in this age, with beginnings of *compensation.*

In the lower stages of growth homicide (or theft) would be followed, if possible, by death. But as property increased, and the chief exercised authority, and it became evident that the full fighting force of the tribe was needed, homicide was compensated by a fine. Pike, Hist. Crime, Vol. I, p. 43.

The Roman Period, 78 A. D. to 420 A. D.—It is not known how far outside of the Roman towns the influence of the Roman laws extended. Pike thinks the Roman law was very generally enforced, and that life and property were relatively secure in South Britain ; while others think the Roman rule was confined to the towns and colonies.

The "English" History beginning with 449 A. D. The people who conquered and perhaps exterminated the Britons were Germans. They were pagan Germans, from the far north where Christianity had not reached. (Green, I.) We must, therefore, study the Teutonic code in respect to crime if we would know how our ancestors treated it.

1. The Old English Period.—This "Old-English" period is divided into two parts : Pagan, 449-596; Christian, 596-1066.

We may follow at this point the course of argument presented by Letourneau, in "Evolution Juridique." The Germanic laws were coarse and rude, like their authors, and correspond to the upper status of barbarism. "The law of vengeance is at the foundation, and that which distinguishes them is the excessive extension of pecuniary compensation and the minute care with which they set a tariff price on all crimes and wrongs. Without doubt the system of pecuniary compensation and penal tariffs has been universally spread over the world, but few peoples have made so general a use of them as the Germans."

Examples of these tariffs are found in the authorities given for the period.

Of Homicide.—The right of vengance had not ceased to be in vigor, but it had already assumed a judicial form. Ordinarily the relatives do not kill the murderer of one of their number; they prosecute him judicially, and this prosecution was itself a duty, as in an earlier age a bloody vengeance would have been. A law of France commanded the confiscation of the patrimony of children who neglected to prosecute the murderer of their father. . . . The compensation was awarded, half to the paternal and maternal relatives, half to the son; in the absence of relatives it goes to the treasury, and in the end the government regularly took a share."

Various prices of "Wehrgeld" were fixed for various circumstances. The murder of a nobleman costs more than that of an ordinary freeman, and the price of a slave is only something larger than that of an ox. Even the values of different kind of slaves are set down; so much for a swineherd, and so much for a carpenter, and so much more for a goldsmith. Nothing could be more rude than all this legislation about murder in Germany. Evidently the legislator does not see in the fact that a man has been killed an act worthy of blame in itself, or immoral; it is in his eyes merely a damage, a material loss, whose price he anxiously seeks to set according to the case and its circumstances. This method of estimating crime is altogether primitive. It carries us back to the origin of human societies with the savages. But all the other parts of the Germanic codes are of the same moral inferiority."

Wounds and Violence.—Like murders, so wounds, injuries, acts of violence, are classified and taxed with a minute care, and, by reason of their great variety, the list of compensations is very long.

Injuries are taxed according to the rank of the person injured. Insults are treated as injuries, and taxed on the same principles. "Nothing is more flatly commercial than all this tariff, and it has evidently replaced the *lex talionis*, as the survivals of that custom distinctly attest, but it could not be so minutely applied save among peoples who held money in high esteem, and this induction fully agrees with the Germanic legislation relative to theft."

Of Theft.—"In the Germanic codes theft holds a considerable place. . . . This exaggerated importance assigned to theft is usual in the legislation of barbarians. It is found in the law of the Twelve Tables. Is it necessary to believe with Sir Henry Maine that this peculiarity results from the form of civilization where the land, the soil, has less value than movable wealth? Rather does it belong with a mental state, still inferior, which makes little account of human life, and much of exchangeable commodities with which one is able to procure a number of pleasures and advantages." The penalty is severe. A robber taken with his booty may be hung or decapitated on the spot. " The Germanic law, like the Twelve Tables, accord great importance to the fact of taking in the act of crime. If once the thief is given over for a time, to kill him afterwards becomes a punishable homicide."

" Regarded from the commercial standpoint the insolvent debtor is scarcely distinguished from a thief : he also is cause of damage and is treated with severity." . . . He may be sold for debt. . . . " Yet he does not fall, if a freeman, quite to the level of ordinary slaves ; the owner cannot sell him, unless he runs away ; he cannot strike him by caprice, only in one case,— refusal to work. If the slave for debt obstinately refuses to work, his master conducts him before the council (Thing) and gives his relatives a chance to liberate him. On their refusal he can kill or mutilate the rebellious slave, ' cut high or low, where he will ;' atrocious cruelty which closely resembles that of the Twelve Tables."

Morals.—Crimes relating to " morals " are regulated by compensation and " amends," with alternative of revenge in extreme cases. Abduction, adultery, seduction and

assaults on modesty are settled for at fixed prices. When
Christianity begins to affect the Teutonic laws the penalties
are rendered more severe.

Crimes against the King and the Church.—At the epoch
when their codes were collated the Germans were under a
monarchical régime, and from this fact comes the aggra-
vation of certain crimes touching the sovereign, and even
a whole class of special crimes; murders, thefts committed
to the detriment of the king's people, either in the palace
or court of the sovereign, acquired a particular gravity:
their compensation rose to double or treble. Unfaithfulness
to the king was an enormous crime, and drew down capital punishment and confiscation of goods. . . . With the
Lombards, when the royal power was strongly fortified,
they went further still: bad thoughts and evil designs
against the monarch were crimes severely punished.

The Church, sovereign of the conscience, enjoyed privileges analogous to those of the monarch, sovereign of the
body. If any man wishes to give his goods to the church, says
the law of the Alemans, let no one oppose him, not even a
duke, count, etc.

The church has the right of asylum. It is forbidden to
take away a man, free or slave, who seeks refuge in the
church. The fine for crimes committed in a church are
higher. Offenses and insults demand double and treble
compensation when they affect an ecclesiastic. The church
imposed the duty of Sabbath rest, and the man who
labored on Sunday lost the ox and the right of the plough
which it drew.

Tribunals and Procedure of Germanic Justice.—The first
Germanic tribunal was simply the assembly of free men of
the clan or tribe. They came armed, and any man could

bring his cause. Under the kings in England the royal court became the last resort for appeals. The process of differentiation went forward, sometimes with halting, or retrograde steps, to our own days.

Penalties.—As we have seen compensation supervened upon direct revenge. In doubtful cases, when, for example, a man accused another without a witness, the accused could demand the trial by combat. This was an early custom, and became more developed in the Middle Ages.

Mr. Green (ch. I, " Short History ") thinks that the two chief changes in the Teutonic government of the English conquerors of Britain, both brought about by war, were kingship and slavery. War united them, and furnished captives for bondsmen.

2. Feudal Justice.—(Letourneau, " Evolution Juridique," ch. XVIII.)

General Characters.— " Regarded in its entirety the justice of the Middle Ages is fragmentary, made up of pieces like the political society from which it results. The law and the society of the Middle Ages were born of the intrusion of the barbarians into the decaying empire. In the Roman provinces the conquering Germans found a judicial organization, centralized, provided with functionaries, which their monarchs accepted with the rest, since all their efforts tended to copy the emperors in an awkward manner. But the old customs of justice were not adapted to this change. For a long time the kings tolerated the assembly of free men who judged by the mediation of designated juries. After the Carlovingians. when the Gallo - Frank kings arranged with their chiefs and instituted fiefs, the titularies of these fiefs, considering themselves as petty sovereigns, demanded and generally obtained the right of higher and lower justice. From that time was opened an era of competition between the chief suzerain, the king and his vassal nobles ; the former attempting to reconquer that which he had ceded of his judicial prerogative ; the others defending their privileges. The advantage finally remained with the king, largely because he was the stronger, and somewhat because the jurists worked for him.

But, for several centuries, the charters intervening between the monarch and his vassal nobles took these latter under their production against the caprices of the suzerain, on the sole condition that they acquitted themselves of the charges of their tenure. The good pleasure of the master was bridled by an agreement, freely debated, and protecting the vassal in a large measure. Between superior and inferior the relations, even the conflicts, regulated themselves with a certain dignity. The jurisdiction of the suzerain was accepted with reserves. In the " Assizes of Jerusalem " the right of appeal is formally recognized ; the plaintiff can refuse the counsel designated by his lord . . . The prince can not, without the consent of the majority of lieges, punish a feudal vassal either in a civil or criminal cause.

But all this protective procedure concerns only the nobility. The multitude of the humble, the serfs, are scarcely able to appeal to the king, and nothing effectually protects them from their lord. Commoners have no defence against the lack of faith in the barons. Finally, there is a jurisdiction against which there is no protection. The church, persecuting with the rage of devotion the crimes of opinion, gives an example of the most iniquitous judicial oppression. As this, so other jurisdictions perform their functions with extreme barbarity ; their great means of receiving information are the ordeal and torture ; their ordinary procedure to decide in doubtful cases is the judicial duel —

the judgment of God.   In the forms of punishment survive
savage customs inspired by the *lex talionis:* the judge
simply taking the place of the offended person, but is not
less ferocious.   "This idea of revenge is persistent — even
in modern times."

**3. English Social Treatment of Crime in the Modern
Period, and Characteristic Changes.**— " To describe the *genesis* of a thing — especially when it is a living thing — is
often the best method of defining it ; it is at least very often
the best method of beginning the search for a definition "
(Mackenzie, Soc. Phil. p. 66).

Interpretation of the Modern Period of Reform.—(1) The
" spirit of humanity " is the immediate cause of all jural,
political and administrative changes.   By " spirit of humanity " is meant that spiritual force whose highest manifestation is seen in the Person of the Founder of Christianity.
The Author of that force is present everywhere, and at all
times, and his energy is the only adequate, and therefore
scientific explanation of humanitarian progress.   Progress
in economic wealth, extension of commerce, mercantile
bonds of interest and amity, improved means of communication are auxiliaries, but not creators of this human
spirit.   Industrial and commercial advance is a phenomenon
which itself needs to be explained by adequate causes of
origin and reasonable ends.   It cannot be historically
shown nor philosophically proved, as some able sociologists
seem to assert, that we require nothing but soil, climate,
sexual appetite, and hunger for food, to explain the infinite
energy and sublime ethical beauty of modern social ideals.
These ideals are as much facts as vengeance and lust in
savages.

It is unscientific either to ignore them or to trace them

to insufficient origins. Soil will explain much in the life of a plant, but it will not explain the life itself. Much that calls itself boastfully " science " simply begs the question of origin, and slips in entire continents of moral values without telling us whence they arose. The " spirit of humanity " manifests itself not only in increasing tenderness toward criminals, but also in the decrease of selfishness, cruelty and insensibility which are the prolific causes of crime.

(2) In consequence of this enlargement of moral *senti-ment* there has been an extension of the field of justice and equity. From being the privilege of a caste or a monarch law has come to be the right of all.

The criminal himself, while under the sentence, is now regarded as still a man, with the rights, duties and responsibilities of a man, limited only by the necessary restraints and penalties appropriate to his conduct, character and attitude to society. " It ought not to be forgotten, although it has been too frequently forgotten, that the delinquent is a *member* of the *community*, as well as any other individual, as well as the party injured himself ; that there is just as much reason for consulting his interest as that of any other. His welfare is proportionably the welfare of the community—his suffering the suffering of the community. It may be right that the interest of the delinquent should in part be sacrificed to that of the rest of the community ; but it never can be right that it should be totally disregarded." J. Bentham, I. 398.

These improvements of sentiment and of law have left monuments of their onward course, and of these we mention a few typical instances. Books are very properly called the " works " of their authors, but they are also " works " of the age for which they voice the best thoughts and inspirations. The last century was marked by the beginnings of great social movements whose force is by no means spent. The abolition of the slave trade and slavery, the humanitarian efforts connected with the Wesleyan revivals, the well - meant changes in the Poor Laws, the removals of ancient wrongs in France through the revolution, were outward signs of the times. But the profound principles and convictions which characterized these movements, find articulate expressions in such books as Montesquieu's "Spirit of the Laws" (1748), Beccaria's "Crimes and Punishments" (1764), "Blackstone's Commentaries" (1765), Bentham's writings (Panopticon, 1791), Livingstone's "System of Penal Law" (begun in 1821).

The conclusion of Beccaria's book marks the chief features of the modern spirit : "In order that every punishment may not be an act of violence, committed by one man or by many against a single individual, it ought to be above all things *public, speedy, necessary, the least possible* in the given circumstances, *proportioned to its crime, dictated* by the *law*."

(3) Not only has law come to be the protection of more people, but it has become more exact and refined. It extends its definitions over more hurtful acts, and relaxes its penalties in the region of thought and faith.

Legislation presses harder upon sexual vice, drunkenness, liquor selling, gambling, lotteries, neglect which issues in damage or death, enforces the responsibility for corporations, themselves enlarged by modern industrial conditions, covers rights of property in intangible possessions, as by patent and copyright laws. "The old common law, originating in an age of unpolished minds, demanded less of fairness than is required by the superior culture and finer moral sentiment of modern times. And the demand increases as we progress in civilization. So that the common law itself has expanded by slow and scarcely observed gradations, and a more rapid expansion has been carried on by legislation, which both adds to the number of crimes and enlarges the boundaries of the old ones. Thence it has resulted that crimes against the individual have been more multiplied by statutes than those against the community." (Bishop.)

The author just quoted declares that he has given the first distinct definition of the relation of corporations to crime. "A corporation, especially as viewed from the standpoint of the criminal law, is an artificial creation of the law, consisting of one or several persons endowed with a part of the duties and capabilities of an unincorporate man . . . . A corporation cannot, in its corporate capacity, commit a crime by an act in the fullest sense *ultra vires* and contrary to its nature. But within the sphere of its corporate capacity, and to an undefined extent beyond, whenever it assumes to act as a corporation, it has the same capabilities of criminal intent and of act—in other words, of crime—as an individual man sustaining to the thing like relations."

But the same refinement of moral sense which demands new restrictions on selfish conduct also takes off burdens where they are useless and harmful. In 1772 was organized the Society for the Relief of Poor Debtors. This is a sign of public interest in the most innocent and helpless class of prisoners. Prison reform began with the amelioration of their condition. The censorship of the press has become confined to inhibition of flagrant violations of rights, of reputation and character. Trials for heresy may burn hot in ecclesiastical circles, where they serve almost to glorify the object of them in popular esteem, but a heretic as such can not be brought before a criminal court to answer for his words. The constitution of the United States embodied the principle of separation of church and state, so that religious thought is free from outward force. This freedom has become education in responsibility, and never before have the educational and spiritual agencies of the church been so active and helpful. The modern age does not show its indifference to religious forces by ceasing to persecute. Zeal manifests itself in our day in self - sacrifice for truth and not in the sacrifice of others for our opinions.

When once the offender has fallen into the hands of justice the *forms of procedure* are more just and equitable. Arbitrary measures are resisted. There is even manifest a tendency to make justice gratuitous, and so within the reach of all. As the judicial and legislative branches of government come to be independent of the executive (king) they are increasingly responsive to the growth of morality, and decreasingly subject to individual caprice of persons in power. The Declaration of Independence marks the transition to modern views of the importance of equitable procedure.

After trial comes punishment. In prison the offender is under the absolute control, economically and spiritually, of the state. The state responds to the new conceptions of universal human rights in its treatment of those who have forfeited liberty and who lie at its mercy. Capital punishment has almost disappeared. Transportation seems near its end. Torture is abolished, both as a means of securing testimony and as a part of the penalty. The element of primitive " revenge " is gradually fading, to be replaced by a rational and dispassionate purpose of righteous retribution, accompanied by a merciful effort to reform the criminal, on the way to protect society. The very names of things have changed,—from " dungeon " to prison, from prison to "penitentiary," and from penitentiary to "House of Correction," "Reformatory," "Reform School," "Industrial School" and even hospital for sick souls.

The following dates will indicate the historic monuments of progress in humane and rational treatment of prisoners. In 1704 Pope Clement XI. built at Rome the prison of St. Michael with its famous inscription, which so impressed the mind of John Howard that he quoted it in his book : "Parum est improbos coercere pœna, nisi bonos efficias disciplina." Peter the Great established what was then, at least in intention, a humane measure, the transportation of criminals to Siberia. In 1773 John Howard was sheriff at Bedfordshire, and came in personal and practical contact with the prison system of the world. In 1774 jail fees were abolished in England, largely in consequence of Howard's disclosures and influence. The year of our Revolution (1776) was marked by the organization of the Philadelphia Society for Alleviating the Miseries of Public Prisons. In 1778 Australia became a convict colony, and Howard's plan for improving prisons was delayed. In 1786 the "Solitary system" was substituted for capital and corporal punishments in Pennsylvania. Simple imprisonment was recognized in France in 1786 as punishment.

In 1818 the Auburn (N. Y.) penitentiary was opened. 1822, the English Jail Act. 1825, the New York House of Refuge for Juvenile Delinquents. 1854, Crofton is on the Board of Directors of Irish Convict Prisons. In 1889 capital punishment was abolished in the land of Beccaria and Lombroso.

In 1816 Mrs. Elizabeth Fry opened a school for women in Newgate. In 1819 John Falk of Weimar organized the "Friends in Need." In 1833 Dr. Wichern founded the Rauhe Haus at Hamburg, to build up boys by "the Word

of God and music. " In 1839 the famous juvenile colony
was established at Mettray to use agricultural labor as an
agency of reformation.   It will be noticed that uniformly
reform ideas begin with a few progressive individuals, and
that they become generally effective by agitation, education
of public sentiment, and last of all by legislation.

The history of the more serious punishments indicates
the course of the stream of progress.

The Death Penalty.—"The punishments inflicted for what
we now call treason and felony, varied both before the Norman conquest and after it.   At some period it was death,
at others mutilation.   Laws of Henry I. speak of some kinds
of theft as capital.   Capital punishment was the law, of the
land " as to *treason* and *all* felonies, except petty larceny
and mayhem, down to the year 1826," subject to exceptions
of " benefit of clergy."

Benefit of Clergy. (Stephen, Vol. I,) p. 459.

" Privilege of clergy consisted originally in the right
of the clergy to be free from the jurisdiction of lay courts."
An ecclesiastic was tried before the bishop and the church
court.   Twelve compurgators could swear that they believed
he spoke the truth in declaring his innocence.

From about 1350 this privilege was extended to all who
could read.   But women (except nuns), as incapable of ordi-
nation, were excluded from the benefit.   In 1576 *purgation*
was abolished.   In 1692 women were put on the same footing as men.   In 1705 the necessity for reading was abolished.
In 1779 branding was practically abolished.   " Even after
1487 a man who could read could commit murder once
with no other punishment than that of having M branded
on the brawn of his left thumb, and if he was a clerk in
orders he could, till 1547, commit any number of murders,
apparently without being branded more than once."

There were two forms of felony which were excluded from benefit of clergy at common law, highway robbery and willful burning of houses. "All this legislation shows that the early criminal law was extremely severe, that its severity was much increased under the Tudors (1485 to 1603) but that it varied little from the time of Elizabeth to the end of the seventeenth century." "Towards the end of the seventeenth century the following crimes were excluded from benefit of clergy, and were thus capital whether the offender could read or not: high treason (which had always been so), petty treason, piracy, murder, arson, burglary, house-breaking and putting in fear, highway robbery, horse stealing, stealing from the person above the value of a shilling, rape, and abduction with intent to marry. In the case of persons who could not read, all felonies, including manslaughter, every kind of theft above the value of a shilling, and all robbery, were capital crimes." "The severity of the criminal law was greatly increased all through the eighteenth century by the creation of new felonies without benefit of clergy. In the second edition of the *Commentaries*, published in 1769, Blackstone says that 'among the variety of actions which men are daily liable to commit no less than 160 have been declared by Act of Parliament to be felonies without benefit of clergy.'" Many of these were particular forms of felony. "However, after making all deductions on these grounds, there can be no doubt that the legislation of the eighteenth century in criminal matters was severe to the highest degree, and destitute of any sort of principle or system." Many who were sentenced, however, escaped by being transported to American, and afterward to Australian, colonies.

"The result of all this legislation as to the punishment of death was in the reign of George IV., as follows: All felonies except petty larceny and mayhem were theoretically punished with death, but clergyable felonies were never punished with death, nor were persons convicted of such felonies sentenced to death.   When asked what they had to say why sentence should be not passed upon them, they fell upon their knees and prayed their clergy, upon which they were liable to imprisonment for not exceeding a year, or in some cases to whipping, or in the case of petty larceny, or grand larceny not excluded from clergy, and in some other cases, to seven years transportation."

The new English legislation seems to begin about 1827. Stephen, Vol. I, p. 473 seq.   In that year "benefit of clergy" was abolished.   "The act of 1827 was followed by several others which were intended to form the nucleus of a criminal code, and to replace the fragmentary and yet indiscriminate legislation of the eighteenth century by laws in which punishments were more carefully adjusted to offenses.   Each of them retained the punishment of death in a considerable number of cases.

Between 1832 and 1861 the punishment of death was abolished in the case of stealing cattle, letter stealing and sacrilege, forgery, rape and abusing children under ten ; robbery with violence, attempts to murder, arson of dwelling-house, sodomy.   The only offences now punishable by death are treason, murder, piracy with violence, and setting fire to dock-yards and arsenals.

The manner of inflicting the death penalty is hanging ; in an early age it was beheading.   "English people, as a rule, have been singularly reckless (till very lately) about taking life, but they have usually been averse to the infliction of death by torture."

Transportation.—(Stephen, Vol. I, p. 480).   "The earliest instance of transportation as a punishment seems to have occurred in the reign of Charles II., when pardons were granted to persons capitally convicted, conditionally on their being transported for a number of years—usually seven. This practice was . . . . greatly extended by subsequent legislation, and particularly by the act of 1768. . . . In the course of the eighteenth and the early part of the present century an immense number of acts were passed by which various terms of transportation, with alternative terms of imprisonment, and power, in some cases alternative and in others cumulative, to order whipping more or less frequently, were allotted to particular offenses." "The punishment of transportation was gradually abolished between 1853 and 1864, principally on account of the objections of the colonies to receive the convicts sentenced to it, and penal servitude, or imprisonment and hard labor on public works, was substituted for it.

The history of the punishment of *imprisonment.* (Stephen, Vol. I, p. 483).

"Imprisonment is as old as the Law of England." A statute of 1166 A. D. (Assize of Clarendon") is mentioned.

"The right of keeping a gaol in and for particular districts was a franchise which the king granted to particular persons." . . . . The gaoler was paid by fees from the prisoners, and, as these were generally very poor, the fees must be extorted by harsh measures. . . . . In 1729 an act was passed which was intended to remedy the mischiefs. It was imperfect. The first great step was taken by JOHN HOWARD, in 1773, when he was sheriff of Bedfordshire. His first effort was to abolish the system of paying gaolers by fees of prisoners, and to substitute salaries.

(6) The Criminal restored to Society.

The criminal, after his discharge, is more carefully watched over by society until he is safely on his way of advance, and restored quietly to occupation and social confidence.

(7) Preventive and Educational.

Not content with humane and reasonable treatment of the fallen, society is earnestly attempting to prevent a fall on the part of those who are in constant peril. Hence all the modern efforts to improve and make universal the advantages of the free public schools, kindergartens, manual training and technical schools. It is believed that it is easier and cheaper to form than to re-form.

The following significant events and facts will further illustrate the growth and spread of rational and humane interest in prison science and all that pertains to the Criminal Class :

"The Congress for Criminal Anthropology should be sharply distinguished from the International Congress for prison and penitentiary systems. The former consists almost entirely of University professors, jurists and scientific specialists ; the latter of prison wardens and others who have had to do with the practical side of the prevention or repression of crime." (A. MacDonald.)

Ellis, p. 316, says: The International Association of Penal Law was founded in 1889, on the initiative of Professor von Liszt. . . . . The conditions of membership involve adhesion to the following propositions : "(1) The mission of penal law is to combat criminality, regarded as a social phenomenon. (2) Penal Science and penal legislation must, therefore, take into consideration the results of anthropological and sociological studies. (3) Punishment is one of the most efficacious means which the state can use against criminality. It is not the only means. It must not, then, be isolated from other social remedies, and, especially, it must not lead to neglect of preventive measures. (4)

The distinction between accidental criminals and habitual criminals is essential in practice as well as in theory; it must be the foundation of penal law.   (5) As repressive tribunals and the penitentiary administration have the same end in view, and as the sentence only acquires value by its mode of execution, the separation, consecrated by our modern laws, between the court and the prison is irrational and harmful.   (6) Punishment by deprivation of liberty justly occupying the first place in our system of punishment, the association gives special attention to all that concerns the amelioration of prisons and allied institutions.   (7) So far as short imprisonments are concerned, the association considers that the substitution of measures of equivalent efficacy is possible and desirable.   (8) So far as long imprisonments are concerned, the association holds that the length of the imprisonment must depend not only on the material and moral gravity of the offence, but on the results obtained by treatment in prison.   (9) So far as incorrigible criminals are concerned, the association holds that, independently of the gravity of the offence, and even with regard to the repetition of minor offences, the penal system ought before all to aim at putting these criminals for as long a period as possible under conditions where they cannot do injury.

The International Prison Congress has held meetings since 1845.   The British Association for the Promotion of Social Science was organized in 1857.   The National Prison Congress met at Cincinnati in 1870; then was organized the National Prison Association.   In 1877 the Societé Générale des Prison was organized at Paris.

This review may be expanded by reading:

F. H. Wines' article on "Prisons" in Lalor's Cyclopædia.
E. C. Wines' "Prisons and Child-Saving Institutions."

Randall, Report of St. Petersburg Congress. Circular of Information, Bureau of Education, No. 2.
Ellis, "The Criminal." Introduction and Appendix.

CHAPTER XXVI.

SOCIAL ACTION ANTICIPATING CRIME.

The forms in which society expresses its convictions are literary, customary, institutional and political. It is only when a conviction has become practically general that it is embodied in effective legislation. It is therefore necessary to study not only the law books, but also the statements of men whose experience, studies and genius entitle them to confidence, and secure for them the esteem due to prophets of what society is likely to do in the future. Bentham has well said : " There are two points in politics very hard to compass. One is to persuade legislators that they do not understand shoemaking better than shoemakers, the other is to persuade shoemakers that they do not understand legislating better than legislators. The latter point is particularly difficult in our own dear country, but the other is the hardest of all things everywhere." Contradictory as it may seem, it seems certain that increased popular knowledge of charity and correction will lead to increased respect for expert opinions.

1. **The Definitions of Jurisdiction** to which the criminal is held responsible have been greatly extended. In primitive time the influence of the code did not touch any persons outside the small group, or clan or tribe. But as tribes became consolidated into states the range of the

criminal law was enlarged in corresponding measure. With a primitive people murder and theft are not only not criminal, but may be praiseworthy if committed against aliens. The growth of large empires, the extension of commercial relations between distant peoples, the blending of interests, the spread of knowledge, the rise of the Christian doctrine of human fraternity and the Fatherhood of God, have had their influence on the definition of jurisdiction. From these conditions have come treaties of extradition. It seems certain that the time is not distant when a fugitive from justice, who has wronged any citizen of any country, will find it impossible to escape from his punishment by taking asylum in foreign countries. The progress of steam transportation between nations makes such measures more and more necessary.

Bishop (Criminal Law) states the American legal position. Jurisdiction of crime as between the United States and foreign nations: "Our territorial limits are fixed by usage and treaties; outside those limits we have no governmental authority; the oceans belong to no one power, but are the common highways of nations; the ships upon them are deemed of the territory of the nation to which they are severally attached; to a limited degree they are so also while in the harbors and internal waters of a foreign nation;—some exceptions."

"Our Indian tribes are independent political communities." "The powers not delegated to United States by the Constitution, nor prohibited by it to the States, are reserved to the States respectively, or to the people."

The St. Petersburg International Prison Congress expressed this judgment: "Treaties of extradition being strictly dependent on the special penal legislation of the different countries, and these enactments at the present time being irreducible to a single type, it would be useless to attempt to introduce in an international convention the names of uniform criminal acts, or a definition of facts which cannot be identical. It would be desirable that special penal legislation should adopt the principle of extradition as a general rule, with all the reservations by which each state would find it necessary to restrict it. . . . A study should be made by a common agreement between criminalists of different countries in view of giving the same denomination and a precise definition to violations of penal law which would be punished by extradition."

2. Powers of Judges.—The regulation and determination of the powers of judges. Laws can never fix in advance the exact measure of ill-desert and the amount of deterrent and corrective penalty suitable for individual cases. Much must be left to the discretion of the judges who hear the entire statement of the case. And yet the danger of partiality and inequality of verdicts is so great, that this power needs to be carefully guarded and defined by legislation. It is imperative that men know, at least approximately, the nature and extent of the penalty assigned to particular violations of law.

The International Prison Congress publishes this judgment: "The maximum punishment for each offense should be fixed by law, and the judge should have no power to exceed it. The law should fix the minimum penalty for each offense, but the minimum can be reduced by the judge when he believes that the offense is accompanied by extenuating circumstances which were not contemplated by the law. When penal law names two kinds of punishment, one for offenses which disgrace, and one for offenses which do not, the judge may, in certain cases, substitute the least severe penalty when he finds in the offense punished, in the abstract, no dishonorable motive."

3. Arrest.—The law governing arrest must seek to protect the innocent from arbitrary and unjust arrest. At the same time it must not obstruct the police in the detection and arrest of dangerous offenders. Criminals are eager to take advantage of legal devices to protect honest men from arbitrary officers of law. Corrupt judges may, in our cities, block the efforts of the police to clear a city of dangerous men. Approximate success is all that society can expect. Between these two perils lies a path of safety which is not very well defined. The principle of law is, that in slight offences executive officers must not proceed without warrant or indictment. But the growth of a crime class with organization and political influence demands a searching investigation of the relation of police magistrates to this group.

4. Crimes Defined.—The particular acts which society regards as criminal are defined by common and by statute law. Men cannot be arrested and treated as criminal unless they commit some overt act which transgresses a definite and published regulation of society. On the other hand, "ignorance of the law excuses no man." While this principle involves individual hardship at times, justice could not be administered without it. The rule is necessary. In American law, "A crime is any wrong which the government deems injurious to the public at large, and punishes through a judicial proceeding in its own name. The criminal law is that department of the law of the courts which concerns crime. The purpose of a civil suit is to compel the defendant to compensate the plaintiff for what

he has unjustly suffered, while that of the criminal is punishment and the cure of a public wrong." (Bishop).   The
statements of statute and common law on this subject fill
many volumes.   We can give space here to a few principles
as illustration of the nature and aims of this part of political action.   To constitute a crime we must find act and
evil intent in combination, the public good as well as ill-
desert, an offense of sufficient magnitude, capacity for
guilt, and a clearly defined law.

The Several Elements of Crime.— To constitute a crime,
act and intention must combine.   "*Act* essential.   The tribunals take notice of wrongs only when the complaining
party is entitled to complain.   And he is so entitled only
when, besides having an interest in the transaction, he
has suffered.   Now, the state, that complains in criminal
causes, does not suffer from the mere imaginings of men.
To entitle it to complain, therefore, some *act must have
followed the unlawful thought.*"

The public good and desert— punishment to combine.— The
law is *practical.*   "In *morals*, the rule for adultery (Matt.
xv. 28) is that the mere imagining or designing of evil is
equivalent to the doing," but in criminal law the act must
be proved.

"In determining whether or not a particular thing is or
should be made cognizable by the criminal law, we are not
simply to look at the morals of it, or even at its practical
enormity, but to consider whether or not to punish the
wrong-doer will, as a judicial rule promote, on the whole,
the public peace and good order."

"The reason for punishing evil-doers is often stated to
be to deter others from crime, and so protect the community; as well as, when the life is not taken, to reform them."
(Refs. Beccaria, Eden, Wayland, Paley.)

"On the one hand, no man is to suffer punishment unless he deserves it in *pure* retributive justice, aside from all collateral considerations ; on the other hand, though it is merited, it will not be inflicted by the governmental powers, which do not assume the full corrective functions of the Deity, unless, presumably, it will contribute to the public good."

The criminal thing to be of sufficient magnitude.— Since the tribunals neither take cognizance of all moral wrong nor punish every remote injury to the community, the evil of such combination of act and intent must be measured in two ways to determine whether it is punishable or not. The one is by its nature, the other is by its magnitude."

The required evil intent.— "In no one thing does *criminal* jurisprudence differ more from civil than in the rule as to intent.   In controversies between private parties, the *quo animo* with which a thing was done is sometimes important, but not always ; *but crime proceeds only from a criminal mind.*   There can be no crime, large or small, without an evil mind.   Punishment is the sequence of wickedness, without which it cannot be.   And neither in philosophical speculation, nor in religious or moral sentiment, would any people in any age allow that a man should be deemed guilty unless his mind was so. . . . .   The essence of an offence is the wrongful intent, without which it cannot exist."

Carelessness and negligence.—"There is little distinction except in degree, between a will to do a wrongful thing and an indifference whether it is done or not.   Therefore carelessness is criminal, and within limits supplies the place of the affirmative criminal intent.   "A homicide may be either murder or manslaughter, according as it was intended or careless."

Necessity and Compulsion. "No action can be criminal if it is not possible for the man to do otherwise." Examples are : acts done in self-defence or in defence of the lives and property of others. It is not settled in law whether taking food to save life is larceny. The command of a superior, as master or parent, is not compulsion to commit crime.

Under the law of capacity and freedom might be studied the coercion of wife by husband, the incapacity of children for crime, if under a certain age, insanity, intoxication.

Judgments of the International Prison Congress on ill-desert in case of intoxication. "The state of intoxication, considered in itself, would not constitute an offense. It gives occasion for repression only in the case when it publicly manifests itself in conditions dangerous to personal safety or by acts of a nature to produce scandal or to disturb peace and public order.

The usefulness of legislative provisions can not be denied in establishing coercive measures, such as confinement in an asylum or a workhouse in regard to persons habitually given to drunkenness who would become a burden upon public charity or private benevolence, and who would give themselves up to a life of beggary or become dangerous to themselves and others.

It is desirable to make the proprietors of wine and liquor shops penally responsible for the sale of strong drink to individuals manifestly under the influence of liquor.

In case of penal offenses committed while in a state of intoxication : The state of incomplete intoxication can not in any case exclude responsibility. As a circumstance having influence on the measure of punishment, this state can not be defined by the legislative authority either as a mitigating or aggravating circumstance. . . . . (St. Petersburg Congress).

Classification of *Criminal Acts.* The acts which must combine with the criminal intent to constitute a crime are described in general terms by law.

The details are to be found in treatises on criminal law, as Stephen, Russell, Bishop, Blackstone and the statutes. All laws of the criminal code may be distributed under the following classes : *

(*a.*) Protection to the *government* in its existence, authority and functions. Here belong laws and penalties relating to treason, malfeasance in office, resistance of officers, contempt of court, perjury, bribery. (*b*) Protection to the relations of the government with other governments, as laws against violation of neutrality, injury to citizens of foreign countries, etc. (*c*) Protection to the public revenue. Laws relating to imports, smuggling, customs regulations. (*d*) Protection of the public health. (*e*) Protection of religion, morals; as laws relating to public worship, the Lord's day, blasphemy, brothels, disorderly conduct. (*f*) Protection of population and wealth of the country; as laws relating to abortion, infanticide, homicide. (*g*) Protection to the public safety and convenience; as laws relating to combustible and explosive articles, offensive trades, dangerous buildings and sidewalks, gambling, brothels, disorderly houses, etc. (*h*) Protection to the public order and tranquillity. Here may be defined riot, disturbance of lawful meetings, unlawful assemblies. (*i*) Protection to individuals. Here are defined offences against personal preservation and comfort; acquiring and retaining propery; personal reputation; offences growing out of combinations to commit private injuries. Here may be mentioned definitions of arson, assault, battery, burglary, embezzlement, trespass, homicide, larceny, libel, slander, mayhem, rape, threats. (*j*) Protection to the lower animals.

Blackstone's analysis is less minute than Bishop's. "All division of crime is arbitrary, a mere device of the author to bring the subject aptly to the comprehension of his readers. The law itself is a seamless garment on the body politic." (Bishop).

5. **Children.**— Modern law aims to protect the children against the selfishness and neglect of unfit parents. In primitive times the world over parental rights were absolute as long as they could be enforced. In our day the doctrine is accepted that parents are the natural and responsible guardians of their own offspring, but that the state, as the institute of, rights, ought to see that the neglected child is not defrauded of its rights by degraded parents.

The International Prison Congress at Rome said : " The Congress is of the opinion that it is for the interest of society that the legislature should guard against the evil consequences of the immoral education of children, by parents. One of the methods recommended is to authorize the courts to declare, for a stated time, the parental rights forfeited when the facts sufficiently justify that course." " The judge should have authority to commit a young delinquent, who has been acquitted as having acted without discernment, to an *educational* institution, or to a reform school. The limit of detention in the institution should be fixed by the judge, who shall retain the right to discharge when the circumstances will warrant it. . . . The judge should have the authority to determine that the imprisonment of the young delinquent should be in an

educational or reformatory institution. This detention
should be only in a public institution." " In developing the
paternal authority, the legislature should be inspired with
the high idea of fully respecting the unlimited authority of
the head of the family when exercised in a manner not
hurtful to the children " (Rome). " Referring to the reso-
lutions of the Congress at Rome, showing that one of the
means advised in order to counteract the deplorable consequences of an immoral training given by parents to their
young children, is to permit the courts to take away from
the parents for a determined term all or part of the rights
derived from parental power, when the facts, sufficiently
verified, justify such a responsibility on their part, the
Fourth Congress recognizes that the state has the right to
ward off the pernicious influence of parents or guardians
upon their children or wards. The court, having proved
the unworthiness or incapacity of the parents of a delinquent child, will fix at the age of majority the term of
tutelary education which it will assign either to the house
of correction, or a benevolent institution, or to public or
private charity. The initiative of measures tending to ward
off or restrain paternal power, will belong to public authority, judicial or administrative, as well as to the institutions
above mentioned, in which the child would be confined.
The minor in whose favor a discharge from a penal or
correctional institution may be granted before the end of
the term of condemnation, or of correction, will continue
to remain under the same guardianship until the end of
the term, unless there be need in such case for a special
decision of the court. The parents should be obliged to
contribute, according to their means, to the expense of
support and education of the children taken away by fault
of the parents from their authority. If the circumstances

which have caused the warding off or restraining paternal
power are changed in such a manner that the child can be
restored to its parents without danger to its morality, a
new judicial decision can reinstate the parents to the enjoyment of their right to the person of the child."—St.
Petersburg Congress.

6. Receivers of Stolen Goods.—The peculiar evils connected with certain kinds of business require special state
and municipal regulations.   In order to prevent the receiving of stolen goods it is necessary :

To enact in respect to certain dealers, such as bankers
or money-changers, jewelers, and furniture dealers, some
regulations to prevent the receiving of stolen goods; to
regard the receiving of stolen goods not as a case of com-
plicity, but as a special offense; to establish a progres-·
sive increase of punishment for a repetition of this offense.
It has been recommended (1) that the police be given
larger powers of entry and search in case of suspects; (2)
that pawnbrokers receive a percentage on stolen goods
recovered; (3) that the hours during which pawnbrokers
may keep open shops should be restricted to daylight; (4)
that they should be forbidden to deal with children.
(Tallack).

7. Modifications of Legislation in respect to *first and minor
offences.*—Imprisonment even for one night is a serious
penalty and injury, even if the person is set free at once.
If a short penal sentence follows for a slight offence the
prisoner is disgraced, he is registered with thieves, he is
affected by their conversation, and is likely to enter a
crime career.   The creation of a deep, bitter and general
sense of injustice among the poor must also be considered

as a distinct social danger and a cause of crime. For these reasons it is to be seriously questioned whether legal measures may not substitute some other treatment for arrest. These suggestions have been made in regard to this class of cases : (1) That the magistrate or police justice should be paid a salary, and should not receive fees, which amount to a temptation to arrest for any cause. It is said that when the legislature of Maryland in 1882 abolished the fee system at Baltimore, the number of arrests for minor offenses in that city, in one year, fell from 12,900 to 7,000, or almost one-half. (2) That arrest and imprisonment before actual conviction should be permitted by law only in those instances where it can be shown that the offender is a dangerous person, or that the offence with which he is charged is of a character so heinous as to require his arrest and incarceration, or the placing under bonds until he is tried. (3) That in such cases of minor offences the person be released under suspended sentence, with counsel and reprimand from the magistrate, and his arrest hang over him until he has shown a disposition to keep out of evil ways. (4) That the police be given by their superiors to understand that their places depend more on the prevention of offences than on the number of poor, youthful and helpless persons whom they arrest. (5) That in case of damage to goods the offender be required to repair the injury in kind, or by an equivalent, as a condition of freedom. Résumé and Historical Sketch of the International Prison Congresses in C. D. Randall's Report of St. Petersburg Congress, Bureau of Education. The proceedings of the Congress of Rome, in French, fill three volumes.

CHAPTER XXVII.

THE CRIMINAL UNDER ARREST AND PUNISHMENT.

1. **The Modern Doctrine of the End or Purpose of Punishment.**—Three statements are made: that the object of punishment is retribution; that it is protection of society; and that it is the reformation of the offender.

Retribution is a rational end of punishment. It ought not to be confused with malicious revenge. It is an impulse which may be absolutely free from selfish taint, and it is an impulse which rises in every sound nature when . confronted with an act of moral wrong. Stephen will hardly be suspected of a theological bias, and he declares (His. Crim. Law, ch. xiv) that the purpose of punishment is to manifest the resentment of society against wrongdoers, and to protect society. He hardly notices the element of reformation and the well-being of the criminal himself.

In N. P. A., 1890, "Penological Papers," Dr. W. T. Harris: "Punishment is thus seen in the purgatorial state of the soul to be a tribute of recognition on the part of the Creator—a recognition of the freedom of the will. Man is recognized as responsible for his acts, as owning his deed. Punishment by imprisonment on the part of the state is a high compliment to the individual criminal, for it assumes that the individual is free in doing his deed." Of course this does not apply to those who, through insanity, are irresponsible for injurious acts, and these are not treated in the same way. Mr. C. A. Collins states the pur-

pose of punishment thus: "The object of criminal punishment is the improvement of the offender. This is the
fundamental principle of modern prison science, the
supreme test of all prison methods. To those who hold the
retributive theory of criminal punishment, and demand pain
and suffering for the offender proportionate to the heinous-
ness of his offense, we say, that there is no pain and suffering more severe than that which necessarily accompanies the
healing process. The lazy man is most severely punished
by being compelled to work, the drunkard by being compelled to keep sober, the dissolute and unclean man by
being compelled to live cleanly. If retributive suffering be
the prime motive in the treatment of criminals, suffering
enough to satisfy the most stringent demands of cold and
merciless justice will be found in the cuttings and burnings
of healing surgery, in the pressing and crowding of the man
of deformed and dissolute habits into the straight jacket of
righteous forms of living.

To those who declare the object of criminal punishment
to be the protection of society from the criminal, we say
that the transformation of the criminal into a serviceable
member of society is the only effective protection of society
against him. The mere temporary caging of the criminal,
as a wild beast, is a protection to society for the time being,
it is true, but if when he is let out of his cage he is worse
than he went in, more inhuman, more brutal, more bitterly
disposed toward his fellows, he may be more wary and cunning thereafter, but he will be more dangerous to society
than before he was caged."

In connection with retribution Dr. Harris adds: "There
is another principle than justice in the divine nature, namely,
grace—and grace subserves and also limits justice. The
deepest principle of Christianity requires us to make the

missionary spirit supreme, and to seek, under all circumstances, to reform and make better all that wear the human
form.   The new penology has therefore by degrees moved
forward to a platform higher than that of abstract justice
which sought merely to return his deed on the doer."

"The essential function of criminal law is to prevent
the offence by intimidation, and this function is conditioned
on elements exclusively *social*.

The secondary function, but very important still, is
to insure the harmlessness of the delinquent at his first
offence, and this function is conditioned on *anthropological*
data.

In a somewhat less degree it has for its end the repar-
ation of the injury which the victim has suffered.

Finally, in the pursuit of this triple result it is necessary
to keep in view the social sentiments of justice, of the
resentment and pity which are manifested on the occasion
of the crime."

M. E. Gauckler, at third Congres d'Anthropologie Criminelle,
Bruxelles, 1892.

"The sentence of the law is to the moral sentiment of
the public in relation to the offence what a seal is to hot
wax.   It converts into a permanent final judgment what
might otherwise be a transient sentiment.   This close
alliance between criminal law and moral sentiment is in all
ways healthy and advantageous to the community.   I
think it highly desirable that criminals should be hated,
that the punishments inflicted upon them should be so contrived as to give expression to that hatred, and to justify it
so far as the public provision of means for expressing and
gratifying a healthy natural sentiment can justify and
encourage it."   (Stephen.)   (Cf. Butler on "*Resentment.*")
Cf. Pike Hist. Crime, Vol. 2, ch. xiii.

2. The Modern Estimate of Obsolete Punishments. — The modes of punishment correspond to the social purpose. Presented in historical order, and admitting the fact of apparent exceptions, the penalties are distinctively marked as vengeance, social protection and reformation.

a) Corresponding to the idea of vengeance, savage and barbarian, we discover in the history of all peoples multiplied ingenious devices for inflicting suffering.

b) Corresponding to the idea of social defence we find the dungeon, exile, transportation; with rigorous deterrent measures, as public executions, humiliations, mutilations.

c) Corresponding to the end of reformation we have imprisonment with instruction, moral influence, discipline, prisoner's aid, with the entire system of division, classification, and indeterminate sentence.

3. Outline of English and American Prison Systems. — The modern ideas of the social treatment of crime are approximately represented in the prison systems. A sketch of two systems, with the criticism of special students and practical leaders will set the facts before our minds in a concrete form.

a) **The English System.** —

Transportation ceased in 1867. In 1878 important changes were introduced. "All the local prisons of England and Wales were then transferred to the General Government." . . . . The number of prisons was reduced from 113 to 59; with improvement in administration and a saving of $420,000 a year. These local prisons receive those convicted of offences for which the punishment is not over two years, while those required to serve five years or more go to the convict prisons. . . . . The discipline in the local prisons and in the convict prisons is similar. Both are under the management of the Secretary for the Home Department and the Surveyor General of Prisons. . . . . A sentence to either prison means a sentence to labor, and in all the prisons work is done almost wholly for the Government. But the local prisons are used also as houses of detention for persons charged with offences before trial, and these persons are treated very differently from convicts. They do not work unless they choose, they wear their own clothing when it is fit to wear, and they are kept entirely separate from the convict inmates.

The system of discipline of convicts has various "progressive stages."

The first stage is that of cellular separate confinement for all convicts with rigorous conditions. "He is put in a cell and set at hard labor and kept in solitary confinement for at least one month, if his sentence lasts so long. The labor is apt to be the tread-wheel, and the task has been made uniform for all those whom the physician finds able to perform it. It is to ascend 8,640 feet at the rate of 52 feet ascent per minute during a period of six hours, divided into two equal portions, in which he works by periods of fifteen minutes' labor and five minutes' rest. Meanwhile the new convict's diet is exceedingly light . . . . for one week. After that he gets a second class diet for a week which is a slight improvement on the first, and later the third, then the fourth class." His bed, which is at first a plank, gradually improves. Other privileges are introduced as rewards of good behavior, or are removed and the severity repeated if prison rules are broken.

"A sentence to penal servitude in a convict prison, which must be five years or more, involves different treatment. The convict is at once taken to the convict prison at which he will serve the greater part of his term."

He is first taken to a local prison — a prison provided for the purpose — to serve nine months of his term in solitary confinement. Some kind of work is provided for him, and he leaves his cell only for a little open-air exercise and to attend chapel. Nothing that the convict can do will shorten his nine months' period of discipline. It is intended to give him a chance to think over the situation and decide on his future conduct. At the end of nine months he is removed to one of the convict prisons, and, if his behavior has been good, put to work with other convicts.

"The convict has now passed the first and severest stage of his punishment. In the meantime he has been on probation, and a careful record of his conduct accompanies him to his new home. The probation period continues three months longer, during which he works with other convicts. If he behaves well and works well all the time, he is then eligible to the graded service. There are three grades, of which he enters the lowest. He must stay in that grade a year, unless degraded for misconduct, when, if his marks are perfect, he may be promoted to the second, and after another year to the first. Each of these grades gives slightly increasing privileges, and industry and good behavior throughout his term entitle him to a remission of nearly one-fourth of his term of imprisonment. It also entitles him to a gratuity of $15 on his discharge. If his record has been especially good he may gain a gratuity of $30."

Women prisoners are granted still larger privileges if they give hope of amendment; and the "star class" of men, composed of those who have never been convicted of crime before, though passed through the same severe discipline, are kept separate from hardened offenders.

The third stage of this progressive treatment is conditional release. Those who have gained good marks may go abroad under the watchcare of the police. They must report each month, give notice of change of place, not be found in company of thieves, and show a purpose to be industrious and law-abiding.

Moral and educational agencies, together with counsel of chaplains, are supplied in all stages of discipline.

After discharge, in the case of most prisons, a society for the aid of discharged prisoners befriends them, seeks employment for them, and encourages them in all possible ways.

Du Cane believes "this system is to be commended, because it appeals to hope more than to fear, diminishes the resort to more drastic forms of punishment, as flogging and reduction of diet, and absolutely diminishes the number of convicts through its deterrent influence. . . .

Reformatory and industrial schools for juvenile offenders form a part of the system. . . . To the reformatories may be committed offenders under sixteen years of age. . . . To the industrial schools are sent youths under fourteen who have not been convicted of crime, . . . found begging or receiving alms or wandering without settled abode or visible means of subsistence, or frequenting the company of thieves, or living with prostitutes. . . . The expense of both reformatories and industrial schools is paid partly by the government, partly by the parents of children committed, partly by school boards, and partly by private subscription. Both are under the supervision of an inspector appointed by the home secretary."

In the English prisons it is sought to give a barely elementary education to those who are illiterate, but no elaborate system of higher instruction is provided.

Labor in English prisons.—The labor performed by prisoners is done directly for the government. They "build fortifications, manufacture supplies for the post-office, the army, the navy, the metropolitan police, for the prisons themselves, and for other government uses." They till farms. It is not attempted to make the prisons self-supporting. The cost, above the meager earnings for the government, is borne by the tax-payers. The industries are not generally conducted in the best way to teach the convicts useful trades. Those who work on farms earn little and cost much to guard, as there are constant efforts to escape. Sir E. F. Du Cane argues from the physical defects of many prisoners, "the absence of the ordinary stimulus which operates on men in a state of freedom, and the inconvenience and prejudice against government trading," that it is undesirable to attempt to make prisons self-sustaining.

The learning of trades is made a reward for industry and good conduct.

"The (subordinate) officers enter the service in the lowest positions, having passed the examination of the Civil Service commission and an examination into their antecedents by prison officials, which is very searching. . . . They are promoted strictly according to merit, and are not in danger of removal unless they deserve it. . . . The men adapted to the work spend their lives in it, and the service is rewarded by a pension." . . . The governors of the prisons are appointed on different principles, often being old army officers. This results frequently in the appointment of men without the proper experience.

Summary of Principles—General Du Cane sums up the principles of the system over which he has been a controlling influence: "(1) That a well-devised system of secondary punishment should provide for subjecting those sentenced to it to a uniform course of penal deterrent discipline. (2) That every means possible should be adopted for developing and working on the higher feelings of the prisoners, directly by moral, religious, and secular instruction, and indirectly by ensuring industry, good conduct, and discipline, through appealing to the hope of advantage or reward, as well as by fear of punishment. (3) That, with a view to deterrence as well as reformation, it is desirable that every short sentence and the first part of every long sentence should be undergone on the separate system. (4) That before discharging the long-sentenced convict to a full or modified degree of liberty, he should be subjected to further training, in which he should be associated, under supervision, while at labor, but separated at all other times. (5) That properly constructed prison buildings, providing among other things for this separation, are all-important requisites for the success of the system. (6) That employment should be provided and industry enforced or encouraged for all. (7) That care should be taken to select and train a good staff of skilled and responsible officials to supervise and carry on the work of the convict establishments, and means adopted to prevent their work being hindered or defeated by the prisoners being brought into close contact on works or otherwise with free men who were under no such responsibilities. (8) That those who on discharge are disposed to follow honest courses should be guided and assisted in their endeavors, and that a careful watch should be kept over all till they have re-established their character."

Since this system was adopted the population of England and Wales increased from 19,257,184 to 26,213,629, from 1853 to 1884 ; while the number of sentences of penal servitude decreased from 2589 to 1428. Whether all this decrease was due to the system must be considered in another place, but it has unquestionably been effective in the right direction.

References : Du Cane, " Punishment and Prevention of Crime."
Tallack, " Penological and Preventive Principles."
J. S. Butler in " Papers in Penology."
Howard, "State of Prisons," (for last century.)

b) *The System of Prisons in the United States*—There is no general system in the nation. Each commonwealth has its own method. Generally there are as many local methods as there are county sheriffs. Uniformity is absent. Errors and abuses disgrace our country, while here and there intelligent and heroic efforts to remove evils and introduce improvements do us honor and encourage hope.

Police—Dr. A. G. Byers (N. C. C., 1889): Urges that the police should be more a preventive than a detective agency. " But this force, under mistaken ideas of its duty, is actually, in most, if not all, our larger communities, in connivance with wrong-doing. We would avoid indiscriminate reflection ; yet the fact remains, that there is scarcely a city in the United States where the saloon, the gambling hell and the brothel, each and all in contravention of law and ordinances, do not carry forward their demoralizing and destructive work under the immediate observation and intimate personal knowledge of the police, while at the same time the honest but hilarious newsboy or bootblack, in giving vent to boyish propensities, is rudely dragged through the public thoroughfares, hustled into the dark and dirty station house, forced into association with the idle and vicious, arraigned, tried, and convicted in the police court, where he is made a spectacle of disgrace in the eyes of those who study law and derive their ideas of public justice from such proceedings. If it were possible to eliminate partisan politics from police organizations, an important step would be taken toward a reform that must precede any well-regulated prison system for the state.

" Adopting the preventive idea, it is certainly practicable to employ sober, industrious, conscientious men on life tenure, liberal salary, and retiring pension, to charge them with the duty of preventing the violation of law and order, and to hold them fairly responsible for misdemeanors and crimes within their precincts."

The chief impediments to efficient police service are: (1) The appointment of policemen for "political" reasons, nominally by Mayor or Board, but really by a local alderman. (2) The system of paying magistrates with fees instead of salary. The magistrate is paid for the papers and trial of a prostitute whom he dismisses without a fine or a small one which is really a tax, and a tax which goes to his private purse and not to the public. The policeman is discouraged from making arrests because he sees it does no good, or he makes arrests in order to divide the spoils with the magistrate. (3) Policemen are burdened with matters which should be attended to by Health and Truant officers. All these matters should be under the control of the police department, with enough special officers to do each special kind of work. (4) Interference by the Mayor and other officials to protect their political friends from arrest. (5) The vices of licentiousness and gambling are hindering and corrupting influences. Prostitutes and gamblers, with the aid of bribes and political influences, often secure license to pursue their degrading ways. (See N. P. A., 1891, p. 107.)

The intelligent and benevolent public may aid the police and encourage them both through legal and voluntary action. Rewards and prizes might be offered to stimulate preventive work — as in service in protecting children, dumb animals and the public health and morality. In England "watch committees," appointed by municipalities, and independent of the police force, have been thought efficient in keeping policemen up to their best work. Various societies have been formed to provide refreshment, recreation, wholesome reading and religious privileges for men on the force. Honor, hope and sympathy are far more efficient agencies in securing the highest service than fear of discharge. Society should both require and honor soldierly service in the defenders of its safety in time of peace as well as in time of war. As the temptations of policemen are peculiarly strong, society is bound to diminish these perils as far as possible, and also to offer all the counteracting influences and motives in its power.

J. P. Altgeld, "Our Penal System and its Victims."

Tallack, "Penological and Preventive Principles." N. P. A. 1888, p. 22.

The Police Station is an important part of the system. It is used for a temporary place of detention for juvenile offenders, for hardened criminals, for persons arrested as suspects, in all organized towns and cities. Too often it is in a bad sanitary condition, dirty, dark and foul with vermin and disease. Around its cells swarm the curious crowd and the associates of the depraved. Separation of classes is frequently neglected and persons of entirely different moral condition are permitted to communicate. There is no centralized method of supervision, and therefore no uniformity of management. Until recently women matrons were not provided, and scandalous occurrences have not been infrequent. It goes without saying, that women matrons ought to be appointed for every lock-up.

The County Jail.—This remains the most disgraceful and dangerous part of our prison system. While there are local jails which provide for a degree of separation of prisoners, there is no uniformity and no system of state supervision in most of the states. Jails are used for the detention of witnesses, of persons of all grades awaiting trial, and for places of punishment by confinement on the judgment of lower courts. Seldom is any kind of work provided. The halls are occupied by drunkards, vagrants, hardened offenders, often young lads, who pass the time of waiting in handling greasy cards, reading what may chance to come, and in gossip such as may be imagined would prevail in such company. The cells are separate unless there is a crowd, but the separation does not prevent easy communication. Absolute separation is demanded by every interest of decency, humanity and justice. The jail is frequently called the high school of crime. It is one of the institutions supported at public expense for the propagation of depravity. A large part of the increase of crime in this country may be charged to this irrational institution.

District Workhouses.—On this much needed element of a prison system Mr. A. G. Byers said: "The next step must include a workhouse for misdemeanants and those convicted of minor offences. Properly constructed and well arranged workhouses are necessarily expensive, so that comparatively few municipalities can afford to erect and maintain them. They should be erected and maintained within certain districts of a state, according to population, and should be under the control of the state. Labor should be imposed, proper industries introduced, and cumulative sentences provided for, so that ultimately the misdemeanant, always an annoyance and frequently a great and growing burden to society, should be restrained of personal liberty and compelled to self-maintenance." The National Prison Association of 1870, on motion of Mr. Sanborn of Massachusetts, passed the following resolution : "*Resolved,* That the district prisons described in the paper of Mr. Byers, intermediate between the state prison and the county jail, are a necessary part of a complete prison system, and, in the opinion of this Congress, such district prisons ought to be established in all states where they do not now exist."

Reform Schools or Industrial Homes.—These institutions illustrate the value of the principle of classification of offenders. Boys and girls of the age of sixteen are placed under the care of the managers of these schools up to the time of their majority upon conviction under the criminal code. In some states the youth may by good behavior be released, on condition that they report to the county agent and the superintendent of the school at intervals. This is the Michigan method. It is essential that during this period the young offenders learn some useful trade and that the officers see that they have employment before they are sent out. Under the head of Preventive Work we may study other methods of caring for juveniles.

N. C. C. 1890, p. 214. Industries in Juvenile Reform Schools.

The State Reformatory Prison. A selected class of offenders may be sent to an institution based on the idea of reformation. Such persons must not be chronic criminals. The most conspicuous example of this grade of prisons in the United States is the famous Elmira Reformatory, under the care of Mr. Z. R. Brockway. In giving the essential characteristics of this reformatory, we give the essential features of the new school of prison managers. To describe it in detail would take more room than we can spare, but the references will guide to more exhaustive sources.

Elmira Reformatory. The prison system of New York is based on the "Fassett Bill" of 1889. The main provisions of that legislation are embodied in the regulations for the prisons. In describing Elmira Reformatory the principles of the statute are brought to light.

To Elmira are committed first offenders of sixteen to thirty years of age. The management of the institution is entrusted by law to a board of managers and a superintendent. The board review the business affairs and decide on cases of conditional liberation. The superintendent has power to control, to appoint and discharge officers. Within the prison there is a careful system of responsibility and division of labor. Prisoners are examined by the superintendent soon after their arrival, to know their character and to decide upon the best mode of treatment. Facts of heredity and personal conduct and character are carefully set down in registers, together with information furnished by the court.

Prisoners are divided into three grades. Each prisoner at first enters the intermediate grade, and may fall by misconduct into the actual criminal grade or rise by "good marks" to the first rank. The marks are based on demeanor, labor and school progress.

The discharge of the prisoner is not made final until after six months of conditional liberation on parole, during which period he must report monthly.

The diet of the reformatory is hearty. Those in the lowest grade are deprived of tea and coffee. Those in the first grade have special luxuries beyond the second. Members of the three grades are also distinguished by their clothing; by the manner of taking their food,— whether at table or in cells; by the size and furniture of the cells; by various privileges in respect to letters and books. In work shops and school the members of all grades mingle on equal terms, and there proficiency alone is honored.

The school at Elmira is an essential feature of discipline. Not only elementary subjects are taught, but also history, literature, geography, political economy, higher mathematics, physiology, practical ethics, and the elements of various trades and technical processes. Each student is treated as an individual, and his culture, physical and spiritual, is taken up at the point at which he left off. A good library of well selected volumes and many magazines and papers is supplied.

The theory of the institution is based on the purpose of reform of the prisoner. If he is physically diseased, feeble or inert, the best known hygienic and medical measures are applied to build up energy and health. Important experiments have been tried with massage, baths, gymnastic exercises and military drill.

The sentence is limited between a minimum and a maximum, with a measure of discretion of the judge. The shortening of the term depends upon the prisoner himself. The statute recognizes the principle that the prisoner should receive a part of the product of his labor for his own sake and for his family.

On both sides of the Atlantic this method has been vigorously attacked. It is claimed by many that it offers a premium to crime, because the condition of the prisoner is made more comfortable than that of ordinary laboring people, and that this is unjust to those who must toil for his support. In reply to this the authorities claim that their method is not lax and luxurious, but that the cleanliness, steady habit of labor, and constant occupation are precisely the things which such persons dread; that the soul cannot be cured of its crime unless the body is sound and vigorous, and the hands trained for useful industry. It is also claimed by critics of the Elmira plan that their reports of success in "reformation" cannot be verified until the Bertillon system of identification and registration has become a part of the state and national methods of dealing with the crime class.

The *financial* plans of the Reformatory have been broken up several times by the public opposition, on the part of business men and trades' unions, to competition with prison labor. At Elmira, under New York laws, the product of any one kind must not exceed five per cent. of the whole product in the state. This has worked to advantage in one direction, since it has compelled the introduction of many trades and so opened a wider field for technical instruction.

> On the New York System and Elmira, see H. D. Wey, "The Elmira Reformatory of To-Day." Papers in Penology, Second Series. Alexander Winter, "The Elmira Reformatory." "Physical Training of Youthful Criminals," H. D. Wey, N. P. A. 1888. N. C. C. 1891, p. 202. On Prison Discipline, N. C. C., 1890, p. 279. On Prison Management, N. C. C., 1889, p. 50.

Reformatory for Women.— Reformatory institutions for girls should be absolutely separated in place and management from prisons for women. Industries adapted to women should be introduced. The management should be in the hands of women. Classification is vital. Discharged prisoners cannot be safely released without watch-care for a certain time. If hardened prostitutes were treated under laws of cumulative sentences their ranks might soon be diminished and their social influence broken. The present policy of short terms for openly disorderly conduct is inefficient and vicious. After all preventive work for girls, and care of demoralized families is most necessary and hopeful.

> N. C. C., 1879, pp. 189–200: *ibid*, 1878, pp. 79, 111.

The State Prison or Penitentiary is designed for those criminals for whom there is less hope of reformation, although prison science is slow to confess that there are any absolutely "incorrigible." The principles of discipline in long term institutions are given below.

A State Central Prison Authority is needed in every State in order to secure uniformity and efficiency; to prevent local abuses; to bring faults into the light of publicity; and to transfer prisoners from one institution to another according to their nature and needs. It is believed that such an authority should be judicial in its functions and powers, and not a branch of the executive department of state or of the administrative force of prisons.

Consensus of Judgments on Prison Management.— Detention of the accused before trial and of witnesses. "It is desirable that special prisons be established for preventive detention as far as it is possible; otherwise that a special part of the institution be designated for the imprisonment of the accused.

Individual separation should be adopted as a general rule for preventive detention, and be replaced by imprisonment in common during the day upon the expressed desire to that effect by the prisoner, if judicial or administrative power authorizes it.

Individual separation should also be applied to minors when they are in a state of detention; it will only be ordered in case of absolute necessity, and it is desirable in principle that minors under seventeen years of age should enjoy liberty until authority decides definitely upon their condition.

Individual separation should be replaced by imprisonment in common for prisoners who cannot endure close confinement because of their health, on account of their advanced age, or physical or mental condition.

The prisoners should be treated on the basis of the common law. Preventive detention should only involve restrictions required to accomplish its purpose, and the desire to maintain order in the prison.

Local administration can be made available in respect to prisoners only by such measure of discipline as is provided for by regulations and restrictions necessary to maintain order and tranquillity.

The supervision of societies of patronage organized for discharged criminals should also extend to persons after acquittal."

Education of Prison Officers.— " The Congress is of opinion that the teaching of penitentiary and criminal science is very useful and much to be desired, and that the scientific study of the application of punishments can easily be reconciled with the requirements of penal discipline.

It expresses the view that a chair of penal science should be established in the universities of different countries, and that the penal administration should create necessary facilities to sustain and encourage that study.

The establishment of libraries of penal science in prisons and for the use of officers of these institutions is desirable." (St. Petersburg Congress.)

" It is of the highest importance for the interests of prison work to insure well the recruitment of officers, employés and agents of the prison service.

With regard to the manner of pursuing that course it is necessary to distinguish between the higher and lower offices.

It is important in the first place to determine the conditions of admission to these positions.   The following should be delegated by preference : To higher offices persons in possession of the general information which the offices require ; to lower offices, as far as possible, old soldiers who have finished their obligatory service. [This last a Continental view.]

The preparation of candidates for the highest offices will include — (a) Certain courses of study and of the theory of penal science ; (b) and the practical study of every detail of prison work, directed by the chiefs of model prisons ; the course finished, the candidates in question will be registered on the lists presented to the administration qualified to make the appointments.

The preparatory instruction for candidates to the *lower* offices will include, above all, practical penal work which will correspond, for example, with the instruction of guardian schools operating in certain countries,this service being directed by experienced prison superintendents in the same places in the department in which the candidate will enter upon his duties.

It is essential to guaranty the officials' emoluments and advantages corresponding to the importance of the work, so honorable and so difficult, which they are carrying on for the good of society. An extreme parsimony could only be detrimental in every respect."

Punishments, Cellular, Progressive, Etc. — " In the infliction of penalties intended at the time to punish the guilty, to place him beyond the possibility of wrong doing, and to give him means to reinstate himself, and the punishments of long duration permitting more than others the hope of the reformation of the condemned ; the organization of these punishments should be inspired by the principles of reform, which regulate punishments of short duration.

Every convict condemned to punishment of long duration should be placed at first in a cell for a certain time.

After the time in a cell, day and night, has expired, when the condemned can be admitted to work in common during the day, he should continue to be confined in the cell during the night.

The administration should organize work, as far as possible, in the open air and in preference public work, but on the indispensable condition that this work will be established in such a manner that the prisoners will never come in contact with the free population.

Conditional liberation will be awarded only with every possible discretion and in following a gradation agreeing with the reform of the prisoner."

Patronages should be established, either by private initiative or by the administration, to protect the condemned during the time of their conditional liberation and to watch over them after their definite discharge while they do not seem completely reformed.

"The progressive system, which begins with cellular confinement with labor, corresponds to the nature of punishments of *medium duration*." St. Petersburg, Randal, p. 177.

"**Incorrigibles**," at least the most difficult cases ; confirmed recidivists.

" Without admitting that in a penal and penitentiary point of view there may be criminals or delinquents absolutely incorrigible, experience shows that in fact there are certain individuals who prove themselves insensible to this reformatory influence, and who return, by force of habit as well as by profession, to the violation of the laws of society. The congress expresses the opinion that especial measures should be taken against such individuals.

In this order of thought, without directing attention to the principles of different legislatures, and reserving the liberty to choose the means corresponding best to particular conditions of each state, the following measures are recommended for study in different countries :

a) Imprisonment, for a sufficient time, in institutions or work - houses where compulsory labor is required, is applicable to certain individuals, as beggars, inveterate vagabonds, etc.

b) Prolonged imprisonment or, according to the case, transportation to certain territories or possessions belonging to interested countries, in order to utilize lost forces ; but always with guaranties that should insure support for those who are deprived of their liberty and a possibility of regaining entire liberty by good conduct, especially according to the system of conditional liberation.

These measures should not be prejudicial to placing in special institutions of assistance persons adjudged incapable of providing for themselves materially by their work."

The suggestion of *transportation* is by no means universally approved.

The St. Petersburg Congress does not admit the existence of this class of incorrigibles.

The proposition is sometimes made that, in the last resort, the instinctive and incurable criminal should be put to death "like a mad dog." It is true that a criminal is like a mad dog, in that both endanger human life, but they differ in this that the criminal is a man and the mad dog is a dog !

Mr. Z. R. Brockway (Randall's Report, p. 124) gives the social reason for declining to kill the hardest cases of criminals : " To incapacitate by destroying them would certainly afford protection as against their further crimes,

and, once accomplished, would relieve society from any
further cost for their maintenance ; but, possibly, the evil
effect of life-taking for incorrigibility might prove worse
than to permit them to live and pursue their criminal calling.   There is much reason to believe that a frequent
infliction of the death penalty for crimes has a debasing
effect upon society at large. . . . It may be said that the
state of public sentiment which, insensible or indifferent to
the cruelty of it, destroys the life of incorrigible criminals,
would also put to death the incurably insane and remediless
defectives of every kind, indicating thus a state of barbarism favorable to crimes, the crimes and the criminals in
turn actually contributing to the public sentiment that produces them."

Motives of Reformation. (St. Petersburg, Randall, p.
175 – 6). "A system of reward and encouragement, material
and moral, for the prisoners, fixed by regulation at the
discretion of the administration, is efficient in the interest
of good discipline as well as reform of prisoners.

The measures indicated should be a reward for assiduity
in work, and of good conduct, as far as may be without
prejudice to the serious character and purpose of punishment.

It is proper to give the greatest scope to all lawful
means of encouragement and reward, such as hope of
shortening sentence, authority to buy books, to send aid to
their families, etc.

In the way of material encouragement, the authorization of better food is admissible, which, without assuming
the character of luxury, appears beneficial in a hygienic
view.

The prisoner can be authorized to make use, for his
material and moral needs, of a share of his earnings in a

measure limited by general regulations, and at the discretion of the director of the institution in each special case.

The part of the competence reserved should be entrusted, at the time of the liberation of the prisoner, to the authorities of societies of patronage, who would charge themselves with making payments to the prisoner by instalments in proportion to his needs.

Disposition by the prisoner of his patrimony outside of his competence can be allowed as a means of satisfying his wants in prison only by the authorization of the director."

Labor in Prisons. Relative to the *correction* and reformation of the prisoner, and the benefit of his family; and relative of prison products to free industries.

" *Labor, useful* and *productive as possible, being necessary* ✓ for *prisoners,* to whatever penal régime they may be submitted, it is in each country proper to examine how, according to the situation, it can be practically furnished and directed in order to answer the rules and different necessities of penal work, whether by the system of labor for the State or by the contract system.

Labor being the important part of penal life should remain subject in its organization and its functions to public authority, which alone has the capacity of securing the execution of penal laws. It could not then abandon them to the promotion of private interests.

In a general manner, but without imposing absolute rules, the system of state labor seems to best facilitate the subordination of work, as of every other part of penal régime, to the end it designs to accomplish. But, on account of the difficulties that the organization of public labor presents, it can be seen that the administration may resort to contracts or private industries, provided that the utilization of manual labor does not constitute the domination of a contractor over the person and life of the prisoner.

In the organization of prison labor, and especially in that of labor for the state, it is desirable that the advantages of prison manual labor be reserved to the state, and the view is expressed that the state be consequently, as far as possible, at the same time, producer and consumer of objects manufactured by prison manual labor.

Manual labor should be utilized, as far as possible, and without doing injury to the necessities of penal work, for the wants of the prisoner and for the use of the prison.

The advantages likely to result from this manual labor should be reserved, as far as possible, to the state, and not contribute to the gains of the management of private enterprises.

The arrangement of the effective forces of each industry in a determined place, the choice of the variety and compensation of these industries, the disposition of salaries and schedules of work, should be so combined as not to allow protection, privileges, or abusive forces to be constituted, capable of depressing corresponding free industries.

Public authority should always preserve, in some manner of organization of work, whatever it may be, the means of warding off every abusive competition which arises, without reducing the prisoners to idleness and without abandoning them to the management or the power of contractors and certain industries."

Mr. C. D. Wright, U. S. Commissioner of Labor, 1885, (summarized in papers in Penology, 2d Series, p. 109,) has given the following survey of the present conditions of this question :

"There are four distinct convict labor systems in this country :

(1) The *contract system*, under which a contractor employs convicts at a certain agreed price per day for their labor, the prisoners working under the immediate ·direction of the contractor or his agents. Under this system the institution usually furnishes to the contractor the power necessary and even the machinery for carrying on the work. (2) The *piece-price* system, which is simply a modification of the contract system. Under this system the contractor furnishes to the prison the materials in a proper shape for working, and receives from the prison the manufactured articles at an agreed piece-price, the supervision of the work being wholly in the hands of the prison officials. (3) The *public account system*, under which the institution carries on the business of manufacturing like a private individual or firm, buying raw materials and converting them into manufactured articles, which are sold in the best available market. (4) The *lease system*, under which the institution leases the convicts to a contractor for a specified sum and for a fixed period, the lessees usually undertaking to clothe, feed, care for and maintain proper discipline among the prisoners while they perform such labor as may have been determined by the terms of the lease."

"The negative and positive results of the applications of these four systems under varying degrees and kinds of circumstances were thus summarized in the bureau report:

The *contract system* is the most prevalent in the United States at the present time. It has the special advantage of being remunerative to the state, and as a rule to the contractor. The convicts are kept constantly employed and the state incurs no business risk. The objection is that the contractors undersell the manufacturers employing free labor, and where a prison having a large number of convicts is devoted to a particular industry its products tend to drive

out of the market the products of free labor in that particular line of manufacture.   This was notably the case in
Chicago," where the cooperage business was very greatly
reduced in proportions, the great packing houses taking
their barrels from the Illinois state prison.

The *piece-price system*, as the bureau sets forth, is simply
a modification of the contract system, the contractor having
nothing to do with the convicts.   It has all the disadvantages of the contract system from the standpoint of the
manufacturer who uses free labor, its sole advantage over
the contract system lying in the fact that the convicts, being
under the full control of the prison officials, may be subjected to reformatory influences.

The *public account system*, the bureau says, is the ideal
system of prison reformers, workingmen, manufacturers and
legislators, as a rule : whatever profit is made in labor and
sales goes to the state.   It offers the best opportunities for
reformatory effort.   But its pecuniary success depends
upon the employment of power machinery ; and as the state
pays nothing whatever for the labor, it will be seen that the
system affects the price of goods in the market more considerably than any other, and the disadvantage is that
prisoners must be laid off in dull times, thus making constant employment out of the question.   It is also a scandal-
breeder.

The *lease system* is the most abominable of all, although
the state gets a fixed sum for the convicts and is relieved of
all responsibility.   The objections to it, as stated by Gov.
Gordon, of Georgia, are included in the bureau's report,
viz :

It places pecuniary interests in conflict with humanity.
It makes possible the infliction of greater punishment than
the law and courts have imposed.

It renders impracticable the proper care by the state of the health of its prisoners, or their requisite separation according to classes, sexes and conditions.

It reduces to the minimum the chances for reformation. It places convict labor in many instances in direct competition with the honest labor of the state.

The report then takes up eleven leading propositions for solving the problem and forms a separate estimate of the value of each. These are discussed in this order :

1. *The entire abolition of Convict Labor.* This is dismissed at once. Experiment has shown that where convicts were not employed, insanity increased at a frightful rate. The expense of maintenance would be enormous.

2. *The establishment of a Penal Colony by the Federal Government.* The bureau says it is not reasonable to suppose that the separate states of the union will take the course necessary for its adoption, and the states as individuals cannot adopt any such plan, because of the small proportion of the prison population of each state. Moreover, says the bureau, the moral sentiment of the nation will never permit the herding of criminals in any section of the land, whether in Alaska, or on any of the islands within the jurisdiction of the United States, for the establishment of a penal colony would entail upon a single community all the evil results now seen to accrue from hereditary taint.

3. *The employment of Convicts on Public Works and Ways.* By this means manufacturers would be relieved of competition, but there would be competition in labor. It merely removes the actual competition from one realm to another. The expense of transportation, maintenance, temporary stockades and guards would be enormous. The chain-gang is a necessity under the plan, and " the demoralizing effects upon communities from witnessing large bodies of crimi-

nals at work openly are objections which the moral instincts of communities clearly recognize." The burden of competition is shifted from skilled to unskilled labor. There is no economy in the plan. It would cost the state a great deal more to do constructive work with convict than with free labor.

4. *The employment of convicts in manufacturing goods for the government.* The radical objection to this proposition is that the entire annual expense of the government for furniture, clothing, mail bags, harnesses, wagons, infantry, cavalry and artillery equipments, clothing for the Indian service, etc., is only about $4,000,000 ; whereas the total product of the prison labor of the country amounts to about $30,000,000.

5. *The exportation of the products of convict labor.* An examination of the statistics of exportation shows that only a small proportion of prison manufactures would be sold in this way.

6. *The prohibition of the sale of convict - made goods outside of the state in which manufactured.* This would be destructive to business in a state like New York, for example, where the prison products amount to about $7,000,000. It would also be impossible to trace the goods. It would be unconstitutional, as interfering with commerce between the states.

7. *Convict - made goods to be stamped "prison - made."* This would lead to an immediate boycott.

8. The payment of wages to convicts. This suggestion has found earnest advocates, but it leads to deficiency in the revenue. The bureau thinks, however, it is worthy serious consideration and study.

9. The reduction of the hours of labor in prisons. This would be a remedy only in a very partial sense.

10. *The substitution of industries not now carried on in this country.* The chief importations consist of fine goods, whereas it is a necessity that convicts be employed upon coarse grades of goods. "A glance at the list of articles imported into this country," says the bureau, "is sufficient to satisfy one of the impracticability of this plan."

11. *The utilization of convicts upon farms.* Gov. Gordon has recommended this plan. The bureau, however, declines to entertain it, believing that the opposition to convict farm labor would be greater in time than that which now exists against the employment of convicts in mechanical pursuits.

Cf. N. P. A. 1888, p. 50 : *ibid*, 1891, p. 202.

Special Topics.—There are questions in which the public can interest themselves only in a limited degree, and which divide even specialists of experience ; " Prison architecture and sanitation ; the prison staff ; mode of appointment of officers ; tenure of office ; prison dietaries ; labor in prisons ; prison schools, including the question of normal schools for training prison employés in their duties ; religious instruction in prisons ; prison libraries ; the correspondence of prisoners ; visits to prisoners by their friends and by other persons ; the rights of convicts in prisons ; the privileges which it is expedient to grant them, and especially the effect of allowing them a percentage of their earnings ; the dress of prisoners ; disciplinary punishments in prison ; prison registers, and the use of photography as an aid to the identification of escaped prisoners, or of recidivists ; prison statistics ; the proper treatment of rich prisoners and of convicts who are or who become insane ; the duration of imprisonment, as it is affected by life sentences, by cumulative sentences, by "good-time" laws, and by executive interference ; the effect of transition from a state of imprisonment to a state of freedom upon the prisoner himself, and the necessity for continued care of him subsequent to his discharge, with especial reference to securing him honest employment." (F. H. Wines in Lalor's Cyclopedia.)

CHAPTER XXVIII.

PREVENTIVE MEASURES AGAINST CRIME.

Identification and Registration. (*a*) The *object* of identification is manifold. It is deterrent, because it hinders the free movement of offenders and makes them feel that detection and condemnation are more certain. It enables prison authorities to measure the relative success of various methods. It promotes the efficiency of the executive departments and instructs the judiciary in the application of the principle of commutative sentences. It is essential to the safe use of the parole and indeterminate sentence systems. No innocent person is injured by it, since the record is not employed except in case of repetition of crime. (*b*) The *method* of identification. The more skillful and permanent officers of law can remember a few of the most notorious offenders, but this is unreliable and local in value. Photography is an important addition to the resources of detectives. But all the best elements have been continued in the system called after its inventor the Bertillon method. Its essential features are two photographs, front and side views of the face ; measurements of the length of certain bones of the body ; noting deep scars and other permanent marks ; classification and registration on such a

plan that a well furnished police office can identify a re-
cidivist in a few minutes.   To become most complete and
valuable it should be adopted by the general government
in coöperation with state and municipal police forces.

A. Bertillon : "Identification Anthropometique," 1893, Paris. *Forum*.
May, 1891.   N. P. A., 1891, p. 64.

2. Patronage or Discharged Prisoners' Aid.—The situation of the discharged prisoner without means and friends
is pitiable and dangerous.   The powerful pen of Victor
Hugo has represented the desperate state of a convict at
large in the sombre picture of Jean Valjean.   In all civilized countries efforts are made, more or less efficient, to see
that the discharged prisoner is met at the door with a
friendly care, offered temporary shelter, occupation and
assistance to secure permanent employment.   In the absence
of such help he may find every door closed against him
except the saloon, the brothel and the rendezvous of thieves
and crime capitalists.   It seems a social wrong of greatest
magnitude to set a man at liberty without some assurance
that he has at least an opportunity of earning a living by
honest industry.   It is at this point that voluntary coöperation with state functionaries is of the highest value, and
here private philanthropy can be sure to do good with the
least mixture of harm.   The spontaneous and unofficial
interest of religious and humane persons has some important advantages over official aid by persons identified with
the punitive agency of the state.   But such societies must,
to be useful, sincerely coöperate with prison officials.

The Prison Congress expresses the opinion : "That
societies of patronage should be established wherever they
do not now exist, and that relations between societies of
patronage or societies of benevolence in different countries

should be established in the general interest of works of patronage, and also in order to bring aid in the most efficient manner to persons needing patronage.

That to this end conventions should be established between different societies which should have for their aim : (a) To issue a regular and reciprocal exchange of experience. (b) To set forth the principle that patronage should extend to foreigners ; regarding always the police regulations of each country. (c) To insure the return home of discharged prisoners, if they so desire, or to secure them work in another place.

That in view of their return home, special supervision should be taken of their earnings, their clothing, and discharge papers, and their free passage.

In the aim of facilitating the establishment of an institution of international patronage, it is desired that societies of patronage which exist in all countries should be united in creating a central national organ." (St Petersburg Congress.)

" It is recommended that societies of patronage should have the opportunity to become interested in the situation of the families of prisoners before they have recovered their liberty. (a) In order to secure, as much as possible, the maintenance of family affections. (b) In order to aid especially the family of the prisoner if his detention has caused serious detriment to minors, the old, or the infirm. To attain this end the societies of patronage should mention it expressly in their statutes, and place themselves in connection with every local authority, administrative or religious."

It is recommended, also, that the society of patronage should seek coöperation with the police. But the police should not follow up those who are under responsible charge of the societies in a way to expose them, intimidate them and interfere with their reformation. (St Petersburg Conress.)

3. **Substitutes for Arrest and Imprisonment.**—The end sought is avoidance of the loss of self-respect, hope and social reputation, which necessarily accompanies imprisonment.

It is proposed that the police should be instructed and trained for warning those who are in the way of becoming liable to arrest ; that judges should exercise a certain discretion with young and ignorant offenders ; instructing, reprimanding and releasing under suspended sentence when it seems to be in the interest of public justice and welfare ; such power to be carefully bounded by law ; that fines without imprisonment and requirement to restore goods or repair damages take the place of incarceration. Such discretion is, as a matter of fact, already frequently used with advantage, and it is proposed to extend the power by careful legislation.

Cf. Morrison, Tallack and Rylands, works cited.
J. F. Altgeld, " Our Penal Machinery and its Victims."
Waugh, " Gaol Cradle."

4. **Juvenile Delinquents.**—Most criminals, as shown by statistics of prisons, begin their crime career very young and come from demoralized domestic conditions. The state seldom notices the child until he has placed himself within the range of criminal law. Experience has abundantly proved the folly and injury of this neglect. An early change of environment, in the case of most children of vicious parents, is all that is needed to turn them from a certain career of crime to a hopeful path of industry and happiness. The most enlightened spirits are turning their

attention, therefore, most hopefully to the subject of preventive work for neglected children who swarm in our cities. The success of Charles L. Brace in New York is remarkable and encouraging, and the diminution of crime in England during recent years seems largely due to the vigor and efficiency of their system of caring for abandoned and perverted children. Similar efforts on the Continent during the century have met similar success.

C. L. Brace, "Dangerous Classes."

Dugdale, "The Jukes." Reform School Work, N. C. C. 1892, p. 166, seq.

H. Folks, "The Child and·the Family." N. C. C. 1892 (explaining the Pennsylvania system of boarding out delinquent children).

The Prison Congress expresses the desire to see generalized, in their different forms of application, the work for children morally abandoned, and measures of protection and of education for unfortunate childhood.

"In accordance with experience, it would be necessary to continue the system of placing in families with that of placing in institutions, the two systems considered separately presenting advantages and disadvantages.

Everywhere it is expedient to conduct the work of the institutions to remove them as far as possible from systems termed "congregate," and to organize them after the principle of family education—that is to say, after the cottage system.

The placing in families can be permitted, especially in the following cases :

a) For the youngest children, especially girls not morally compromised and of a healthy constitution.

b) For children morally neglected or guilty, after a sufficient lapse of time, when they will have been improved or corrected in an institution.

c) For children whose correctional education is finished and who are still under patronage.

For the interest of education in families it is recommended that free organizations of education or societies of patronage or competent committees established by public authority should make it their study : (a) to make a judicious choice of the family in which they can intrust the children ; (b) to direct these families; (c) to supervise their education ; (d) to regulate supervision after established principles. It would be desirable that on one side the heads of houses of education, and on the other side the committees of family education of each district, should establish between themselves a cordial understanding, in order to be able to exchange protegès and to combine thus two kinds of education after the individual needs of the latter."

5. Checks upon Hereditary Supply.—But the education of vicious children must be followed by the attempt to cut off the hereditary supply of such children. If society is to take care of the anti-social element it has a right to use reasonable measures to cut off that element or to reduce its magnitude as far as possible.

No adequate measure has yet been proposed, and probably no one means will ever be found sufficient. The extension of the term of imprisonment until it becomes a life sentence for recidivists of the most confirmed type would help to reduce the supply of morally deformed offspring.

Marriage laws, prohibiting the issue of licenses to persons of unfit character, can hardly be supposed to help much, as sexual laws are seldom influential with this class of people.

The same thing is true of education. While in the circles of the most intelligent and moral, the insane, the consumptive and the syphilitic continue to marry and propagate diseased children what can be expected of the crime class? And yet, while the educational process is slow it seems the only method which will finally avail. Cf. Part IV., "Domestic."

6. Immigration Laws.—Our country has the right to protect itself against the unfriendly and injurious act of other peoples who make our country their penal colony. If Australia's plea against England was valid ours must be, that to transport criminals is a nation's crime against another nation. Cf. Part I., ch. vi.

7. The Education of the Public in Prison Science.—At many points the ignorance or prejudice of the public interferes with prison discipline. No system of reformatory labor, for example, can be successfully conducted in face of boycott and adverse legislation in obedience to a popular demand. Nor can rational means be used to help discharged prisoners unless the community understand the differences among criminals and the necessity for lending a helping hand. The voluntary visitation of prisoners, under regulations, is of high value, but requires both interest and intelligence on the part of religious people.

"In order to interest the public in penal and preventive questions, it is desirable,

That ministers of different religions should coöperate in this work by devoting a Sunday in addressing their congregations in regard to prisoners.

That the support of the press should be given to the solution of these questions.

That competent men should organize conferences and publish special articles upon the questions of public interest mentioned.

That members of every social class should join patronage or prison aid societies."   (St. Petersburg Congress.)

"Les crimes sont les maladies du corps social. Comme les maladies physiques du corps humaine, elles varient dans leur intensité, dans leur nature, dans leur caractère, dans le plus ou moins de danger qui en résulte, dans le plus ou moins d'espoir qu'elles laissent."— MOREAU-CHRISTOPHE.

The "social body" is the most complex organism known to us. Its diseases affect a vast network of organs, tissues, bodies, souls, lands, houses, institutions, laws, sentiments. Having regarded dependents, defectives and delinquents as extra-social or anti-social beings we ought now to study them from a new point of view, as organic members of the great social body.

No one but a social quack will offer a panacea for all the ills to which the social organism is heir. It is precisely here that the sociological method is seen to be superior to all others and adapted to displace charlatanism with a complete, systematic and harmonious method which will assign its true place and value to each rational agency of public welfare.

It is proper to deny that sociology, as art or science, has as yet given to its material a perfect analysis and arrangement. But it is not proper to assert that its teachings are merely theoretical guesswork. The recommendations in these pages come from men who are familiar with the costly social experiments of the past and who have subjected them to the test of present experience in dealing with the unfortunate and the lawless. This experience of thousands of years must be worth something, and certainly it has cost much. History has left us problems to solve, but it has also supplied us many data for the solution.. A systematic arrangement of such certified conclusions may be regarded, so far as it is true to the facts, a *scientific* work.

In the social body the individual may be compared to a molecule or a cell in the physical body, or to a member of the body. Both figures are imperfect. An individual human being is movable, while a cell or a member cannot change place in the body. A person is conscious, intelligent and free,— if a normal person,— and so can make a contract. A person may belong to many organs of the social body: in industry a mechanic; in domestic life a father and husband; in art life a singer; in church a deacon; in politics a partisan and office holder. If a man is anti-social he carries his defect into all the organs of society of which he forms a part; and, on the other hand, the defects in social functions affect him.

To give an orderly and systematic treatment of social reforms for any class we must, therefore, consider the pathological states of each organ and institution and the appropriate remedies. As the science and art of medicine are based on a knowledge of anatomy and physiology, structure and functions, of the body, so social remedies must be based on a consideration of the normal structure and functions of society. The restoration of a dependent pauper or an anti-social criminal is a restoration to his place in relation to all the social organs, and to do this all social agencies must be set in motion.

But society is a " moving equilibrium:" it develops. The extra-social members must be taught and disciplined to adjust themselves to this fact of progress or its wheels will crush them.

The concluding chapters of this book have for their aim an exposition in outline of this method of dealing with social remedies. Nothing more than a sketch can be offered, with a few illustrations under each head. At the same time the sign posts of reference will point the way to the houses of interpreters where all the wisdom and knowledge thus far gained may be found.

It is desirable that every citizen should have a fair knowledge of the entire field, and should be taught to see the place and relative importance of each effort to promote the common health and welfare. But there will be room still for specialists, and even for hobby-riders. While every citizen should seek intellectually to survey the whole field as from a tower, when actual work is undertaken it must be limited to special forms of activity. Time, strength and means are soon exhausted, and only a little surplus of each is left, after the individual wants are satisfied and family life provided for, to bestow upon general social interests. But for the most humble and obscure philanthropist there is inspiration and direction in the study of the general movement of modern times, and in being conscious that the section of the army which he leads is an organic part of a great organic whole.

Ref. J. Bascom, "Sociology."
Mackenzie, "Social Philosophy."
R. T. Ely, "Social Aspects of Christianity."
F. Wayland, "Moral Science."
E. G. Robinson, "Principles and Practice of Morality."
D. J. Hill, "The Social Influence of Christianity."

Literature on Social Hygiene and Therapeutics.

W. S. Jevons, "Methods of Social Reforms."

Schulze, "Gaevernitz, Zum Socialen Frieden."
Wood's, "English Social Movements."
Martineau, "History of the Peace."
McCarthy, "A History of Our Own Times."
Toynbee, "Industrial Revolution."
Rogers, "Six Centuries of Work and Wages."
H. C. Adams, "An Interpretation of the Social Movements of Our Time," (*Journal of Ethics*, Oct. 1891).

Fiction.—Mr. Charles Zeublin, Ph.B., has suggested the following list of Social and Economic Fiction : More, "Utopia ;" Bacon, "New Atlantis ;" Lytton, "The Coming Race ;" Dickens, "A Tale of Two Cities ;" Eliot, "Middlemarch ;" Reade, "Put Yourself in His Place ;" Martineau, "Hands and Machinery, Illustrations of Political Economy ;" Kingsley's, "Two Years After," "Alton Locke ;" Besant, "Children of Gibeon," and "All Sorts and Conditions of Men ;" Mac Donald, "There and Back ;" Wood's, "Metzerot, Shoemaker;" W. A. Jones, "The Middleman;" W. Morris, "News from Nowhere;" Mrs. Stowe, "Uncle Tom's Cabin ;" Bellamy, "Looking Backward ;" Mark Twain, "Connecticut Yankee in the Court of King Arthur."

French : Balzac, "César Birotteau," "Père Goriot," "Eugenie Grandet ;" Hugo, "Les Miserables ;" Ohnet, "Le Maître de Forges ;" Zola, "L'Argent " (Money).

German : Immermann, "Die Epigonen ;" Freitag, "Soll und Haben " (Debit and Credit); Spielhagen, "Problematische Naturen," "Hammer and Amboss," "Was Will Das Werden ;" Sudermann, "Frau Sorge," "Die Ehre."

Norwegian : Ibsen, "Brand," "Pillars of Society," "League of Youth."

Russian : Turgenieff, "Fathers and Sons," "Virgin Soil," "The New Generation," "Smoke ;" Tolstoi, "Anna Karenina."

Polish : Sienkiewicz, "With Fire and Sword."

CHAPTER XXIX.

POPULATION AND TERRITORY.

The basis of social life is the people and the land they occupy.

1. **Social being and well - being** depend first of all on adaptation of population to territory. There must be sufficient land for the people, and it must be of a certain quality in order to sustain a society. There must be a proper distribution of the population over the territory. There must be free access of the population to the land.

2. **Symptoms of pathological conditions** are over crowding of the territory as a whole; congestion in cities and desertion of farming lands; artificial hindrances to free use of available lands, as by laws, customs, and defects in modes of taxation. Weigh these facts: 28 of our largest cities increased 44.86 per cent. in 10 years, while the same number of English cities increased 11.2 per cent. Our urban population grew from 12.5 per cent. in 1850 to 27.7 per cent. in 1890. In ten years an increase of 60.5 per cent. in urban population of 10,000 and over. Yet there is much waste land even in New England and New York.

3. **Remedial.**—A general and diffused knowledge of the conditions of healthy social life as taught in biology, economics, and politics. Biological science determines the physical necessities of family well - being; economical science discloses the actual arrangements of population

with reference to the territory and points out the elements of improvement ; political science coöperates with individual and associated enterprise to amend the conditions according to the principles of biology and economics. In carrying out improvements the technical sciences, as of engineering and agriculture, are auxiliary. It is obviously impossible to introduce within our limits the bulky material of these subjects ; it is enough to indicate their importance in relation to the cause and cure of the pauper and delinquent elements.

Social agencies for adjustment of population to territory. Illustrations of this movement may be seen in the colonization plans of European countries, the societies which aid emigrants, the effort of Canada to encourage immigration, the state agencies in the hilly regions of New England to sell abandoned farms and homesteads, the efforts of Children's Aid Societies to remove neglected children to the country, the circulars of information from the South and West, inviting attention of capitalists and mechanics to the opportunities presented in the sparsely settled regions, the reports of the U. S. Bureau, the advertisements of railroad lands, etc.

References. Marshall's Principles of Economics. Ch. II and fol.
J. S. Mill, Political Economy.
Henry George, in "Progress and Poverty," and elsewhere has pointed out many of the evils under this head.

CHAPTER XXX.

ECONOMICAL.

1. **Economical conditions of social health.**—The material necessities of life are food, clothing and shelter. A certain

minimum of these is essential to existence, and a higher average minimum is necessary to health, to progress. Without a surplus above bare necessity, the domestic and spiritual life cannot develop. If there is no progress there will be danger even to life. Non - progressive peoples are in the way to extinction.

Latent in all men are æsthetic, intellectual, social and religious needs and cravings. To gratify these aspirations wealth is required.

The essential and general conditions of the exchange and production of means of life and culture are discussed in political economy. The special modes of obtaining these ends are treated in technical science and art, and are practically learned by serving apprenticeship in the productive callings of society.

The appropriate state agencies for promoting these ends are discussed in political science. But the state agency for production of wealth is late and restricted. Most productive enterprise is carried on without any interference or help from government.

The normal production and equitable distribution of the means of life and well - being depend upon the diffused intelligence, the acquired technical skill and the appropriate habits and morals of the people. This law must lie at the foundation of all reforms. Wealth cannot be directly given to people without ultimately impoverishing them. It is only what they earn which helps them. Philanthropy must increase the wealth of the people, the physical basis of their welfare and progress, by increasing their intelligence, skill and morality. Even political agencies, subject to the popular will, are helpful only as they are the expression of popular wisdom and virtue. Taking " Education" in this broad meaning, we may accept Mr. Ward's declaration that all progress waits upon popular education.

2. Pathological Economic States.— "Give me neither poverty nor riches." Extreme poverty and luxury are prolific sources of physical and moral decay. It is among the proletariat and the idle rich that the most dangerous vices arise. The demoralized family is the first product of unnatural and unjust economic conditions. When the home is defiled the streams of custom, morals and sentiments which issue thence are polluted. The rate of prostitution in London rises and falls with the price of bread. (Schäffle.)

It is not extreme poverty alone which degrades family life and arouses social and political strife; it is even more a belief that economical and political arrangements are inequitable. The demand for a fair share of the increasing wealth and advantages of modern improvements is socially justifiable and encouraging, since only by the diffusion of material advantages, can knowledge, taste and refinement increase.

Schäffle, "Bau und Leben," Bnd I.
Marshall, "Economics," pp. 2, 590, 594–95.

3. Remedies — Utopian, Experimental and Practical.— *Socialism* is a hypothesis "in the air." Thus far it is hardly a "working hypothesis." But it cannot be ignored and its essential propositions are by no means absurd. The advocates of state socialism claim that the end of all social evils would be greatly hastened by constructing society on a new basis.

(1) *Socialism defined.* The socialistic state would be one in which all the instruments of production are owned and controlled by the government. Socialism does not propose to hinder the freedom to use commodities accord-

ing to individual choice, except so far as such use would interfere with the equal rights of others.

Socialism does not propose to prevent the saving and accumulation of private property. Here socialism is opposed to communism which would abolish private property.

Socialism does not, necessarily, interfere with the right of inheritance of family property.

Socialism might provide for means of savings and insurrance, but could not offer interest - bearing bonds.

Socialism would not, of necessity, prevent gifts of philanthropy for social welfare, or for church work.

Examples of socialistic methods already applied are : State ownership of railroads, mines, etc.; municipal ownership of water works, street car lines, electric and gas lighting, etc.

Socialism is sometimes called " *Nationalism*," a political rather than economic term. " Collectivism " is the economic term.

(2) The *probable effects of socialism* on dependency and crime. We never can know the result of socialistic methods until they have been tried. But judging from the local experiments of small communities and from known laws of human nature and society it seems *probable:*

That no great change could be made in respect to those unfit for social life, as the infirm, the aged, the insane, the anti - social defectives. These are already cared for by the state. Improvement in their treatment is made with the progress of social knowledge and sentiment.

In respect to the lazy pauper, socialism could not improve his condition without persuading, inducing or compelling him to work.

It does not appear that a socialistic state would be superior to the present method in dealing with the pauperism which grows out of the vices of drunkenness and licentiousness.

It seems impossible to foresee how the friendly relations between the strong and the weak would be affected by the proposed changes in modes of production.

The unemployed. " Here socialism, to the degree in which it is practicable, would effect a complete remedy. The unemployed class would be eliminated from the ranks of pauperism. Certainly the line of poverty would be raised. The only question at this point would be whether this result was gained at too great a cost to society." (Professor Tucker in And. Rev.)

Bellamy, "Looking Backward."
Dawson, "Bismarck and State Socialism."
Rae, "Contemporary Socialism."
"The Fabian Essays."
Webb, "Socialism in England."
Laveleye, "The Socialism of To-day."
Schäffle, "The Quintessence of Socialism."
Gunton, "Wealth and Progress."
Paulsen, "Die Ethik."
For special study, the writings of Marx, Lasalle, Proudhon should be consulted.

The probable effect of socialism on crime. — Under Socialism the temptation to theft would be greatly reduced, but not entirely removed. There would be household property, though not capitalistic property. Every man would be obliged to work or starve, and he would be given work to do. Socialism would not remove the sources of crime which begin in abnormal sexual impulses or in tendencies to intoxication, although it might reduce the temptations from these causes. The crimes which arise

from resentment would not be much affected by the
arrangements of a socialistic state.   Coöperation would be
compulsory and not voluntary.   But the arrangements
between laborers and employers can hardly be called
"voluntary" in any strict sense of the word even now.
Legally, contracts are free ; economically, the poor and
unskilled laborer is not free.   Even in trades-unions there
is very imperfect approach to conditions where a really
free bargain is possible.   Unorganized laborers have no
real industrial freedom ; they are compelled to accept what
is offered, and discussion is not permissible when a contract for labor is made.

We can only guess what Socialism might effect.   Society
does not like to experiment very far with guesses.   For
this reason we call the propositions of pure Socialism
"Utopian."   If it is ever to come it will grow, and no
violent attempts to introduce it can succeed.   Revolutionary
methods would inevitably produce reaction.   Socialism is
a subject for study, not a scheme for immediate action.
At the same time many of the measures advocated by able
Socialists are being accepted and employed in all modern
countries.

Nationalization of land.—Mr. Henry George's plan of
practically confiscating private property in land must be
classed, along with pure Socialism, as Utopian.   While
almost every American is trying to buy a home, and while
millions own land, a movement in this direction can hardly
be practicable.   And yet the discussion in its favor is
resulting in important modifications of abuses in the law
relating to the ownership and transfer of land.

Experimental government insurance is still in the condition of hypothesis.

In England several schemes have been proposed, but

no legislation has been reached. In Germany an elaborate plan has been adopted, but the experiment is too young to furnish reliable data.

It is evident that the chief sources of anxiety to wage earners are the helplessness of indigent old age, the care of dependent members of the family after death, the maintenance of the family in cases of sickness, accidents and enforced idleness from want of employment.

If provision can be made for these needs without depressing manhood and independence of spirit ; and if sources of enjoyment now requiring wealth are opened to all by associated effort, then life would be comfortable to millions who now are anxious or even desperate.

As experiments on the living body of society are costly and perilous, and involve a kind of vivisection, our age is inclined to move cautiously, and to test the bridge before trusting everything to its structure.

Old age pensions. All modern Christian states have adopted the general principle that all helpless indigent persons, in old age, are to be supported at public cost. They are sometimes relieved in the poor house, sometimes in families through out-door agencies. The *doctrine* on which such legislation rests was thus stated by the German Emperor, November 22, 1888 : "I do not indulge the hope that the distress and misery of mankind can be banished from the world by legislation, but I regard it as the duty of the state to endeavor to ameliorate existing economic evils to the extent of its power, and by means of organic institutions to recognize, as a duty of the commonwealth, the active charity which springs from the soil of Christianity."

In Germany, under Bismarck's leadership, a system of insurance for workingmen provides for indigence caused

by sickness, accident or old age. The fund is raised by a
tax laid upon the workman, the employer and on the
empire at large. No provision is made for the unemployed,
the lowest class of the "proletariat." See Dawson's
"Bismarck and State Socialism."

In Austria the principle has long been adopted that
dependent old age is entitled to be supported by the young
and strong. The Emperor Joseph II "decided that at
sixty a man should have the right to claim from his native
town or commune a pension equal to one-third of the average daily wage he had received during his working years.
This pension was to be regarded in exactly the same light
as a soldier's pension — not as a charity, but as the reward
for past services. This is still the guiding principle of the
Austrian Poor Law." (Review of Reviews, March, '93,
p. 208).

In *England* various plans of pensions for old age have
been proposed : a universal compulsory pension scheme,
the fund collected by the state from all the poor (Blackley) ;
a voluntary assessment scheme (Chamberlain) ; an old age
endowment scheme (Booth). But Parliament has as yet
acted upon none of these schemes, and looks to the Poor
Law alone for care of old age. See Rev. of Revs., 1892,
p. 271. Con. Rev., March, '92. Quar. Journal of Economics, July, '92.

"General" Booth's Salvation Army Scheme. In this vast
dream of help, economical, moral, philanthropic, and religious elements are blended and mixed. It does not look
for direct political aid, but relies on individual gifts of the
rich for its funds. Its management depends on the execu-
tives of the Salvation Army. Its characteristic elements are :
(1) food and shelter for every man in the city, with work ;
(2) employment bureau to secure work for the unemployed ;

(3) the Household Salvage Brigade, to collect and utilize waste scraps of food, clothing, books, etc.; (4) the transfer of the unemployed to farms; (5) rescue work, — "Slum Sisters," traveling hospitals, prison gate brigade, watch-care of drunkards, open-door houses for penitent fallen women, preventive work for young girls inquiry, office for lost people, industrial schools, asylums for moral lunatics; (6) assistance in general; — improved lodgings, model suburban villages, the poor man's bank, the poor man's lawyer, coöperative schemes for purchase or production, matrimonial bureau.

All these elements have been tried by various organizations as well as by the Salvation Army. The permanence of the work depends on the cohesive power of a comparatively new and limited organization. The scheme has many able friends and foes. Some of the objects, apparently, cannot be secured without state and municipal action. Those who incline to enlarge the powers of the state and extend its activity, favor referring the measures to the municipality.

A. Experimental and practical.— Proposed Remedies Depending Primarily on Individual Initiative of Capitalists.

Many of these are described as actually in beneficent operation in the United States, by Pidgeon, "Old World Questions and New World Answers." In every city the employers of labor, influenced both by philanthropy and enlightened sense of duty and interest, are improving the conditions under which their employés labor.

Profit-Sharing depends on the good will of capitalists. But it seems probable that the lessons of experiments now being tried may prove that self-interest is directly involved. With the growing power of trades unions, the margin of income for superintendence and capital is being cut down to narrow limits, while it is often claimed that there is a great fall in the productiveness of labor.   If a system could be devised by which the workmen would have a direct interest in increasing the product, as they now have in shortening the hours, raising the pay and diminishing the energy of labor, many believe that the capitalists would be personally interested in promoting such a scheme.   Fortunately, the experiment is being conducted under favorable auspices in all civilized lands, and a happy issue may reasonably be expected.

N. P. Gilman, "Profit - Sharing Between Employer and Employé."

B. Voluntary Coöperation in Purchase and Production promises great relief to the multitude of those who live on the margin between plenty and necessity.   The English coöperative societies have shown that there are decided advantages in associated efforts to secure good articles at a reduced price.   In the United States similar efforts have been rewarded with a high degree of success, especially building and loan associations when operated under carefully devised laws.

It cannot be said that large bodies of laboring men have shown ability to conduct manufacturing enterprises on their own account.   Hopeful beginnings have been made on a small scale, as among Minneapolis coopers, but they cannot be regarded as more than harbingers of a better day.

In life insurance, hopeful results have been worked out by coöperation in mutual benefit societies ; but here there are many dangers and losses, and the whole field requires investigation.

Cairnes' "Some New Principles of Political Economy."
Baernreither's "English Associations of Workingmen."

History of Coöperation in the United States. (Baltimore, American Economic Association ; 1888.)

Holyoake G. J., Manual of Coöperation. J. B. Alden, N. Y.

H. S. Rosenthal, "Manual for Building and Loan Associations."

C. D. Wright, "Coöperative Distribution in Great Britain," and "Manual of Distributive Coöperation." A. H. D. Ackland, "Workingmen Coöperators." T. Hughes and E. V. Neale, "Manual for Coöperators." C. Barnard, "Coöperation as a Business." S. Dexter, "Treatise on Coöperative Savings and Loan Associations."

"Coöperative Credit Associations in Certain Foreign Countries." U. S. Department of Agriculture. Miscellaneous Series, No. 3. *Atlantic Monthly*, Feb. 1887 (by R. T. Ely.) Miss Beatrice Potter, "The Coöperative Movement." Wood's "English Social Movements," Ch. 1.

Trades Unions aim to secure higher pay, shorter hours and improved conditions of labor. They are self-protecting, but their tendency is to diffuse the advantages they gain for themselves and make these universal and customary. Their most devoted and intelligent advocates do not teach that these unions have reached their best form or are free from serious defects. Their militant organization is a temporary effort to meet the military conditions of the capitalistic organization of productive enterprise. The relative and temporary value of trades unions must be estimated in view of the history of past conditions of unorganized labor, the situation which confronts them, and the possibility of their becoming an agency of common welfare.

On the uses and abuses of Trades Unions see :

Cairnes' " Some Principles of Political Economy."
Toynbee's, " Industrial Revolution."
Baernreither's, " English Associations of Workingmen."
T. Roger's, "Six Centuries of Work and Wages."
G. Howell, "The Conflicts of Labor and Capital."
Woods' " English Social Movements," Ch. I.

The Extension of Municipal and State Ownership of monopolies is demanded by a growing conviction of our times and resisted by a resolute and able school of economists and statesmen on grounds both theoretical and practical.

If efficiency and honesty of management can be secured equal to that of individual enterprise it seems to be conceded that there would be a decreased cost of many necessities of our civilization,—as lighting, heating, water, street transportation, railroad service, telegraph and telephone communications, etc. This would be equivalent to an increase of income for all the families of a community so far as the affected industries are concerned. The only question is as to the possibility of securing competent and honest public officials to conduct these industries for such salaries as the public might be willing to vote them.

Refer. "A Plea for Liberty," (opposed to extension of state control).
W. Graham, "Socialism, New and Old."
S. A. and Mrs. Barnet, "Practicable Socialism."
W. Donisthorpe, "Individualism, a System of Politics," (adverse to Socialism).
T. Kirkup, "Inquiry into Socialism."
Rae, "Contemporary Socialism."
"Fabian Essays in Socialism."
S. Webb, "Socialism in England."
E. de Laveleye, "Socialism of To-day."
Woods' "English Social Movements," Ch. II.

Municipal regulations of the physical conditions of health and well-being, or coöperation with non-political organizations.

Unsanitary conditions of alleys, streets, houses and sewers produce feebleness and sickness, and thus indirectly increase pauperism and crime. Private initiative and voluntary organization can combat these evils with a measure of success, but the power of the " Collective will " is required in dealing with ignorant or selfish landlords, their agents, and the degraded occupants of rented tenements.

Industrial Education has a direct bearing on the earning power, and thus on the social status of youth. It is believed by an increasing number of competent educators that the more general introduction into public schools of sloyd and manual training courses, and the establishment of technical and trade schools would tend to remove many of the perils of pauperism and delinquency. No help can be given to people unless it leaves them with increased skill and habits favorable to useful industry. It seems reasonable that the methods found essential for the reformation of delinquents ought to be useful in the normal formation of those who are in danger of becoming delinquent. Merely literary and mathematical education, without physical and technical discipline, cannot be regarded as adequate for the average child of industrial communities. Want of skill is the immediate cause of failure to secure employment. Said the head draughtsman of one of the largest tool-making establishments in the country, "Our object is to make machines that any fool can use and that no fool can break."

Provident Schemes.—Political, philanthropical and coöperative.

As the possession of property is partial security against dependency and delinquency remedial measures must aim to foster and encourage thrift. In large cities the savings banks perform an important function in gathering the small savings of the poor and returning a small rate of interest. But their usefulness does not extend beyond centers of population, and the capital so collected is not available for productive coöperative enterprise. In Germany, philanthropy has sought to connect the savings of the wage earner with commercial and manufacturing enterprise; and similar experiments are being tried in America. The provision of capital and of efficient management must precede successful productive coöperation in which wage earners share the advantages of capitalists.

As the very poor are compelled to pay extravagant rates of interest when obliged to borrow on such security as they can give to pawn-brokers and chattel mortgage brokers, the "Provident Loan" plan has been recommended and is being tried. In such associations the company accepts the security offered to small brokers and content themselves with a return of six per cent. on their investment. (Charities Review, March and June, 1892.)

Postal Savings.—In order to extend the advantages of the small deposit system to persons to whom the city savings banks are not accessible it is proposed to copy the English system of government postal savings. On this plan almost every postoffice would become a place of deposit, ample security would be given by government, and the habit and custom of thrift would be cultivated even by children and those who otherwise are improvident.

W. Lewin's History of Postal Savings.
Edinburg Review, Oct., 1892.
Charities Review, June, 1892, (Article by J. Wanamaker.)

Employment Bureaus.—Under the head of Economic Amelioration should be considered the means of securing employment for those who are involuntarily idle. (See Part I, The Unemployed.)

"Bureaus of Justice" may help to secure wages unjustly held back and to protect the poor against voracious and unscrupulous money lenders.

Report Boston Association of Charities, 1892, p. 29.
Additional references; Woods', "English Social Movements."
Syllabi of Prof. E. W. Bemis (University of Chicago) on "The Labor Question" and "Some Methods of Social Reform."

CHAPTER XXXI.

DOMESTIC RELATIONS.

1. Conditions of Health.—The outward conditions of a sound domestic life are—a sufficient economic basis, a healthy house in a clean neighborhood, adequate provisions for intellectual, æsthetical and spiritual development, and the protection of a fair, impartial and intelligent government. The personal conditions of a sound domestic life are moral and regular sexual relations in marriage, and the rule of affection and its bonds between parents and children. These natural bonds must be idealized and purified by the infusion of æsthetic, moral, and religious culture, if they are to be most pure and permanent.

2. Pathological Phenomena of Family Life.— When a family is impoverished it is a seat and seed of social disease. Extreme poverty may arise from the weakness, inefficiency, laziness or vices of the parents; from the fraud or violence of external persons; from the ravages of war, pestilence or famine; from the improvements of machinery displacing acquired skill; from sudden change of an industrial center; from unjust methods of dividing the products of common industry; or from bad government. When a large number of families have been reduced to a condition of misery, history leads us to expect an increase in beggary, theft, attacks on property, assaults on the person. The education of children is neglected among the proletariat, and infant mortality rises to a dreadful height. With growth of coarse and cruel impulses come industrial strife and political revolutions. When the family is impoverished the social body is in peril.

Relations between parents and children. The natural affection of parents and the obedience of children under parental care are rudely shaken by the proletariat condition. When mothers are compelled to earn the living, and young girls go too early to the factory, true womanhood is stunted and deformed, education is neglected, household order is impossible, cleanliness and neatness are unknown, and bitterness engenders violent and anti-social feelings. The neglect of children by parents at the other extreme of wealth is also notorious, where mothers surrender their offspring to ignorant attendants and spoil their own lives in a wild round of frivolity and excitement. The allurements of unhealthy society lead to a revulsion against the duties of maternity, and the means of avoiding those duties are often the way to crime.

Disorder of the relations of the members of the family is part of the social malady. Here may be mentioned the enforced or voluntary neglect of marriage at a suitable age. From this is certain to arise unnatural sexual vices, prostitution, crimes against morality, insanity, and serious economical disturbances. From precarious livelihood, rudeness of manners, cruelty and abandonment arise the numerous divorces among laboring people. The growth of a set of idle rich young men, near to a population of very poor girls, means seduction and ruin,—an evil which is condoned in a society where wealth hides a multitude of sins under the gay mantle of the title "youthful folly."

The "regulation" of prostitution is not even a palliative remedy, but tends to destroy the moral feelings which promise a real cure. Under cover of "legal regulation" our "Christian" states offer to lust hecatombs of corrupted girls, a more hideous example of human sacrifices than those of the heathen.

Marriages for money are part of the same evil and tend to social demoralization, for adultery is a too common result.

Illegitimate children are brought into the world with tremendous disadvantages. They are born in unusual peril and their rearing is in neglect and shame. (From Schäffle.)

3. **Remedial.**—*a*) As the family is the organization through which society is renewed and maintained it has been proposed that the state prevent the increase of pauper and delinquent members by the heroic measure of *sterilization* of incorrigibles. (Boies, "Prisoners and Paupers.") The proposition is favored by many eminent writers, and is by no means absurd.

Several considerations, however, should be weighed. In the first place it is almost impossible to discuss the subject in a way to carry the public without injury. Furthermore, mutilation is condemned by modern sentiment and will be approved only in most aggravated cases of crime. Therefore only inveterate offenders who, probably, have already become parents, would be affected by this measure. Only a small minority of paupers and delinquents would be touched.

It would appear that this measure, though humane, is unnecessary, since it is always in the power of society to isolate the incorrigibles and to require them to support themselves by productive labor. It has been shown that crime may be steadily reduced, as in England, by repres-

sive and preventive agencies. And, even if the measure
under consideration were adopted, these repressive and
educational efforts would still remain necessary. On the
whole, therefore, while the proposition is sound, and even
humane in these days of anæsthetics, it cannot be regarded
as offering a panacea. It comes too late.

Social institutions organized to restore the fallen women
are to be counted among palliative, remedial and prophylactic agencies. In most cities are found refuges for outcast and ruined girls who desire to abandon their vicious
career. Foundling Hospitals give temporary relief to
unmarried mothers and their unwelcome offspring, and
Maternity Hospitals aid in bringing back hope to the
desperate. But peculiar obstacles make these agencies
perilous, and at best they are palliative.

The National Divorce Reform League is a non-political
organization, with a basis broader than its name. It makes
a thorough historic and scientific study of the family,
diffuses its information, educates public sentiment, influences opinion and custom on the subject of marriage
and domestic virtue, and seeks to modify legislation, both
state and national. The patrons of this society render a
valuable service to mankind.

The preventive and educational work of caring for
neglected and abandoned children has been considered in
Part I.

Dwellings.—The health and morality of a community
are greatly affected by the condition of the dwellings of
the poor. It is demonstrable that a "let-alone" policy
here is destructive. The ignorance, filth and lust of
crowded families are not self-corrective, and competition of
landlords, each of whom holds a monopoly of his own
tract of land, cannot be relied on for improvement. By

combining voluntary with municipal action it has been found possible to improve unhealthy and crowded tenements. The enforcement of sanitary regulations, governing the size of rooms and the conditions of cleanliness, has been a distinct help. Syndicates of philanthropists have found a reasonable return upon investments by buying up such property, improving the houses, and requiring a moderate rent. Octavia Hill's great name is conspicuous in this connection. In the last resort, municipalities might be justified in purchasing the land of infected and depraved districts, and assuming the functions of the landlord in the common interest.

Harper's Magazine, April, 1884 (of Octavia Hill).
Riis, "How the other Half Lives."
A. T. White, "Improved Dwellings for the Laboring Classes."
Octavia Hill, "Homes of the London Poor."

The Family is the primary organ, not only of renewing the population, but of transmitting the æsthetic, scientific and spiritual culture of the race from generation to generation, and from class to class. Whatever the School, the Church, the Press, the State can do to enlarge, enrich and elevate the family life is returned to each social institution, augmented in power and consecrated by tenderest associations. All the fundamental forms of knowledge, of accurate speech, of æsthetic refinement, of moral ideals, of religious fervor and exaltation must be wrought into the plastic nature of children by parents. The Public School, the College, the Church, the Newspaper can never effectually give culture to children whose home life is vulgar and wicked.

See the articles of Dr. S. W. Dike (Auburndale, Mass.) and other publications of National Divorce Reform League.

CHAPTER XXXI.

THE INSTITUTIONS OF CULTURE,—INTELLECTUAL AND ÆSTHETIC.

This title furnishes us a new point of view.

1. Health.—It may be said that the fundamental conditions of social health in this sphere include at least these factors : that every member of society have a certain minimum of education in the elements of learning, and a certain degree of preparation for a productive calling ; that an increasing number of the more capable members of society have higher opportunities of developing their native capacities in special courses of higher culture ; that a few be supported by private means or at public cost to push out upon the frontiers of science and discovery ; that all adult members of society have means and opportunity (by "University Extension" and Night School methods) of securing the wider outlook of the social sciences and literature ; that the agencies of culture,—Press, Pulpit, Parents,—be normally active, and be trained for their functions.

2. Pathological.—There are entire strata of society in our great cities where the children are not sent to school. If they did go there would not be seating room and teaching force to supply their wants. The officers charged with enforcing the compulsory education law are hindered by the ignorance and neglect and hostility of parents. One great obstacle in the way of extending the culture of adults is the length of the working hours. Frequently the distance from labor consumes much time and strength. Before "University Extension" methods can do much for the "laboring classes" the pressure of long hours and Sunday work must be relieved.

In the South and in sparsely settled regions of the West educational systems are hindered by the absence of interest and curiosity, and by the industrial situation.

It is generally admitted by educators that our public school system is defective in its failure to provide training for the hands in connection with literary studies. As improvements cost money, and their meaning is not understood by the average city legislator, progress is very slow.

3. **Signs of Progress.**—Already many cities and towns have introduced kindergartens, sloyd and manual training schools, and trade institutes, either by municipal or coöperative action.

Mr. Ward (" Dynamic Sociology") urges that knowledge has little social value until it is generally diffused, and that the chief social need is not research but popular instruction in what is already known by a few. There are large tracts of socially dead information. Many libraries and museums are like the Campo Santo — holy cities of the dead. But the Chautauqua schools, the University Extension and settlement methods promise to make a great part of this socially dead material a part of the circulating nutriment of the social body. The free public library has unrevealed possibilities in this direction. When lecture courses by experienced teachers are clearly connected with them their usefulness is vastly enlarged.

On University Extension, Woods', English Social Movements, Ch. IV.

"University Extension," by Mackinder and Sadler.

"The University Extension World," Chicago.

CHAPTER XXXII.

INSTITUTIONS FOR PROMOTING SOCIAL WELFARE.

There are many social organizations, not directly professional, industrial, ecclesiastical or political which tend to reduce the evils of dependency and crime, although they do not have this for their avowed end.

1. **Societies for Mutual Benefit.** — In great cities and large towns numerous clubs of working men, women and girls are formed for common advantage. They originate in churches, mission, "settlements," like the "Hull House," or among the more ambitious members of the wage-earning classes. The primary object may be social, musical, literary or political. Liable to perversion as they may be, their multiplication is, on the whole, a hopeful element of modern life. Courtship, for example, is rendered more sane and rational when it is conducted in connection with refining social influences, of which the lives of the very poor and crowded are so barren. It is a disadvantage to have clubs for men which destroy family life ; but many such organizations promote friendly intercourse of all the members of the families in a neighborhood. The churches may promote this movement by giving the use of their buildings during the week for such wholesome objects. As too many such clubs rent of saloons, philanthropy might well be joined to business by building and leasing suitable halls and offices for a moderate rent to societies of this nature.

Classification of Mutual Benefit Societies according to their ends; and estimate of their social value according to the worth of the end and the adaptation of the means to the governing purpose. The name of those social groups is legion, for they are many. One society may have many objects. Some have a merely local membership and others are national in extent.

Those to which the title "Mutual Benefit" is most properly applied have for this organic purpose some form of economic advantage, as insurance in case of accident, sickness, or death. But thousands of other societies are organized by the "social" instinct, which is itself a very complex motive composed of many elements. The most valuable of these societies are those devoted to the cultivation of taste in music, literature, science and social questions. Societies organized ostensibly for mutual entertainment, card playing, dancing, and the like, are sometimes turned to more serious purpose by tactful and superior minds ; but usually a club will not shoot higher than it aims.

Pathological.—Some of the clubs and societies are means of indulgence in vices without interference of law or public opinion. Drinking, carousing, gambling and occasionally licentiousness are fostered by such associations. Occasionally associations are formed with distinctly criminal purposes, but they can hardly exist on any large scale or continue for any length of time.

Where men belong to many lodges, and give much attention to them, they are frequently led to neglect business, domestic duties, philanthrophy, civil, political and religious service to the community. This neglect is fostered, in a degree, by the tyranny of a phrase, "*Benevolent* Society" for " Mutual Benefit Society." It is so easy to regard the payment of a monthly insurance premium as a gift of good will to mankind. This is not an argument against the existence but against the abuse of such organizations.

2. **Societies for the Benefit of the Community.**—Another group of organizations has this common feature, the purpose of promoting some specific social end. The National Red Cross Association, of which Miss Clara Barton is the renowned President, is organized to care for public interests in times of general social calamities, as in war, flood, famine, pestilence. It was founded in 1881. The county fair associations, the state expositions and the vast international exposition companies, in varying degrees, seek to promote more or less extended interests common to many persons.

In cities, associations are formed to secure improved sewerage, better school privileges, clean streets and alleys, to beautify parks and grounds, and effect any object which touches the members of the community generally. The influence of such efforts on the volume of social evils may not be directly perceived, but may be rationally estimated. Indeed, many social evils, like many physical diseases, are prevented or cured more by tonic and food than by specific dosing and local applications. The opening of a large park for a town may appreciably lower the rate of infant mortality.

3. **Philanthropic Societies.**—Members of one social class may combine to help members of a less fortunate social class. Their work may be to relieve the distress of dependents and defectives, to reform and assist the delinquent, to prevent the beginnings of social maladies or to promote various economic, domestic and educational enterprises.

Many of these have been mentioned and their methods and functions noted in Parts I, II and III. They are so numerous and varied that a bare mention of their names, with an outline of their organization fill a considerable volume in such cities as Boston, Philadelphia, New York, and Chicago. They are mentioned here to indicate their place as palliative and remedial agencies in a scheme of social reform and progress. Their chief good is not in relieving temporary distress but in keeping alive social sympathy and justice, in laying bare the extent and causes of misery, and in conducting society to more radical and efficient methods of reform.

CHAPTER XXXIII.

POLITICAL.

CIVIL SERVICE REFORM.

" He rooted out the slothful officer
Or guilty, which for bribe had winked at wrong,
And in their chairs set up a stronger race,
With hearts and hands, and sent a thousand men
To till the wastes, and moving everywhere
Cleared the dark places and let in the law."
TENNYSON, " Geraint and Enid."

De Greef has shown the relations of the political organs and functions to the other organs and functions of society, and has illustrated their dependence upon the customs and beliefs of the economic, domestic, æsthetic and moral life. The political machinery does its work in response to the actual habits of conduct and feeling among tradesmen, merchants, fathers of families, and members of general society. Statesmen may as teachers influence the conduct and opinions of men, but as statesmen they can do nothing but register the popular or collective will with a rude approximation to accuracy. The legislation in respect to commerce has first become custom in trade; and the popular view of marriage and divorce determines both law and degree of efficacy of law in respect to domestic affairs.

But it is also true that, by slow and minute increments, the judgments and sentiments of the people may be affected by legislative measures, as when, through state - collected information and state schools, knowledge is diffused among the people. And when a certain degree of intelligence and morality has become general the outlawed minority may be repressed or even partly educated out of their relatively inferior position. This is but an example of the general principle of society, that each organ is at once both means and end, that it is effect and cause. Intelligence creates schools, and schools increase and diffuse intelligence. Justice creates government, and good government secures finer discipline in justice. There is no contradiction here, but simply fact and law.

To describe all the evils of our popular representative government and the proposed remedies would be to traverse the ground covered by such works as Woolsey's " Political Science," Bryce's " American Commonwealth," De Tocqueville's " Democracy in America," Lieber's " Political Ethics" and " Civil Liberty," etc.

The comprehensive principle in relation to the subjects of this work is that injustice in government increases misery and crime, while fair and honest administration of wise laws tend to remove the causes of these social evils. While this summary of the case seems void of contents, it suffices to show that we cannot touch a social nerve without communicating with the entire system, giving pain or pleasure. The reformation of partisan politics and of municipal government would help reform members of the criminal class. The notorious corruption of the city halls provides powerful examples and motives for a life of crime. Civil Service Reform is one of many efforts to make the institutions of justice a terror to evil doers rather than a social agency for rewarding the robbers of society with the spoils of office.

Prophylactic measures to secure political peace and order.— The propositions urged by Lombroso (in La Crime Politique et les Révolutions) include almost all the experiments offered to secure social peace and political security ;—universal suffrage and democratic institutions ; substitution of an interest in the business for bare wages (profit-sharing); productive and distributive coöperation ; provision by associated effort, with capitalistic and state aid, for sickness, premature death, old age, and accidents ; societies for mutual benefit ; rational socialistic measures, tentatively introduced and cautious trial of the most hopeful suggestions, as prevention or protection of child labor, weekly rest, inspection of factories, liberty of striking, gratuitous medical assistance, protection of coöperative societies, substitution of arbitration for industrial and international war, abolition of standing armies, etc ; limitation and taxation of inherited and accumulated wealth ; arrangement of systems of taxation so that the burdens may fall on those best able to bear them ; protection of workmen from injurious and unwholesome conditions of toil ; state direction and provision for insurance of the poorer classes ; councils of conciliation and arbitration, selected from the professions interested, and endowed with authority by the state ; emigration directed and assisted by the state to relieve an overcrowded population ; aid, private and public, for desperate need.

Further measures Lombroso recommends, which require the coöperation of private and public agencies ; the regulation of the alcoholic traffic and war against its evils ; the rigorous extermination of all societies whose purpose is to commit crime or endanger public order.

He suggests, with De Greef and others, that an effort should be made to have the various trades and professions represented in the legislatures, instead of giving to lawyers a vast preëminence out of all proportion to their numbers ; that minorities should be represented, and that the despotic absolutism of majorities should yield to a more just arrangement of political power ; that the higher education by the state should be freed from the despotism of classical traditions and time given for such new sciences as biology, anthropology, and sociology ; that the principles of Froebel rule in primary instruction, and that manual training lead up to technical discipline for the majority of the youth ; that the feeble and poor members of society should have able advocates at the bar of justice, and so be accustomed to feel that the state is friend of all ; and that the right of *referendum*, as known in Switzerland, give to the people at large a direct power over the laws by which they must live.

<hr />

CHAPTER XXXIV.

THE CHURCH,—THE INSTITUTION OF IDEALS.

1. **The Church of Christ** is the chief organ of the Kingdom of God. That is its Ideal. And while no historical church, local or national, has in any age fulfilled its ideal

purpose, no other social organization has even approached it in efficiency, breadth and spiritual exaltation. It is not necessary to depreciate any auxiliary social organ to bring honor to this, and it is not wise or honest to ignore the follies and the crimes committed in the name of religion either by hypocrites or fanatics. The value of the normal service of the church will be estimated very much according to the view held of the teachings for which it stands. To those who regard all religion as a transitory superstition or unverifiable " metaphysics," all worship and religious teaching must seem to be so much waste of time and wealth which ought to be turned to social account. This is not the place to consider this position. Writers on Christian Apologetics and on Christian Theology and Philosophy, together with the Christian poets, have furnished such evidence of the reality and value of the Faith as can be placed in human language. There are others who have no care for the religious truths and hopes of the Church, who value it for its services in relation to charity, education and social progress. They are willing to give, sometimes very cheerfully, their aid to the churches because of these services.

Believers in Christianity will continue to hold, what is here taught, that the spiritual contents of this Faith are, in themselves, the supreme good of mankind, and generally it will be seen that a social organization for the expansion and propagation of spiritual truth is reasonable and necessary.

But the very fact that the religious life has brought together powerful social organizations implies corresponding responsibilities. Power means duty, and duty is determined for the church by its creed of love and by the needs of the world in which it is planted. It is not conceivable that a church can exist with such a creed and not feel under obligations to use all practicable means of diminishing the evils connected with pauperism, misery and crime. The unrest of conscience, the sense of glaring inconsistency between creed and deed, and the pressure of educated communities forces the church to take hold of the "social problem."

That the churches have become conscious of the necessity of helping men physically and socially in order to bring them into the Kingdom of God is shown by the universal modern movement of living Christian societies toward philanthropic work. No man ever became a leader in the church who had a stronger faith in bare preaching than Rev. C. H. Spurgeon, and yet his appreciation of the meaning of the New Testament made his church the center of a vast scheme of charities. Many Englishmen complain, however, that he cut off his work from the work of others, and by isolation weakened other social movements without enlarging his own. But there can be no question that he saw clearly that Christianity is meant to touch all human need. Woods says of the English Church: "There is probably not a single church of the establishment in any working·class district in London· but that has definitely abandoned the plan which makes a church merely an association of people for the culture and spread of the religious life." It would be strange if the professed followers of Him who healed disease and fed hunger should regard the temporal needs of society as beneath the dignity of religion.

Freemantle, "The World the Subject of Redemption;" Mackenzie, "Social Philosophy;" D. J. Hill's "The Social Influence of Christianity;" Martensen's Ethics; Paulsen, "Die Ethik;" Schäffle, "Bau und Leben;" Woods' English Social Movements; Baptist Congress Rep., 1892; C. L. Brace, "Gesta Christi;" R. S. Storrs, "Divine Origin of Christianity."

The service of mere relief of physical wants is a small part of the future social work of the church. In modern nations the state has taken over much of this relief work, and the church is a distributor of only a small part of the total alms of the community. Organized charities and state supervision are needed even to prevent abuses of ecclesiastical charity. As wealth is more diffused and the economic condition of workingmen rises church patronage will be resented as an insult rather than hailed as a blessing and a kindness. The church will be compelled to touch the average man at a higher level of his nature or lose contact with him. The laborer will not ask so much for bread as for books, for leisure to read, for social justice, for a hearing, for a voice in control, for democracy in social fellowship. He will abhor "missions" more and more, and spurn advances of the self-styled "superior classes." Thus, while there will long be use for Salvation Army and "slum" work, the really great social work of the church in the future will lie in personal fellowship on terms of equality in genuine churches where the best talent is employed. And this advance movement is necessary to save the church from extinction and the people from slow but sure descent to a godless social state, without a sky and without a moral ideal.

The transformation of city life, morally and religiously, waits on the Church of Christ. There must be a general and carefully planned readjustment of population. It is essential that there should be in every neighborhood a few residents who are willing and able to stimulate the higher life and help the people fight their battles for health, sociability, beauty, culture, order, and faith. This work cannot be done at long range, nor by hired missionaries. It must be done by men and women, filled with the religious spirit, who are known in each neighborhood as belonging to it, suffering with its suffering, personally interested in having its alleys clean, its sewage in order, its atmosphere pure, its politics honest and efficient. Such leaders would find many humble and unlettered folk ready to gather about them and recognize them as friends and equals. The people must rise by their own endeavors, and must create and maintain their own institutions. If each rich, strong church would plant small colonies of suitable persons, perhaps sometimes without children, in dangerous localities, their influence on the conditions of life would soon be felt. Those who undertook the work would find a mission which would give worth and dignity to their existence. Such a career would not require money as much as intelligence and enthusiasm for humanity. The people would generally support the work themselves. The suggestion is not utopian, because it has already been joyfully acted upon by many people in many cities. Toynbee Hall in London, Miss Dodge's work for girls in New York, Miss Adams' "Hull House" in Chicago are simply signs of a social movement into which thousands of well-equipped persons have already entered.

So far as these social measures advance the well-being of the Progressive Class, they are not to be considered here. But there is not one of them which does not, at least indirectly, tend to diminish the number and the influence of the Dependent, Defective and Delinquent Classes. Indeed, when we regard the whole of society and its vast future, we see that these preventive and educational measures are the only ones which give satisfactory promise of bringing these forms of misery to an utter end. How great this hope is, depends largely on one's own temperament and on his religious or philosophical beliefs. An optimism which looks for the end of pauperism and deformity without patient, earnest and prolonged effort and sacrifice, is an optimism not justified by history, and it is practically both foolish and wicked. But the relative success already attained in every branch of remedial, preventive and educational effort of philanthropy gives rational ground for a sober hope, a burning zeal and a deathless strife with error, pain, disease and pauperism.

The treatment of these special and forlorn members of the race is a part of the universal movement of human history. If we regard these classes as the foot, down in the mire, we may so far adopt the figure as to say that the foot is still a member of the social body ; that while the foot suffers all the members suffer with it ; and that until the foot is extracted from the mire, the head will be hindered in its journey of progress. May we not partly explain the frequent outbursts of savage traits in the refined circles of society—as bestial lust and drunkenness, selfish greed, barbaric osten- tation, fondness for display, murderous indifference to the suffering of employés — by the near presence of a neglected portion of the human family? The hovels of neglected paupers furnish the nidus for germs of plague, and in the same hovels are prepared moral temptations for the sons of the elect. The atomistic notion of society, which regards each individual as a separate unit with whom we have no relations, is only evil and cause of evils. To prevent dependency and to diminish the number of defectives, society must learn to move together and work all its insti- tutions of school, family, church and state in conscious harmony toward a purposed end.

Relation of our Subject to Philosophy and Religion. — Pessimism and-agnosticism deny that we really know that

the " ground " of the world's life is the Ideal One — per-
fectly holy, just, good : the will that wills for us all perfect
happiness, beauty and goodness.   But none can deny that
we possess the ideal, for the denial itself must restate the
ideal.   We have traversed in these lectures the most difficult and rocky regions, the darkest valleys, the most sombre
caverns of human experience.   We have analyzed and measured with such precision and completeness as statistics and
other special sciences can furnish the saddest elements of
human life.   And even here, when faith and philosophy
alike pass into eclipse, we have discovered facts which point
to the *ultimate* justification of man's noblest beliefs.   Human
beings once regarded and treated as hopeless idiots, wild
and soulless brutes or demonized outlaws, are now regarded
and treated as human brethren, capable of gaining thought,
love, happiness and beauty.

It is the *faith* in the *unseen ideal* which has given the
courage and the patience of Howe, Wilbur and the other
uncanonized saints of our age.   The evolution of the race,
the victory over evil, the prospect for the entire disappearance of the pauper and defective stock, the very hope itself
born of past achievements, indicate that we are moving
toward an age when it will be far easier to hold unqestion-
ing and unclouded faith in the absolute and eternal truth,
love and beauty of God.   To this highest achievement of
reason all the special sciences contribute — sociology among
them — and the arts of life serve in the same rational ministry toward the same end.

The conclusion of our own studies is practically this :
We are not merely to medicate and dress an ever open sore
of pauperism and insanity and idiocy and crime, but to *cure*
it.   It is in that faith we began our lectures with the ideal
of a divine kingdom, with increased faith we close.   Dante

passed through Inferno and Purgatory, and came out at
last into the effulgent glory of Paradise. Dante's sublime
song is the story of human history : believe ; love ; act.

> " Take heart ! The Waster builds again ;
> A charmed life old goodness hath.
> The tarés may perish, but the grain
> Is not for death."

> " God works in all things, all obey
> His first propulsion from the night ;
> Wake thou and watch ! the world is gray
> With morning light."

> " Aid the dawning, tongue and pen ;
> Aid it, hopes of honest men ;
> Aid it paper, aid it type ;
> Aid it, for the hour is ripe ;
> But our earnest must not slacken
>   Into play ;
> Men of thought and men of action,
>   Clear the way !"

THE WORLD'S AGE.

> " Who will say the world is dying ?
> Who will say our prime is past ?
> Sparks from Heaven, within us lying,
> Flash, and will flash to the last.
> Fools ! who fancy Christ mistaken ;
> Man a tool to buy and sell ;
> Earth a failure, God forsaken,
> Ante - room of hell.

> Still the race of hero - spirits
> Pass the lamp from hand to hand ;
> Age from age the Word inherits
> ' Wife, and Child, and Fatherland.'

While a slave bewails his fetters ;
While an orphan pleads in vain ;
While an infant lisps his letters,
Heir of all the age's gain ;
While a lip grows ripe for kissing ;
While a moan from man is wrung :
Know, by every want and blessing,
That the world is young."   C. KINGSLEY.

THE END.

INDEX.

www.ingramcontent.com/pod-product-compliance
Lightning Source LLC
Chambersburg PA
CBHW020512270326
41926CB00008B/846